D0771853

Black
City
Politics

DAVID FELLMAN
Vilas Professor of Political Science
University of Wisconsin–Madison
Advisory Editor to Dodd, Mead & Company

Withdrawn by
Whitman College Library

Black
City
Politics

by
ERNEST PATTERSON
University of Colorado

DODD, MEAD & COMPANY
New York   *1974*

PENROSE MEMORIAL LIBRARY WHITMAN COLLEGE

E
185
.615
.P34

Copyright © 1974 by Dodd, Mead & Company, Inc.

All rights reserved

No part of this book may be reproduced in any form
without permission in writing from the publisher

ISBN 0-396-06901-0

Library of Congress Catalog Card Number: 73-15388

Printed in the United States of America

DESIGNED BY JEFFREY BARRIE

To Johnnie

Contents

Preface

This book reflects a black man's concern about the powerlessness of black Americans. It is a well-publicized fact that in many American cities the number of citizens, both black and white, who are discontented with municipal government has been growing markedly over recent years. Where there has been a gradual decline in trust in the system among whites, the level of trust among moderate-to-upper-income blacks is falling more rapidly. In fact, political estrangement is growing more rapidly among those blacks whose incomes allow them to live in middle-class neighborhoods than among the many lower-class blacks who are forced to live in hemmed-in black natural neighborhoods. With so many black people questioning the legitimacy of city government, blacks are no longer asking whether traditional municipal institutions have the ability to solve the multitudinous problems of large cities, but whether those institutions are willing to attempt to meet legitimate black needs.

In addition to examining some myths and harsh realities of black-white relations, this book explores the probability that black citizens are being shortchanged by a closed decision-making process. It is clear that if the elite does not want to risk the possibility of society coming apart at the seams as the United States moves into the mid-1970's, it must find ways to satisfy the discontented and convince them that the system *is* legitimate and does serve them. This can be accomplished only if many policy-making and executing bodies are restructured and become more representative and responsive. Therefore, those conventional structural arrangements that do not and cannot work for blacks, except to help provide day-to-day survival benefits, are identified; and a fundamental structural change is offered that holds the potential to benefit all of America.

Since this book is the product of the thinking of many years, it is impossible to acknowledge and thank individually all of the many persons who cooperated with and aided me in its writing. Yet a debt of gratitude must be expressed to four people. Political scientist William O. Winter's sharing of his wealth of knowledge pertaining to urban government and politics in general, his reading of the manuscript, and his providing of constructive criticism were of indispensable assistance. Political scientist Shelby Lewis Smith's natural and acquired knowledge of black thinking helped me to better portray past and present thinking of both the black masses and the black bourgeoisie. Economist Earl W. Phillips' suggestions made possible a better focus upon racial-economic problems.

My final but most important expression of gratitude goes to my wife, Johnnie L., whose skillful editing clarified concepts and sentence structure and greatly improved the readability of *Black City Politics*. But of greater significance, her patience and devotion allowed me to survive the ordeal of completing what at times seemed an impossible task.

ERNEST PATTERSON

Introduction

The realities of government in contemporary American cities are not well understood by the typical citizen, black or white. Since the black citizen in this country today is by all odds likely to spend most of his lifetime in an urban community, this book, written from the perspective of intimate knowledge of big city black cultural experi˥ces, is designed to help him gain a serviceable understanding of the operation of city government and politics. Operative knowledge can help the black citizen better devise strategies that will enable him to gain a greater voice in shaping the policies that directly affect black people.

Ethnicity (race, religion, or national origin) remains as a major determinant in American big city politics. In this book ethnic political factors are examined in Atlanta, Chicago, Cleveland, Cincinnati, Detroit, Los Angeles, Miami, New York, Philadelphia, and St. Louis. In particular we examine the illiberal standards used historically by elites to choose black leaders who were unable to effect beneficial economic and political changes in behalf of black people. We show how immigration, housing patterns, strength of the dominant political party, and a city's electoral structure allowed blacks in some cities to gain elective office earlier than blacks in some other cities, and how these elements or circumstances can affect today's black political activity. Also, because some blacks consider that coalition politics should be part of an arsenal of successful electoral strategies, we examine the dear price black people pay to be part of a coalition, especially if a city operates with nonpartisanship.

We investigate the period of the early 1960's when many blacks began to regard themselves no longer as docile perpetual losers in a lifelong, generation-to-generation struggle with authority and took steps to utilize ad hoc protest organizations. The results of our in-

1

quiry, hopefully, will show what may be expected from the upper part of the elite if black political activists of the 1970's use protest organizations in an attempt to eradicate political and economic racism. We show how the highest ranking individuals in a power establishment are able to utilize legal machinery as political chicanery and manipulate institutions of public order so as to induce a concomitant decline in black faith in legalism as a weapon to help advance black people. Our examination of political racism includes devices used to prevent blacks from winning citywide offices. We also show why black people need not necessarily expect black voters to support black candidates just because of race.

Blacks and whites who in the 1960's were very persistent in their efforts to oppose institutional racism actively through creative protest politics were not very successful in bridging the gulf between the racist "is" and the idealistic "ought." Because much of their strategy was greatly influenced by the highly questionable assumption that the low status accorded blacks in America represents nothing more or less than a century-long lag of public morals, we examine their failure from a perspective that views black-white relations as an aspect of human power relations.

We present an example of black political unity by examining an occurrence whereby a St. Louis bank took an obstinate stand and attempted to punish and make examples of political protesters, creating a confrontation which so united the black community that blacks were able to organize politically and influence the selection of a mayor and a governor. However, black people must be made aware of the fact that when they become organized and help elect a white candidate, there always remains the possibility of making a costly error. Black political support given to help a white man become mayor does not necessarily mean that blacks are helping to elect a mayor whose administration will give top priority to the pursuit of legitimate black demands. In presenting evidence which indicates that when black people decide to support a white candidate for office they should distrust him, we show how the ability of collective black communities to survive and enhance themselves politically depends, in large measure, on the development of a "healthy" black political paranoia which entails maintenance of a high degree of suspicion toward the motives and actions of every white politician.

Black aspirations toward meaningful participation in the political life of cities are coming at a time when political participation, without major system change, could result in very few gains and an increasing sense of frustration. This probability provides both the framework and approach of this book. Thus we examine the institutions and processes of big city government and address specific proposals concerning how to help effect the necessary structural changes. Based upon the fact that current holders of power have demonstrated unwillingness to relinquish meaningful power to citizen groups, our findings confirm the urgent need for effective use of a cohesive black vote that is not attached firmly to any particular party. In particular, our disclosures indicate that black people can influence presidential and congressional elections with vigorous urban organizations built upon the foundations of amoral power. Urban organizations are a necessity because of the concentrated black population in 89 cities that have total populations of 50,000 or more; black people must come to view city politics as the central nervous system of black political activity.

We give attention to technological advances and the magnitude and nature of the population shifts in urban America. These make it imperative that most existing political institutions and structural arrangements be modified to the extent that they will allow greater inputs from noninfluential and/or subordinated black natural neighborhood citizens. Inputs or legitimate demands of powerless citizens must and can be handled so that in most big cities such citizens will not have to resort to threats or politics of violence to be heard. Since blacks (as well as browns and poor whites) find city government remote and unresponsive to their needs, and thus question the legitimacy of city government, the need for natural neighborhood government takes on new urgency.

America's crisis of legitimacy *can* be alleviated, before it becomes more serious, by effecting structural changes that will open avenues leading into the political system for those people organized around different values from those previously regarded to be the only acceptable ones. Easy entrance into the political system tends to increase the loyalty of new groups to the system and helps the old dominating elites maintain much of their status even though they lose some of their power. This type of resolution of a crisis of legitimacy will result in a high measure of tranquility and stability, thus making the society more secure. At the same time, the elite's continued failure to recognize the necessity of taking steps to make local government more meaningful for noninfluential citizens could increase the polarization between the races.

Further polarization would be very easy since most white ethnic neighborhoods remain essentially leaderless, unlike the black communities in which a homegrown leadership cadre gradually emerged during the 1960's. Such further polarization could be very unfortunate. Recent research indicates, for example, that as black men increase their educational and income levels there is a tendency for them to see violence as a necessity for social change. Before the elite decides to block meaningful natural neighborhood government, it should recognize that in any big city on any given day a very small band of black urban revolutionaries with increased educational and income attainments could ignite the fuse in an attempt to effect social change.

This book gives particular attention to the belief of many people that because increasing numbers of poor blacks came to cities they are generally responsible for the financial predicament of cities. In showing that this predicament is partly owing to the increasing strength and militance of city employee unions, we show this to be an erroneous assumption. We also present a theory of black migration as inducing a momentous derangement in the administration and financing of city services, thus modifying political relations. Central to this theory are recognition of the existence of organized white producer groups and recognition of the exclusion that caused blacks to become volatile and force the national government to undertake an unprecedented part in big city politics. Thus we are able to offer a major reason why there emerged in the 1960's a series of federal service programs directed toward black natural neighborhoods, and why federal spoils were spread in a manner similar to distribution under old big city machines.

The blatant corruption and spoilsmanship of the past have, in the main, given way to governmental services generally being performed by technical specialists. We examine this fact from the black perspective to help provide guidance for black people, since it is now clear that neither the democratic ideology of equality of opportunity nor good government notions concerning "public-regarding" motivations are automatically served by civil service and/or merit. Indeed, we explore ways in which civil service and/or merit help secure bureaucratic autonomy, shield patterns of institutional racism, and help exclude already underrepresented blacks from the bureaucracy. We, accordingly, present specific schemes that will help overcome black bureaucratic underrepresentation and reduce white fears pertaining to loss of employment.

Since American big cities have reached the critical financial juncture, we show why it is imperative that urban black power-seeking organizations gear themselves to influencing governors and state legislatures. We base our opinion upon the fact that cities will increasingly become more financially dependent on state governments (and the national government) for portions of their funds. Municipal governments can only petition the higher governmental levels for necessary funds, thus allowing for greater state and federal intervention in urban politics generally, and in natural neighborhood politics particularly.

Not only must there be increased and more effective political activity on the part of urban blacks, but the private sector must cease and desist in some of its practices if blacks are ever to become a part of the American system. For this reason we look into the problems created when businesses and industries that have jobs for people possessing limited skills relocate outside the central city.

The political activism that was partly responsible for the civil rights legislation of the 1960s did not produce basic change in the economic opportunities for blacks. Consequently, we hope that this book will serve to help those who seek to enhance black people politically and help those who seek relative peace and a greater degree of tranquility for American big cities to come to recognize the need to work for acquisition of the type of political power that will also help advance black people economically. Unless political and economic opportunities are fairly distributed during the 1970's there will remain the strong possibility that discontent could pull the society apart at the seams.

CHAPTER 1

Distribution of Authority in St. Louis

In studying big city government in the United States, one will generally find that most major decisions are made by a plural elite or a ruling (pyramidal) elite. In a plural elite city, power relationships do not necessarily persist over time and the distinction between elites and the masses may be quite blurred. Supposedly, individuals move in and out of the ranks of decision makers with relative ease, depending on the nature of the decision. In a ruling or pyramidal elite city, power and influence are structured to the extent that such relationships tend to be steadfast for long periods. Over the years, many issues will confront a city and many elections will be held, but due to the structural nature of power and influence, the same elites will remain dominant.[1]

St. Louis is an example of a ruling or pyramidal elite city. Therefore, whether one studies a period when St. Louis city government was dominated by Democrats, or a period when it was dominated by Republicans, the same forces can be seen to greatly influence public policies. The dominant elite has been and continues to be composed of a downtown economic aggregation of men who are primarily concerned with broad policies for the city which affect industrial development and taxation. These industrial, banking, and commercial leaders usually receive support from the two daily newspapers in their efforts to effect public policies. Generally, one will find that most middle and upper-middle income St. Louisans, professionals, religious leaders, and educational administrators identify their interests with the downtown group. Together they make up the city's social elite.[2]

Politically, St. Louis is not unique in that it is a long way from being run in the aggregate by the elected politicians and bureaucrats. Here, as in America at large, city officials frequently receive help as well as hindrances from citizens who hold no political office and possess no chartered authority in making many important decisions.[3]

Some of the elites who comprise the American power structure conspire consciously to oppress and exploit the rank and file. On the other hand, many members of the power structure may be "public-regarding" in their mentality and make decisions which they believe are in the best interest of the masses. If a power structure's strongest current is self-seeking, it may be influenced to respond to the needs and demands of the many less powerful because of election results. However, regardless of whether the establishment is structurally open or closed, competitive or consensual, pyramidal or pluralistic, if it is not responsive to the demands of the masses, it could be responsible for the failure of "democratic" America's survival. Schoolboy fiction teaches that democracy is government by the people. But the people do not make public policy. Therefore, the policy-making elite must effect equitable management of public affairs to ensure that this form of government will live longer.[4]

The elite might defend its prerogative to determine the survival of this form of government by suggesting that it is busily engaged, well informed, and enlightened.[5] However, it could be dangerous for one to accept elitism complacently and to feel that following elite guidance is the best position for America to find itself in, particularly if the elite fails to become open enough to include and accept inputs from blacks (and browns) who will reflect the needs and wishes of their people.

Public-regarding elites resist entrusting America's future to the masses because they are aware that America's survival depends, in part, upon a high degree of openness to and acceptance of theoretical democratic values. Not only is there a question as to the extent to which the masses can shed their apathy and become well informed and enlightened, but there is a greater question as to whether or not the masses can become public-regarding. Historically, the white masses' commitment to theoretical democratic values that would have effected a measure of individual dignity for blacks (and browns) has not been very strong. In regard to equal opportunity, as well as in regard to freedom to express oneself and to dissent when in opposition to established policies, the masses have followed the lead of that element of the elite that has been intolerant.[6] However, one could counter this line of argument by pointing out how intolerant the elite has been with blacks, browns, and New Left whites who dissent from its established procedures and practices. The position of the dissenter in this country is generally perilous. Since the elite is committed to the preservation of the existing normative and institutional arrangements, it usually attempts to establish rules that penalize those who deviate from established patterns. In their defense, the elite might say that effective, more meaningful public policies can be better designed by a public-regarding establishment than by a governing group in which there is wholesale participation on the part of the masses because the more views represented, the less likely the possibility of reaching agreement on any single comprehensive public policy.[7]

Banfield and Wilson attribute the style and structure of many city governments to whether or not one or the other of two conflicting ethos prevail (white Anglo-Saxon Protestant ethos vs. immigrant ethos). Most people in urban areas are greatly influenced by the political ethos predominant in a given city. Where the public-regarding, white Anglo-Saxon Protestant middle-class ethos prevails one can expect to find that the city has moved from bossism and spoils toward merit systems and technical specialists. According to the WASP ethos, especially in Eastern and Middle Western cities, the establishment places emphasis upon its members' obligations to participate in public affairs and seek the good of the community "as a whole," which implies, among other things, the necessity of honesty, impartiality, efficiency, and no favoritism. The lower-class immigrant ethos, on the other hand, whether brought with the immigrant group or acquired by them as a result of interaction between their predispositions and the conditions of life they found in this country, identifies with the ward or neighborhood rather than with the city as a whole. Those who adhere to the immigrant ethos look to politicians for "help" and "favors" and are less interested in efficiency and impartiality in conducting the public affairs of city government than in its readiness to confer material benefits of one sort or another upon them.[8]

When the municipal reform movement became active in the United States, apparently the St. Louis establishment was able to adopt the WASP middle-class ethos of the reformers and stress what it considered to be public-regarding virtues rather than the private-regarding values of Boston's Mayor Curley's "newer races," bosses, and machines. This is ironic, for generally speaking, St. Louis has fewer upper-income and more lower-income people in proportion to total population than any other big city outside the South; therefore, according to theoretical views concerning public-regarding vs. private-regarding political ethos, it should be one of the worst governed cities in the United States. The structural form of the city's government was also out of line with middle-class reform ideology. Instead of electing its aldermen through nonpartisan at-large elections, St. Louis elects twenty-eight of its twenty-nine aldermen by wards. Some people believe that ward-based elections do not contribute to viewing problems citywide; neither do they contribute to honesty, efficiency, and impartiality. When St. Louis was predominantly middle class, a generation or two ago, it was notoriously corrupt.[9]

The non-office holding elite in St. Louis seeks to obtain its goals by maintaining a great measure of influence over the office of mayor, the comptroller, and the president of the Board of Aldermen.[10] This particular structural combination is most significant because collectively it becomes the Board of Estimate and Apportionment, which submits requests for operating funds for all city departments, boards, and offices to the Board of Aldermen. Although the Board of Aldermen may reduce recommendations in the appropriation bill that do not pertain to amounts fixed by statute, ordinance obligation, or the payments for principal or interest of the city debt, it cannot increase items or insert new ones.[11]

Since the downtown group concerns itself with civic reform, it has a high degree of interest in the budget, because there most basic policy decisions come to a head. As a result, the non-office holding part of the establishment ensures that there is comprehensive press coverage of the campaigns for mayor, comptroller, and president of the Board of Aldermen. These three positions are filled by citywide elections and these campaigns generally cost a good deal more than for other elective offices.[12]

Competing within the party dominating St. Louis politics in any given era, one generally finds neighborhood business representation, lesser downtown interests, labor unions with vested local interests, and those who are usually found at the bottom of the economic ladder. This "neighborhood" wing of the party addresses itself to precise issues that help determine actual day-to-day survival: jobs, stop signs, spot zoning, treatment by civil authorities, and the like. This element of the party is usually well represented on the Board of Aldermen, which is composed of its president and one alderman from each of the twenty-eight wards.[13]

St. Louis is not part of any county, but as a consolidated city-county, it has traditional county offices, powers, and functions. These county offices attract the patronage-minded group; and city-wide elections for such offices are held in November, along with general elections which do not receive the publicity of a spring mayor's election. Each of the twenty-eight wards has a committee-man and a committeewoman, for each party. With well-organized ward machinery, strong committeemen of the dominant party actually determine who will hold such county offices as Treasurer, Sheriff, Magistrate, Constable, Collector of Revenue, License Collector, and Recorder of Deeds. Neither the mayor nor the City Charter has any direct control over these offices. On the other hand, the approximately one-thousand jobs outside of civil service serve as part of the cement that helps bind ward organizations. Frequently, ward committeemen themselves hold various county offices.[14]

Some evidence suggests that office holding and patronage are important ingredients of ethnic politics; therefore, the intense battles for the elective county positions and control of the jobs outside of civil service indicate that ethnicity persists in St. Louis politics. Apparently, some co-ethnics derive varying degrees of psychological benefit when a member of their particular group holds elective office or secures a patronage job. On election day such co-ethnics are inclined to support the party that is responsible for so recognizing their ethnic group.[15] This helps explain why in some St. Louis wards, party apparatus remains effective.

There is little doubt that this type of ethnic group-party relationship in St. Louis made it possible for various ethnic groups to come by many day-to-day survival benefits. However, those co-ethnics that held elective office or patronage jobs hurt their own people when it came to long-term substantive benefits involving education, health, taxation, and welfare. This was so because they usually lived up to party expectations by discreetly making sure that other members of their groups would not make demands that could strain or disrupt the party.[16]

Even with the persistence of ethnicity, these two diverse interest groups (dominant downtown and spot zoning), wearing the same party label, are not so antagonistic as to produce strife. Those whose point of convergence is the mayor's office (dominant downtown group) are not interested in spoils and patronage, but support extension of civil service. The politically-oriented people (spot zoning group), on the other hand, are mainly interested in the specifics mentioned above. It is possible for both groups to remain within the same party, primarily because they need each other; and there are many areas in which each group is willing to permit the other to dominate. The spot zoning group would find its political machinery falling apart without financial aid from the nonpolitical group, which in turn is in need of the neighborhood-oriented groups—the precinct workers and the delivery ward vote. Unless labor becomes monolithic, this arrangement has the potential to exist indefinitely.[17]

However, although still functioning in St. Louis, the arrangement became strained during the 1960's as blacks began not only to fight for day-to-day survival benefits, but demanded long-term substantive benefits in the areas of education, health, and welfare. Although these black demands strained and disrupted the party, they had to be taken seriously because the city's black population was increasing as many members of the city's most numerous white ethnic group were fleeing to the country.

Until the first decade of the second half of the twentieth century, St. Louis residents of German parentage were by far the most numerous in the city. Italians and Irishmen were easily identifiable as sizable ethnic groups; and other smaller, recognizable groups were Russians, Polish, English, and French.[18]

Although there is evidence that ethnicity persists as a major factor in American politics instead of being short-lived and only associated with initial immigration,[19] Democrats in St. Louis apparently believed by the late 1960's that ethnicity had a lesser impact upon the city's political culture than in the past. In February of 1968, the City Democratic Central Committee went so far as to abolish the requirement that both German- and English-speaking persons be available for political meetings. Committeemen were also relieved of the responsibility of making comprehensive plans to facilitate naturalization.[20]

During the years that these aforementioned ethnic groups were dominant in the earlier years in St. Louis politics, that city, like other cities in the United States, was experiencing a great influx of southern and rural black people. By the 1960's, this flowing into central cities by blacks reached such proportions that it began affecting traditional politics. In 1940, black people constituted 9.8 percent of the total United States population and 9.5 percent of the population of America's central cities. By 1950, black people were 10 percent of the total United States population and 12.3 percent of the central cities. Ten years later, in 1960, 10.5 percent of this country's total population was black and black percentages in central cities had increased to 16.7 percent. Black percentages in St. Louis jumped from 13 percent in 1940 to 18 percent in 1950 to 29 percent in 1960.[21]

However, black people were well represented in St. Louis prior to 1940–60. From the time when servants and slaves provided the labor for Laclede and Chouteau pioneer outposts, there has been a sizable St. Louis black population. Moreover, black people have always suffered from racism in this city. Outpost days saw the emergence of "a pattern of segregation, social exclusion, low wages and limited educational skills . . . imposed upon the local Negro community from the beginning."[22]

Despite patterns of exclusion, black people increased their numbers in St. Louis at the peak of the steamboat era, between 1870 and 1880, because their services were sought in menial capacities as roustabouts, cabin boys, deckhands, and the like. But by 1890, that portion of St. Louis' 22,000 black people dependent upon loading and unloading for a livelihood was replaced by the mechanical hoist. Yet there soon developed another period of increased black migration. The demand for maids, cooks, butlers, and porters created when thousands poured into St. Louis for the 1904 World's

Fair, served as the magnet to pull additional black people to the city.[23]

During World War I, increased numbers of blacks came to St. Louis, anticipating that their lives would materially change because of the demand for unskilled workers to produce for the war. It is possible that many of these blacks improved their economic lot, but being at the bottom of the ladder, they lost even this insecure foothold when the great depression occurred in 1929.[24] Many found themselves on the relief rolls and struggled to survive until World War II. But even with the war there was no significant improvement in their lives, since the World War II's production techniques required a relatively low percentage of unskilled workers. Most black people did not receive adequate opportunities to receive training that would help them acquire marketable skills. On the other hand, many black people with training were not employed to the same extent as whites. Therefore the fight to secure the employment of blacks in St. Louis during the war was not very successful.[25] Consequently, by the time blacks challenged Germans for their position as the dominant ethnic group in St. Louis, many black people were receiving low wages and many others were on relief despite their having cooperated politically with the dominant elites over the years. All had experienced social exclusion, and the vast majority were faced with inadequate educational opportunities for training that could have provided marketable skills. These racist factors ensured that ethnicity would remain as a major element in the city's politics.

NOTES

[1] Thomas R. Dye and L. Harmon Zeigler, *The Irony of Democracy: An Uncommon Introduction to American Politics* (Belmont, Calif.: Wadsworth, 1970), p. 10.

[2] Robert H. Salisbury, "St. Louis Politics: Relationships Among Interests, Parties, and Governmental Structure," *Western Political Quarterly*, XIII (June, 1960), pp. 499–503.

[3] Edward C. Banfield and James Q. Wilson, *City Politics* (Cambridge, Mass.: Harvard University Press, 1963), pp. 243–45.

[4] Dye and Zeigler, *op. cit.*, pp. 1–2.

[5] *Ibid.*

[6] *Ibid.*

[7] See this view expressed pertaining to planning by James Q. Wilson,

"The War on Cities," in Robert A. Goldwin, ed., *A Nation of Cities: Essays on America's Urban Problems* (Chicago: Rand McNally, 1968), p. 19.

[8] Banfield and Wilson, *op. cit.* (n. 3), 35–46; 329–33. See also Raymond E. Wolfinger and John Osgood Field, "Political Ethos and the Structure of City Government," *The American Political Science Review*, LX (June, 1966), pp. 306–26; Robert L. Lineberry and Edmond P. Fowler, "The Effects of the Reform Ideal on Policy," in Edward C. Banfield, ed., *Urban Government: A Reader in Administration and Politics* (New York: The Free Press, 1969), pp. 335–36; and Timothy M. Hennessy, "Problems in Concept Formation: The Ethos 'Theory' and the Comparative Study of Urban Politics," *Midwest Journal of Political Science*, XIV (November, 1970), pp. 537–64. Also see James Q. Wilson and Edward C. Banfield, "Political Ethos Revisited," *The American Political Science Review*, LXV (December, 1971), p. 1049. Because certain inferences have been made about the terms and because there has been confusion among some scholars about them, there is a move under way to refer to WASP or public-regarding as "unitary" ethos and immigrant or private-regarding as "independent" ethos.

[9] Edward C. Banfield, *Big City Politics* (New York: Random House, 1965), p. 121.

[10] Salisbury, *op. cit.* (n. 2), pp. 499–503.

[11] City of St. Louis, Missouri; *Charter*, Article XVI, Sec. 3.

[12] Salisbury, *op. cit.* (n. 2), 503.

[13] *Ibid.*

[14] *Ibid.*, pp. 502–503.

[15] Raymond E. Wolfinger, "Some Consequences of Ethnic Politics," in M. K. Jennings and L. H. Zeigler, eds., *The Electoral Process* (Englewood Cliffs, N.J.: Prentice-Hall, 1966), pp. 47–52.

[16] *Ibid.*

[17] Salisbury, *op. cit.* (n. 2).

[18] Mary A. Flannery, "Significant Trends in National Elections in the City of St. Louis Between 1944 and 1948" (unpublished master's thesis, Saint Louis University, 1950), pp. 2–4.

[19] Edgar Litt, *Beyond Pluralism: Ethnic Politics in America* (Glenview, Illinois: Scott, Foresman, 1970), p. 2.

[20] *St. Louis Post-Dispatch*, February 4, 1968, p. 3A. Henceforward in footnotes the *St. Louis Post-Dispatch* will be referred to as *Post*.

[21] See *Sixteenth Census of the United States:* 1940, Population, Volume IV, Part 3, Table 2, p. 340; *Seventeenth Census of the United States:* Census of Population, 1950, Volume II, Part 25, Table 33, p. 67; *U.S. Bureau of the Census. U.S. Censuses of Population and Housing:* 1960 Census Tracts Final Report PHC (1)–131 Table P-1, p. 15; and Table P-4, p. 131.

[22] *Community Race Relations Institute of Greater St. Louis Proceedings*, 1946, pp. 51A–52 (mimeographed).

[23] Nathan B. Young, ed., *Your St. Louis and Mine* (St. Louis, Mo.: N. B. Young, 1938), pp. 32–33.

[24] *Community Race Relations Institute, op. cit.*, p. 37.

[25] *Ibid.*

CHAPTER 2

Elite Selection of Black Political Leaders

The patterns of overt and covert exclusion in St. Louis, which dated back to outpost days, fell under attack when the city's black people began agitation for political recognition in the form of black representation. This political consciousness developed partially because the black population began to increase after the turn of the century. At first, this pressure was felt more by the Republicans than the Democrats because St. Louis blacks voted overwhelmingly as Lincoln Republicans until 1932.[1]

Partially because of the developing black political consciousness, it appears that some members of the St. Louis elite decided in 1918 that it would be good Republican politics to have a black elected official. Would not that generation of black people recognize and remember that the first and only elected black public official in the city of St. Louis and the state of Missouri was a Republican? From such reasoning came the decision to run Charles Turpin, a black man, for constable.

This decision must have caused the elite to experience some resistance from its political arm, especially from the low-ranking element which manned the election machinery. With the political arm of the establishment in control of the election machinery, the first canvass of the ballots after the election showed Turpin losing. However, it was revealed that the more influential and powerful members of the elite supported Turpin's candidacy when the police department deputized and armed black men who were Turpin supporters so that they could guard the ballot boxes around the clock until there was a recount. The recount revealed that Turpin had won by more than a two-to-one margin.[2] Thus, low-ranking white political hacks were prevented from stealing an election from a black man.

And so a black man who was born in Georgia, lived in Mississippi, and was a gold prospector and one-time jewelry salesman in Mexico became the first black man to be elected to public office in the city of St. Louis and the state of Missouri.[3]

Two significant factors in Turpin's election were not unique to this St. Louis election of a black man. First, black people did not select Turpin. He was chosen and staunchly supported by the elite, so much so that black men were given guns to assure his election. Secondly, he looked white. To show how similar selection techniques were used elsewhere, we will examine Chicago and the election of a black congressman in 1928.

The 1928 congressional election in Chicago was psychologically important to black America because blacks had had no congressional representation between 1901 and 1928. George H. White of North Carolina was the last of the black men who came to Congress after the Civil War. In what amounted to his farewell address in 1901, he predicted that blacks would again serve in the United States Congress. Representative White had been elected during the Fusionist campaign of 1896 and was reelected in 1898 despite a racist campaign. Between 1896 and 1901, twenty black men had served in the United States Congress. But so little regard was paid them that they were virtually powerless and none of them was able to obtain the passage of important legislation in behalf of their race. During Congressman White's two terms, black people were subjected to defamatory utterances from various congressmen,[4] not all of whom were from the Deep South. One of these congressmen was David A. DeArmond, Bates County, Missouri, who served in the United States Congress from 1893 until he perished in a fire in 1909.[5] In April of 1898, this Missourian contributed to the vilification when he described black people as being "almost too ignorant to eat, scarcely wise enough to breathe, mere existing human machines."[6]

More than a quarter century after Congressman White made his prediction, black people in this country, in many ways, were pleased to see a black man going to Washington as a member of the House of Representatives. They were pleased despite the fact that earlier black congressmen were held in so little regard and were so powerless that they were unable to effect passage of any major effective race legislation between 1869–1901. Still, there were relatively few blacks that did not regard Oscar DePriest's election to Congress in 1928 as an event of the greatest importance.

From 1904 until 1928, voters in Chicago's First Congressional District had sent a white man, Martin B. Madden, to represent them in Congress. During the latter years of Madden's career, more and more black people moved into his district, and he began to receive challenges from black men in the Republican primaries. In 1920, 109,458 or 4.1 percent of Chicago's population was black, and 49,224 lived in the First Congressional District. This represented 44.7 percent of the district's population. Two years later, a black man challenged Madden in the Republican primary and only received 17 percent of the Republican primary vote. Black people continued to move into the First Congressional District and Madden's 1924 black Republican primary challenger received almost 40 percent of the vote. By 1930, there were 233,903 black people in Chicago, or 6.9 percent of the city's population, and 54,606 black people lived in the First Congressional District. This meant that 58.0 percent of the district's population was black. Two years earlier in 1928, it was assumed that blacks were in the majority within the district. It was in 1928 that Madden and other Republican party leaders in Chicago, both black and white, were made to feel uncomfortable by a major challenge from a black insurgent.[7]

William L. Dawson, a black man from Georgia who had been educated at Fisk University and the Northwestern University Law School, used a strong racial appeal against Madden in the 1928 Republican campaign and highly disturbed black and white party officials. Such a campaign holds the potential to strain and disrupt traditional political party machinery. When Dawson brought the issue of race into the open in 1928, he sounded little different from some black politicians running against a white incumbent today: "By birth, training and experience I am better fitted to represent the district at Washington than any of the candidates now in the field. . . . Mr. Madden, the present congressman, does not even live in the district. He is a white man. Therefore, for those two reasons, if no others, he can hardly voice the hopes, ideals and sentiment of the majority of the district."[8]

When the votes were counted, Dawson had only received 29

percent of the Republican primary vote, but white politicians had been put on notice. It might be mentioned also that Dawson, who was an outspoken and vigorous champion of racial causes in 1928, allowed party constraints to cause him to be called something other than a race man later in his career.

Congressman Madden died shortly after he won the 1928 primary election, and the Chicago local elite handpicked a black man to run as a Republican to replace him. One can never be sure just what, if any, effect Dawson's 1928 primary campaign strategy had on this decision. It possibly would not be erroneous to assume it helped determine the selection of a black man, Oscar DePriest. But there may have been other causes for this decision. Just as Constable Turpin of St. Louis did not possess physical traits normally attributed to most black men, DePriest was sandy haired, light complexioned, and had blue eyes.[9] Could it be possible that both Turpin and DePriest were chosen by white power structures because they differed less than other black men from the standard used by whites to judge others? If so, were they considered to be less inferior than their darker brothers? It is said that "everywhere in the world men and women [use] the standard of their own people to judge others and [think] that people who [differ] from this standard [look] funny or ugly,"[10] in other words, inferior.

Chicago's Mayor "Big Bill" Thompson was in a position to exercise much influence in the selection, but he did not make the decision alone. Legally it was necessary for him to consult the Congressional District Committee, which was composed of ward committeemen who belonged to his faction of the Republican party. Despite his control over the party machine, he consulted with the committee members. When possible, a successful political leader will cause his followers to feel that they have helped make important decisions. In addition to helping morale, this tactic could become politically expedient when a bad decision is made.

Not only was DePriest the Mayor's choice, he was also a member of the committee. (Other committee members included Daniel Serritella, an associate of Al Capone; Dan Jackson, a black gambling king; and John "Dingbat" Oberta, who was later assassinated in a gang war.)[11] The committee's decision was foreordained: DePriest was chosen to fill Madden's shoes.

With an associate of Al Capone, a black gambler, and a person who was later killed in a gang war helping to make the decision as to who would represent black people of Chicago in Congress (theoretically, black people nationally), it should come as no surprise that the type of man chosen did not please all of the members of Chicago's black community. Shortly after DePriest's candidacy was declared, a number of black people announced support of another black man, William H. Harrison, as an independent candidate. In order to illustrate how the elite will impose a black man of any morality, who has strings attached to him, upon black people as their leader, the early career of DePriest will be examined.

It appears that prior to 1910, when there were relatively few black people in Chicago (no more than 3 percent of the population) and no law governing the selection of candidates, it was possible for a black man to obtain nomination in the Republican County Convention and secure office in the general election to the County Board of Commissioners by an electorate that was more than 90 percent white. Straight-ticket voting and a lack of awareness of the ethnicity of all candidates by most whites allowed blacks to be elected. In this manner, a black man was elected to the County Board of Commissioners in a countywide, at-large election as early as 1871; and he was reelected in 1872 for three years. However, no other black man held the post until 1899. In 1904 and again in 1906, Oscar DePriest was nominated by the Republican County Convention and elected in the general election on a countywide basis to the County Board. However, by 1910, the new law pertaining to primaries meant that greater publicity and revelation of race would make it extremely difficult, if not impossible, for black politicians to win elective office in countywide elections.[12]

Shortly after DePriest was reelected as County Commissioner in 1906, he became involved in a factional fight and sided against Congressman Madden. He could not survive the charge that he had been disloyal to those most responsible for his political advancement. As a result of having chosen the wrong side, his dreams of returning to the County Commission and going to the state legislative body were not realized in 1908.[13]

During the seven years that he did not hold an elective office, between 1908 and 1915, DePriest became an opportunist and made enough money to become an investor in real estate, stocks and bonds, and to return to elective politics. He accomplished this comeback by returning to the Madden fold and remaining most loyal. He also devised and executed a scheme whereby he could cheat and rob black people and remain respectable. His successful scheme included becoming a contractor, decorator, and real estate agent. In some neighborhoods where white people feared inevitable black "invasion," DePriest capitalized on such fear because of his morality (or lack of morality). It allowed him to take advantage of black people who desired housing. He leased buildings totally occupied by whites, and as they fled, he doubled the amount of rent for his own people who moved into the previously white occupied buildings. According to one account: ". . . when the migration began he would lease whole buildings in sections where white people had lived and were paying $20 a unit rent and rent them to colored for $40, while his obligation for the same unit ran about $10, thus leaving a $30 profit. Negroes weren't aware of being overcharged anyway. Times were good and they didn't mind. And if DePriest hadn't gotten it, someone else would have."[14]

The census data reveals that Chicago's old Second Ward was 70 percent black in 1920. Therefore, the 1918 belief circulated in Chicago's political circles that there were more black than white voters in the ward was possibly accurate. At any rate, the white alderman from the Second Ward who was elected to the state senate in November of 1914 apparently voluntarily relinquished his aldermanic seat. Then three black men and five white men actively sought to become Second Ward Republican alderman. However, one of the black aspirants, Oscar DePriest, had become so politically socialized that no other aspirant stood a very good chance of winning. With his acquired know-how and the money that he had taken immorally from black people, he was a much stronger candidate than in 1904 or 1906. His strength as a candidate was so evident that by December of 1914 he was being supported by the regular Second Ward Republican organization. Such support almost automatically assured his election. Actually, DePriest had worked so hard and effectively in his own behalf that the regular organization did not have much choice other than to endorse him:

Many months before the primary he was busy securing endorsements and holding meetings. By the end of November, 1914, an appeal was presented to Congressman Madden, Second Ward Committeeman, which contained the endorsements of thirty-eight precinct captains, the Hotel Waiters' Association, the Chicago

Colored Barbers Association, Ministers of the Chicago Baptist Churches, Ministers of the Chicago Methodist Churches, women's church clubs, the Physicians, Dentists and Pharmaceutical Club, and many individual party workers.[15]

DePriest secured the Republican nomination and defeated a white Democrat and a white Progressive in the general election.

While serving as alderman, DePriest attempted to look after what he perceived to be the interest of his constituents. The press and the Municipal Voters' League were not particularly pleased with him. In keeping with true WASP ethos, the nonpartisan Municipal Voters' League was interested in efficiency and economy and not in DePriest's efforts to secure jobs for black people. Its twenty-second annual preliminary report stated:

Oscar DePriest—finishing first term with bad record; no alderman in Chicago's history piled up a more notorious record in so short a time. . . . Alderman DePriest's voting record is important only as showing how such aldermen vote; he voted against giving finance committee an expert staff, against keeping city expenditures within income, against business methods of hauling ashes and garbage, against publicity on "60-day" jobholders, against prohibiting aldermen soliciting jobs from public service corporations, against compelling school board to disclose facts about its finances and against non-partisan organization of council; one of the "budget aviators," not a candidate.[16]

Among other factors, the Municipal Voters' League's preoccupation with efficiency and the like caused it to be anti-DePriest. It considered that the only significance that could be attached to his voting record was to show how such aldermen voted. In reality, DePriest's voting record revealed much as to why many politicians of that day failed to support expert staffs, business methods of hauling ashes, and publicity on 60-day jobholders. DePriest had adopted the prevailing political morality of that day, which was closely akin to what we have called the "immigrant ethos." Actually, many politicians and much of the general public at that time accepted the idea that jobs and favors were parts of American political life. DePriest was alderman until 1917, and as late as 1923 William B. Munro could write that in Europe, unlike America, municipal employees were chosen because they possessed those qualifications established by law or tradition and not because of political influence.[17]

Actually, DePriest was possibly more a product of American

historical development than he realized. Historically, the European Plan had been given ample opportunity to establish itself in United States cities, where in some cases early mayors and or councilmen had power to select municipal employees. However, political party organizations in America began to exert influence early in the choice of municipal employees. This was not too difficult a task for party organizations to accomplish since many mayors and councilmen were dependent upon party apparatus and efforts for nomination and election to office. What better way to show appreciation and gratitude and help cement and strengthen the party?[18]

It is possible that the political morality which motivated DePriest and many other politicians of that era would have had a much more difficult time establishing itself if the seeds of Jeffersonian theory had not survived, developed, and grown during the Jacksonian period. As a result, there evolved the political myth of Jacksonian democracy, which greatly influenced the style of government in American cities until the end of the nineteenth century, and which still influences a sizable minority of twentieth-century city politicians.[19]

The Jacksonians believed that, from its inception, the government of the United States had been run by a relatively small elite group of aristocrats and that, by 1824–28, it was time to introduce new blood into the political system. Jacksonians were not greatly concerned with the education or background experiences of the "new blood" since they so thoroughly believed that one man was as good as another. They specifically believed that common men were as good as aristocrats and deserved to play an important role in developing and executing public policies.

Since the Jacksonians believed that no special qualifications were needed for office holding, it followed logically from their egalitarianism that universal manhood suffrage was a central political necessity. This would make it possible for any man to run and be elected to office (at least theoretically). They perceived public office holders as servants of the people. Therefore, the people should exercise a great measure of control over them. To effect this control, they advocated and were largely successful in having most top-level state and local offices filled by election for short terms rather than by appointment. This resulted in the long or "bedsheet" ballot and also facilitated Jacksonian desires to effect turnover in office and inject new blood to prevent the same people from holding office indefinitely. This movement was underway when, in 1822, Boston and St. Louis made the office of mayor elective. The floodgates were opened and elective city offices spread rapidly thereafter.[20]

Thus, popular acceptance of the idea of "passing the rewards around" and not permitting the same people to hold office indefinitely helped the spoils system to develop firmly. This idea rested upon the very stable assumptive foundation, due to popular acceptance, that all Americans were equal by nature and law; therefore they were equally capable of governing.[21] Those who accepted the assumption could have defended it by asking if there were any good reasons why every man should not have a try at making and executing public policy since all men were equal.

The Jacksonians intended that their emphasis on equality would effect a return to the principles of the Declaration of Independence. Whether or not America ever previously had adhered to the fundamental principles contained in the nation's "birth certificate," there is evidence that the Jacksonians did not realize their intentions. For approximately the thirty years immediately following 1825, there was much violence perpetrated upon various individuals and groups in America. Some were beaten; others were tarred and feathered; and there were riots. Here we are not including black men and women as victims since black people were already suffering the most inhumane violence—slavery. (But even free blacks were regularly victims of mobs.) The victims during this era, among others, included Irish and German Catholics, who were hated by some Americans because of their divergent religious views and hated by others because of fear of economic competition.[22] The lesson that some white people learned during this period has haunted the vast majority of black people since the violence which transpired between the states.

Some whites learned that the violence perpetrated against individuals and groups in direct disregard of the principles stated in the Declaration of Independence and the guarantees stated in the Constitution, and of laws passed to protect citizens by both Congress and state legislative bodies, was indicative of the fact that many local elected authorities of that period were unwilling or unable, or both, to help safeguard rights of victimized individuals and groups. Also, the period of Jacksonian democracy helped point out that professed principles and formal rights are valueless if there is no governmental effort to enforce legal guarantees against physical violence.

If, since 1776, the accepted doctrine of America has been that "all men are created equal," possessing such "unalienable rights" as life, liberty, and the pursuit of happiness, then much of America's behavior did, indeed, deviate to a considerable extent from the fundamental doctrines professed. Many victims of violence lost their lives, and it is highly doubtful that those who suffered beatings felt very secure in their "pursuit of happiness."

Of course, we may be accepting the words written in the Declaration of Independence too literally—especially when we consider that in Thomas Jefferson's original draft of the document the only substantive change made was the deletion of a denunciation of the slave traffic as one of the several complaints against King George III, leaving the simple proclamation that "all men are created equal."[23] That deletion possibly meant that the document was to be taken less seriously than we have subsequently taken it since Jefferson believed that the document attempted to express the American mind,[24] and we are aware that the American mind has historically accepted violence as part of the political process, despite the fact that some Americans have used selective historical sources to arrive at the belief that violence is abnormal in this country.[25]

Propagation of the egalitarian theme contained in the Declaration of Independence profoundly shaped the black concept of equality in America. According to black psychiatrists William H. Grier and Price M. Cobbs:

Black people feel bound to the concept of equality. It is a belief which allows them to live. It cannot have merely an occasional hortatory meaning for black Americans—it must be seen as a universal truth. No other conviction can sustain black people in this country. It is absorbed in childhood and built on the child's conception of fairness. Public pronouncements of every kind find a responsive affirmation in black breasts if they only include the word "equality." The idea of all men's equality lies at the deepest level of the black man's conception of social organization. Slavery and the post Civil War experience have made this concept dear indeed.

It extends from the broad social meanings to its implementation in everyday life. Black children are acutely sensitive to the undemocratic formation of "exclusive" groups and social bodies. This conviction finds support in the concept of brotherhood. We are not only brothers but brothers keenly aware of our equal status.[26]

The fact that DePriest and many other politicians adhered closely to something akin to what we have called the "immigrant ethos" does not mean that they had violated the tenets of Jacksonianism. Their style of politics meant that their low-income level constituents did have some representation in local governing circles. The net effects of Jacksonianism was not the advancement of absolute equality, but the obtaining of a more open elite system whereby the new rising middle class west of the Alleghenies became assimilated into America's governing circles along with the established Republican leadership in the East. Therefore, in reality, DePriest and similar politicians, as well as Jacksonians, sought to advance special interests.[27]

No doubt DePriest would like to have had support from the press, which was not particularly pleased with him, and also backing from the Municipal Voters' League, which attacked him. However, it is doubtful that he felt that he owed the good government-oriented Municipal Voters' League an apology because it criticized him for soliciting jobs from public service corporations. He no doubt sloughed off the criticism because he saw his actions as being part of the system—a system that forced men who desired to enjoy political success to find and obligate men to them who had the ability to carry precincts. Because DePriest's future with the party was to be partly determined by his ability to help the party win elections, rather than by his receipt of praiseworthy editorials and favorable statements from Municipal Voter's League speakers, he sought jobs for his constituents.[28]

DePriest was not atypical. It was common practice for politicians to seek jobs for their constituents with public service corporations.

Appointment in the public service is not the only patronage available for the boss in rewarding party workers. There are jobs with public service corporations or private business concerns which may be secured by the boss for his workers. This is a means by which the upper world of business may repay him for services rendered and privileges received. Paving contractors;

dealers in coal, fire-fighting apparatus, and street cleaning machinery; and street railway, bus, telephone, gas, electric lighting and taxicab companies, as well as banks, hotels, office buildings, and even factories, are fertile fields in which the boss may find employment for a deserving party worker.[29]

Whereas DePriest was not Chicago's political boss, he was part of the "ring" (as matters pertained to black voters), the inner circle that guided the machine along paths designed to maintain power.

Upon the expiration of his first term as alderman in 1917, DePriest did not seek reelection because a month before the primary he was indicted by a grand jury. Part of his troubles began in 1912 when he supported the Democrat Maclay Hoyne in Hoyne's successful bid to become State's Attorney. However, in 1916 DePriest worked against Hoyne and for Mayor Thompson's nonvictorious candidate for State's Attorney. In January of 1917, Hoyne was able to repay DePriest for his lack of loyalty. Hoyne, with written confessions from a police captain and an underworld figure, was successful in having the grand jury indict DePriest and some other people for bribery of police officers so as to help protect gambling houses and houses of prostitution.[30]

During the trial, it was revealed that several policemen had been demoted because they had raided places that received syndicate protection, and one of DePriest's agents told of collecting graft money from gambling clubs and paying it to the alderman himself. DePriest himself, on the witness stand, admitted that he had received $1000 and had reduced some detectives in rank. Clarence Darrow and E. H. Morris, DePriest's defense lawyers, interjected race into the case but primarily based their case on the ground that the money which DePriest received was not for police protection but merely a campaign contribution, part of which was turned over to the Thompson candidate for State's Attorney, Hoyne's opponent.

DePriest was acquitted and in the long run the trial did not prevent him from enjoying future success as a politician. With the passage of time, which caused the details brought out during the trial to fade into generalizations, he was helped to become known as a man who could stand up under fire. He acquired this politically advantageous reputation partly because some black people felt that he had been persecuted and that by being acquitted, the trial proved that he had defeated his persecutors. It would be very difficult for us not to admit that DePriest had become a political mechanic. Even with good luck, it would be extremely difficult for most politicians to survive such a trial.

When the establishment selected a man of Oscar DePriest's background to replace Congressman Madden as the Republican Candidate for Congress in 1928, it was not surprising that a group of black people announced their support of William H. Harrison as an independent candidate. Harrison stated that he had made himself available because he did not desire to see black people represented in Congress by a disreputable black man of the gangster, gambler, grafter type. Based on the revelations about DePriest cited in this chapter alone, Harrison would have had sound reasons to make such a statement. However, even if Harrison and/or his followers had known nothing about DePriest's past, the accusations circulating at that time pertaining to him were enough to warrant such a statement. In fact in 1928 DePriest was indicted for "aiding, abetting, and inducing" those racketeers who operated "gambling houses and disorderly places" on the South Side by helping to protect them from the police.[31] These charges were similar to the charges of DePriest's indictment in 1917.

Even with the 1928 indictment, the handpicked candidate of the elite did not withdraw from the campaign for Congress. During the campaign, racism emerged in the form of a letter distributed to white people throughout the district urging them to support the white Democratic candidate. Despite this letter and Harrison's candidacy, DePriest was the plurality winner. Some white Republicans refused to vote for either black candidate and voted for the white Democrat. DePriest won by 3800 votes, where two years earlier Madden carried the district by 14,000 votes.[32]

During the campaign the Harrison forces asserted that even if DePriest were to be elected he would not be seated. However, the Harrison people underestimated the influence of a determined elite. A few days before Congress convened, the case against DePriest was dismissed by the court because the prosecution announced that it had insufficient evidence to bring the newly elected black congressman to trial. Thus a potentially embarrassing and politically damaging public trial was avoided. Nevertheless, it was necessary to take other behind-the-scenes steps to ensure that Congress would not invoke article I, section 5, clause 1 of the Constitution, which empowers each house to be the judge of the election returns and qualifications of its own members. Here, the widow of Medill McCormick, who had served as a United States Senator from 1919 to 1925, played a major role. Mrs. McCormick, Illinois' representative-at-large, was a close friend of Mrs. Alice Roosevelt Longworth, the wife of the Speaker of the House of Representatives. Taking advantage of this personal friendship as well as that of other Republicans in Washington, Mrs. McCormick helped devise a scheme to thwart those Southern congressmen who were rumored to be ready to object to DePriest's taking his seat. The Speaker was persuaded to abandon the usual practice of administering the oath to members grouped according to states, in order to prevent any member who had been sworn in from objecting to any member in a subsequent group. Speaker Longworth therefore announced that because of the disorder that could accompany administering the oath in the traditional manner it would be a more dignified ceremony if he were to administer the oath to all members at once. This move caught the anti-DePriest congressmen off guard, and DePriest was sworn in along with all the rest before there was an opportunity to raise objections.[33]

Thus the Honorable Congressman White had correctly assessed the future of American congressional politics when, in 1901, he predicted that black faces would again be seen in Congress: "This, Mr. Chairman, is perhaps the Negroes' temporary farewell to the American Congress; but let me say, Phoenix-like he will rise up some day and come again. . . ."[34] Whether one could classify DePriest's going to Congress as a Phoenix-like return is debatable, since it was the second restoration of white supremacy, and not the black Congressmen's own actions, which caused them to be consumed by fire. But, more important, the various events revealed above which led to DePriest being elected and seated in Congress, indicate how far the elite is willing to go in behalf of its handpicked "Negro."

NOTES

[1] St. Louis Board of Election Commission, 1932.

[2] Herman H. Dreer, *St. Louis Argus*, January 21, 1966, p. 38. Henceforward the *St. Louis Argus* will be referred to as *Argus*.

[3] Nathan B. Young, ed., *Your St. Louis and Mine* (St. Louis, Mo.: N. B. Young, 1938), p. 39.

[4] Rayford W. Logan, *The Betrayal of the Negro: From Rutherford B. Hayes to Woodrow Wilson* (New York: Collier Books, 1968), pp. 98–101.

[5] State of Missouri, *Official Manual*, 1957–1958, pp. 1402–03.

[6] Logan, *op. cit.*

[7] Harold F. Gosnell, *Negro Politicians: The Rise of Negro Politics in Chicago* (Chicago: University of Chicago Press, 1935; 1969), pp. 78–81.

[8] *Ibid.*, p. 79.

[9] *Ibid.*, p. 166.

[10] Ruth Benedict and Gene Weltfish, *The Races of Mankind*, Public Affairs Pamphlet No. 85, Public Affairs Committee, New York, Sixteenth Edition, October, 1956, p. 6.

[11] Gosnell, *op. cit.*, p. 80.

[12] *Ibid.*, pp. 81–83.

[13] *Ibid.*, p. 169.

[14] *Ibid.*, p. 169.

[15] *Ibid.*, p. 170.

[16] *Ibid.*, pp. 171–72.

[17] William B. Munro, *Municipal Government and Administration: Vol. II, Administration* (New York: Macmillan, 1923), p. 31.

[18] *Ibid.*, pp. 31–32.

[19] Charles R. Adrian, *Governing Urban America: Structure, Politics, and Administration* (New York: McGraw-Hill, 1955), pp. 50–51.

[20] Alan P. Grimes, *American Political Thought* (New York: Holt, Rinehart and Winston, 1960), pp. 51–52.

[21] *Ibid.*, Ch. 8.

[22] Richard Maxwell Brown, "Historical Patterns of Violence in America," in Hugh D. Graham and Ted R. Gurr, eds., *Violence in America: Historical and Comparative Perspectives*, A Report to the National Commission on the Causes and Prevention of Violence, June 1969 (New York: Signet Books, 1969), pp. 50–51.

[23] Bradford Chambers, ed., *Chronicles of Black Protest* (New York: Mentor Books, 1968), pp. 46–49.

[24] Grimes, *op. cit.*, pp. 88–89.

[25] See *Violence in America: Historical and Comparative Perspectives*, *op. cit.*

[26] William H. Grier and Price M. Cobbs, *Black Rage* (New York: Basic Books, 1968), p. 119.

[27] Thomas R. Dye and L. Harmon Zeigler, *The Irony of Democracy: An Uncommon Introduction to American Politics* (Belmont, Calif.: Wadsworth, 1970), pp. 64–66.

[28] Charles M. Kneier, *City Government in the United States* (New York: Harper & Brothers, 1947), p. 520.

[29] *Ibid.*, pp. 525–26.

[30] *Ibid.*, pp. 172–73.

[31] *Ibid.*, pp. 182–83.

[32] *Ibid.*

[33] *Ibid.*, p. 184.

[34] See Gosnell, *op cit.* (n. 7), p. 78; Logan, *op. cit.* (n. 4), p. 100; and the *Congressional Record*, 70th Congress, 1st Session, February 2, 1928, p. 2485.

CHAPTER 3

Emerging New Leadership in St. Louis

Despite St. Louis' having a small-ward system, black people in that city suffered from the same political and economic powerlessness as their sisters and brothers elsewhere in America. However, beginning in 1960, increasing numbers of younger blacks in St. Louis began to change their thinking, like younger blacks in other parts of this country, because of their rising consciousness as to how the total United States political system exerted a pervasive influence upon their lives. They began to regard themselves no longer as docile perpetual losers in a lifelong, generation-to-generation struggle with authority and its spokesmen. This, in part, explains why throughout this country "a shift occurred in Negro leadership, away from accommodationist civil dignitaries, tapped by whites as liaison spokesmen for the Negro subcommunity. . . ."[1]

The rising consciousness of these young black people helped produce a crisis for most old-line black leaders. The handpicked accommodaters held their positions primarily because they were acceptable to the white elite. To further aggravate their plight, they had traditionally only been endured by black people because the pervasive accommodationist mentality, now losing its grip, had previously been accepted by blacks as a way to get along with the elite. Now old-line blacks found their days numbered.

The rising black consciousness helped spark a series of protest demonstrations throughout the land. Those demonstrations were manifestations of the impatience on the part of many young blacks with the snail-like pace and lack of meaningful economic and political progress in the system. A type of tension was produced that helps explain why in many areas of the country the "middle-class leadership of the National Association for the Advancement of Colored People (NAACP)[2] and Urban League . . . [were] supplemented and jostled into new militancy by the direct-action protest organizers. . . ."[3]

The 1960 militant direct-action group in St. Louis was the Congress of Racial Equality (CORE).[4] Black St. Louis CORE members shed themselves of the accommodationist mentality and ceased to be of a mind to harmonize their aspirations and behavior by acquiescence to the status quo. Unlike old-line black St. Louisans, they no longer believed that they could—by solely utilizing discussion, negotiation, and compromise—effect immediate relief from the racist practices that had caused black St. Louisans to suffer so severely. As a result, they added another weapon to their arsenal by taking to the streets to make themselves heard.

In the late 1950's, several organizations and many well-known local blacks were responsible for negotiations in attempts to advance black St. Louisans. And there is ample evidence to indicate that before the mood of some young blacks in 1960 became one of impatience, they had waited optimistically in good faith as their elders negotiated. However, tendencies of anticipating progress from negotiations over time changed to loss of confidence and hope. Young blacks acquired an obstinate determination to seek an end to their galling state of quasi freedom and provided the incipient thrust that led to a measure of progress for black people in St. Louis. Their 1960 sit-in activities also made it easier for CORE to recruit new members.

But neither CORE nor the old-line black leaders provided the spark that helped usher in the new militancy. It was provided in the fall of 1960 by unnoted eighteen-year-old Arthur Shaw, a Vashon High School senior, and his nineteen-year-old classmate, Cecil Wright. These two young men began receiving citywide attention shortly after having been arrested twice in a twenty-four-hour period for restaurant sit-in demonstrations. The Shaw-Wright sit-in-movement attracted scores of other high school students, and many were arrested in the various demonstrations.[5]

Arthur Shaw had a North Leonard address and did not come from one of the so-called nice middle-class Negro families. Nevertheless, he was a manful, stouthearted, respected leader to those students who followed him. The manner in which young Shaw was treated by some black organization leaders caused some people to question whether or not black advancement in St. Louis was hypocritical. Was it to be a movement dominated by middle-class blacks to secure privileges and rights for themselves? Or was it to be a movement for all black people?

However, it is noteworthy that long before it became politically popular in St. Louis to become active in the "movement," one William L. Clay, a young black politician, was arrested in 1959 for his movement activities against one of the restaurants being picketed by Shaw.[6] Clay was to become the dominant black politician in St. Louis.

The *St. Louis Post-Dispatch* well documents that during the early stages of the "Shaw Movement," young Shaw and his followers received criticism from some people within the black community itself. Apparently not realizing that no plebeian movement is identical in different geographical areas, Shaw and his supporters were accused of not following behavior patterns established by those utilizing sit-ins in some Southern cities. In addition, initially, no organization would admit Shaw's movement was supported by it, or that he belonged to any organization.[7]

Evidently the demonstrations helped to create a situation whereby traditional segregated eating was being held together by a type of tension that disturbed unity among restaurant owners. Some of them began to recognize that there must be an irrevocable break with past racist practices. This was evidenced when one owner suggested that blacks be served under a system we would call a type of "continuum." According to the continuum plan, in the beginning only very fair or extremely light-skinned black people would be served. Gradually, from light to dark, bodily pigment would determine when each group of blacks would be served. It is difficult to see at what point along the "scale" the line would be drawn. Theoretically, it must have been assumed that black people's dissimilarity is based solely upon color. This suggestion was received by CORE as being so obnoxious that not much time and discussion were required for its rejection by blacks.[8]

By November of 1960 the then Mayor of St. Louis, Raymond Tucker, moved behind the scenes and effected an agreement whereby six operators of fourteen large cafeterias and restaurants removed color bars. It then became popular to support Shaw, and it was announced that he was part of the "youth arm" of the St. Louis NAACP. There is evidence that this must have been a most ambivalent period for some prominent St. Louis blacks. Some who had criticized young Shaw's techniques now readily and publicly stated that Shaw and his followers should receive credit for bringing things to a head after more than a decade of persuasion by individuals and groups had failed.[9]

Stirred by the Shaw Movement, St. Louis' black politicians intensified their efforts in behalf of black people, and by May of 1961, the Board of Aldermen had utilized the authority of the city's licensing and police powers to hammer out a public accommodation ordinance. The ordinance prohibited discrimination in public places because of race or religious beliefs, and its administration was assigned to the St. Louis Council on Human Relations. William L. Clay was one of the aldermen responsible for introduction of the bill.[10]

It has been shown that the power structure in St. Louis, that group which actually formulates and implements broad courses of action, consists of the dominant downtown business interests, office of the mayor, and other interests associated with these two. Black St. Louisans had made slight political progress through the 1950's but had failed to become a part of the power structure. They fought primary election battles for committeeman, alderman, and the like; but holders of such positions exercised comparatively little influence when it was time to decide which major policies would be adopted by the city.

Analysis of that period in St. Louis which stretched from the Liberty League days of the 1920's (see Chapter 4) through the 1960's reveals that the nature of the strategies of those black politicians who won elections had been and continued to be influenced and shaped by the citywide political system. And as black people sought more political control over their lives in the 1960's, whether or not the traditional citywide political system could adjust so as to include blacks in the group that formulated and implemented policies became a crucial point. Some believed that St. Louis' traditional process of selecting black leaders excluded them from exercising any great measure of influence when the city formulated broad

courses of action. As early as 1937, some black St. Louisans complained that white people selected those blacks as leaders who advocated what white people believed was good for black people.

> Colored St. Louis in part has accepted that pet trick of
> the white folks that was employed so successfully back in
> slavery—the setting up of a "one-man leader." It has been advo-
> cated and attempted here both civically and politically. The favor-
> ite advice of certain white leaders (not leader) has been: "you
> folks select your leader and send him to us," and when that event
> does not come about, they say, "well, well, you folks can't get
> together, so we'll have to do what we think is best." And they
> select some Negro who represents what they want represented.[11]

Also, as early as the 1930's blacks in St. Louis realized that some
blacks were chosen by whites to represent black people, not because
of any specific knowledge or technical skills they might have possessed, but because the elite found it desirable for various agencies
to have a black face on the payroll in order to legitimize decisions
affecting blacks made by the agency. Such token leaders did not
represent the militant elements in the black community, nor did
they speak for blacks who confronted their agencies with specific
issues. The fact that black people in general (correctly or not)
believed that the agency black possessed an agency viewpoint helped
cause them not to rely upon him to push their issues.

> Rarely is the token leader assertive on race issues in his capacity
> as a member of the public agency, and rarely does he take a
> position in opposition to the public agency on some matter of
> presumed concern to the race. The token leader justifies his actions
> by arguing that he was selected for his position not so much
> because of his race but because of his qualifications, that the prob-
> lems with which it deals are too complicated to be judged solely
> on the basis of racial factors, and that a wider perspective than
> race is necessary to discharge one's duties in a manner that will
> contribute to the public interest.[12]

This practice of not taking grassroots black leaders into consideration for appointments, and appointing only those who were suitable
according to white middle-class standards and who expended insignificant efforts for the total black community after appointment,
became reprehensible to many black people.

Whether we refer to St. Louis, Chicago, New York, Atlanta,

or some other American city, token leaders, especially those associated with some agency, are inimical to the black community since
they are usually nonassertive and not selflessly devoted to the black
community. Moreover, since the 1960's they have further reduced
their potential effectiveness by developing a justified insecurity.
When a black person with inept knowledge and no expertise re-
ceives an appointment because whites are of the opinion there is
a need for a person of color, such an appointee realizes that there
is a great likelihood that he will be challenged from within his
community. Therefore such an appointee will go to great lengths
to protect his insecure position and possibly come dangerously close
to acquiring Reverend Charles Merrill Smith's "Old Black Joe"
protectionist mentality.

> It is a genuine asset, in fact almost a necessity to have a Negro
> member of your church these days. . . . "Every church needs
> to have a pet nigger." And while we wouldn't want something
> like this said so crudely (in public) he may be right.
> The idea is that one Negro member works for you and makes
> your church look liberal, decent, christian in attitude, and inte-
> grated . . . so bold a step . . . might encourage the idea that your
> church actually wants and welcomes any and all Negroes who
> care to join. This . . . would be disastrous if colored people in
> any significant numbers took advantage of your goodwill.
> Make certain that you pick the right kind. Avoid at all costs
> the educated, professional, superior type of colored man who
> is a pace setter in the Negro community. Where he leads others
> follow.
> The very best kind, for your purposes, is a coal black, poor,
> semiliterate Negro bachelor, the "old Black Joe" type. He is no
> threat whatever to any of your people (a Negro schoolteacher,
> for example, would be better educated than some of your staunch
> members and they would resent this bitterly). And he would
> remind them of the days when racial relations were clearly defined
> and tranquil, not ambiguous and tension-filled as they are in our
> present society. In short, he would be looked on with affection
> as a pet. He would be cuddled, protected and prized. And he
> would not encourage other Negroes to follow him because they
> would be a threat to his privileged position.[13]

Insecure token leaders generally perceive of other blacks as
threats to their positions, whence there ceases to be honest contact
with their black brothers. On the other hand, it is highly possible

that counterfeit relationships help prevent nonagency blacks from knowing their weaknesses, thereby helping the token leader feel a measure of security. It has been shown that as early as 1937 blacks in St. Louis deplored whites selecting black leaders who represented white viewpoints. Then, as in the 1960's, the token leader had no rapport with black masses and no sizable following. Middle-class blacks would smile in his face, but they did not respect him; therefore he was a leader of no consequence. In the early 1960's, white St. Louis found it necessary to meet face-to-face the possibility that while it was selecting "Negro leaders," it was simultaneously sowing seeds which helped provide one of the causes for unrest in the black community.

This raises questions pertaining to black leadership in St. Louis. Did St. Louis blacks of the 1960's have leaders who selflessly devoted themselves to causes which would benefit black people as a race and as a community, or leaders that represented what the "white folks" wanted represented? Pertaining to an earlier period in Chicago, it was said "that there are 'no good' Negro leaders—leaders who are selflessly devoted to causes which will benefit Negroes as a race and as a community."[14] If one were to view many of the *St. Louis Defender*'s editorial cartoons for 1963 and 1964 depicting many St. Louis black leaders, it would be easy to conclude that those remarks pertaining to Chicago's black leadership could be considered very mild when applied to St. Louis black leadership.

In July of 1963, the *St. Louis Post-Dispatch* ran a series on the St. Louis black leadership's quandary and divisiveness because of the new black tactics. Evidently, in a general sense, there was no division as to goals. Apparently all involved in the intense struggle to lead generally agreed that educational policies, employment practices, and housing patterns should be changed so as to be more favorable for black people. In 1963 the vast majority publicly supported some form of direct action. The younger and more energetic black leaders were designated as the Clay-CORE group, later called the "young Turks."[15] Among its adherents were high school and college students, a few people past fifty, ministers, elementary and high school teachers, janitors, unskilled laborers, physicians and others associated with medical services, including anesthetists, lawyers, maids, steelworkers, unemployed men and women, postal workers, college instructors, and politicians. These people, along with their liberal and/or religious white associates, strove to improve black people's lot.

William Clay and several other CORE members were part of various ward political organizations. However, under CORE's umbrella, they were able to function as and present an almost united front. Some of those who directed CORE in 1963 and 1964 had formerly been members of the NAACP. And some had been very active in the civil rights movement prior to 1960. As a result, they were sufficiently well informed and experienced to direct CORE. There will possibly continue to be a controversy over whether they left the NAACP solely because of its accommodating practices or whether the less direct action-minded NAACP did not welcome energetic young people.

In addition to relying on Bill Clay's administrative and organizational abilities, CORE was aided by an energetic, comely black woman whose magnetism served as a cohesive element. Marion Oldham was also very active in various other community organizations, and therefore she was able to garner additional support for CORE. Her husband, Charles Oldham, at one time had served as the white national president of CORE and had played a role in helping formulate goals and strategies for St. Louis CORE.[16] Three young black lawyers were also active. They, along with Charles Oldham, Adam Casmier (teacher), and other politically minded members, helped develop part of St. Louis CORE's ideology. "Freedom now" to them included political opportunity and political rewards. They sought political gains not primarily for their own sakes, but as a means of obtaining enhanced economic opportunities, more meaningful education, and improved housing for black people. Also high on their list of aims was for blacks to hold citywide elective offices and to receive bureaucratic appointments with the same fringe benefits received by whites. Within this group, very little public attention or credit has been given to one whose influence permeated the organization. A little known postal employee, Walter Hayes, serving as treasurer, did much more than read the financial report at each meeting; he greatly helped keep the organization functioning.

Such people, along with others, directed CORE, and they were not dictatorial and dominating. The style of CORE meetings, a far cry from NAACP meetings, was so democratic that the give-

and-take which resulted helped hold together its diverse membership. The professional people who were part of this group showed
no arrogance toward less affluent blacks. It was common, for example, to see informal conversations and discussions with both professionals and nonprofessionals participating. In 1963 and 1964, it
was not unusual for 100 or more people to attend Sunday CORE
meetings; frequently there were not enough chairs. Every person
in attendance had an opportunity to speak, and votes were taken
in the public meetings. Possibly the only resentment expressed toward other blacks was that which CORE members held toward
those identified as representing the police, and toward James Q.
Wilson's "adviser" type of black person who was paid to supply
"intelligence" pertaining to the black community.

Those black leaders who were opposed to the young Turks were
much older and were generally well established in the community.
Most were associated with the NAACP; and the Clay group accused
a few of them of being what we have described as "advisers,"
thus impairing their effectiveness as leaders. Others were charged
with having the type of political ties which caused them to be
"committed to seek improvements for Negroes through channels.[17]
However, some members of old established groups charged that
Clay himself was associated with the AFL-CIO Steamfitters' Union
Local 562, which withdrew its manual from an apprenticeship training program in St. Louis schools when the first two blacks were
enrolled in the course. Assuming this to be an accurate charge,
later policies designed to recruit black men for the steamfitters
seemed to enhance Bill Clay's stature.[18]

The disunity of these two groups had political implications. Generally speaking, those blacks who had confidence in negotiations
were aligned with what has been identified as the dominant downtown elite. The activists were generally aligned with the spot-zoning
groups. But despite political, ideological, and tactical disagreements,
and despite their leadership positions being challenged, some members of the old guard gave Clay credit for fighting for black people.
Accordingly, some members of the old group stated that "even
if Clay is advancing himself politically through the race issue, he
is at the same time doing an excellent job of fighting for equal
opportunities for Negroes."[19]

Despite disagreements with the Clay-CORE group, the older

group did not openly challenge or frequently criticize the young Turks publicly. Aside from fearing possible ill effects if such a challenge were made and lost, some believed an open fight with the young Turks would have been detrimental to blacks in general. Regardless of reasons, failure to challenge indicated that what had transpired was more than just a split in black leadership, that there was actually new black leadership emerging.

New black leadership meant that St. Louis' elite would have to learn to deal with blacks whose not-so-accommodating style reflected a shift in the mood of the black community. Aggravating the situation for the elite was the fact that the ascendance of the new leadership did more than just displace old-line leaders. Many of those who formerly advocated gradualism desired to maintain some type of leadership status, and in order to do this they found it necessary to become more aggressive and less cooperative with the elite. Thus, the appearance of younger black leaders in St. Louis marked the beginning of a drive strongly predicated on the idea that it was necessary to pressure and annoy the establishment in order to open its eyes.

Politically oriented and alert young Turks becoming ascendant in St. Louis was possibly made easier by the death of committeeman Jordan Chambers in 1962. As a young man, in 1932, Chambers left the Republican party and helped George L. Vaughn lead black people into Democratic ranks. His power was continuously augmented until he became St. Louis' most powerful black politician. With the death of Chambers, and the inability of any of his contemporaries to acquire enough power to become dominant, the young Turks were in a more commanding position. It was not accidental that no established black leader could become dominant after 1962. Bill Clay and the young Turks bitterly denounced the established black leaders for being too responsive to the desires and wishes of the elite and for supporting Democratic candidates who were opposed or indifferent to the needs of black people.[20]

St. Louis' new black leaders held title to what seemed to be a different concept concerning communication between the races. They believed "that there . . . [was] no real communication between the white and Negro communities. Existing lines . . . [were] between white leaders and white appointed Negroes who . . . [did] not represent the masses." They were convinced that "the

problem . . . was that of 'Uncle Toms,' white-controlled leaders
who insidiously preach gradualism."[21] Thus, the establishment was
placed in a position where it became necessary for it to reevaluate
its communication ties with the black community. Reevaluation
was especially imperative because of the breakdown in communications that had occurred between the races; however, in a sense
this breakdown had occurred only because of unilateral action on
the part of the power structure.

Actually, in St. Louis in particular, and in America generally,
there never has been any communication between the establishment
and the black community. The only communication that had transpired in St. Louis prior to the 1960's was between the power structure or its representatives and those old-line blacks who were noncontroversial and who often operated in some clandestine manner
and accepted the view that whatever the elite decided was good
for black people was all right. With few exceptions, this has been
historically true for blacks in all of America:

> With exceptions such as Nat Turner, Harriet Tubman,
> Sojourner Truth, and Frederick Douglass, the Negro leaders of
> their time were passive, meek, and exceedingly solicitous of the
> white man's approbation. . . .
> The impoverishment of Negro political power is best reflected
> by the national Negro leadership of the early Twentieth Century.
> After Douglass, there seemed to be no national spokesman to whom
> whites could turn to find out what the Negro was thinking. But
> in 1896, they found one who would gladden their hearts. . . .
> Booker T. Washington quickly became the national Negro
> spokesman, and he said precisely what America's whites wanted
> to hear and believe. Washington's brand of head-scratching, shoe-
> shuffling accommodation to segregation angered the more militant
> Negro leaders, such as W. E. B. Du Bois. . . .[22]

By the early 1960's old-line noncontroversial, head-scratching,
shoe-shuffling blacks were increasingly no longer endured by the
black community regardless of how acceptable they were to whites.
But the power structure and its representatives unilaterally refused
to deal with the ascending militant black leaders, who before receiving publicity because of their direct action techniques, had been
anonymous ciphers as far as the establishment was concerned.[23]

The elite had no desire to deal with these new leaders because they were uncompromising and unwilling to communicate in an accommodating fashion. So, in this sense there was a breakdown in communications. This is the type of situation discussed by Charles Silberman.

> . . . Negro leaders are determined that "the white power structure" recognize them and negotiate with them—that public officials, businessmen, and civic leaders come to the bargaining table not as patrons but as equals. They are insisting that whites recognize the leaders selected by the Negro community itself, whoever they may be or however distasteful the whites may find them. . . .
>
> . . . For nothing rankles Negroes quite so much as the white power structure's habit of choosing the Negro "leader" whom it wants to reward or with whom it wants to deal. The habit is strongest in the South, of course, where the almost total lack of communication between the races makes it easier for whites to deal with Negroes through colored intermediaries . . . through straw bosses of their own choosing. And the whites naturally enough have chosen only Negroes willing to accommodate themselves to white interest.[24]

Where prior to the 1960's established black leaders dominated the NAACP in St. Louis, a viable CORE grew up in the 1960's that was not under their control.[25] As CORE became more influential and respected in the black community of St. Louis it came to be unavoidable, in regard to many matters, for the elite to deal with several blacks previously unknown outside of the black community, blacks who like their leader, Bill Clay, were determined not to echo sedulously the words of the establishment.

NOTES

[1] Dwaine Marvick, "The Political Socialization of the American Negro," *The Annals of the American Academy of Political and Social Science,* CCCLXI (September, 1965), p. 112.

[2] Henceforward the National Association for the Advancement of Colored People will be referred to as NAACP.

[3] Marvick, *op. cit.,* p. 112.

[4] Henceforward the Congress of Racial Equality will be referred to as CORE.

[5] *Post,* October 20, 1960, p. 1.

[6] *St. Louis Crusader,* October 28, 1969, p. 1.

[7] *Post,* November 4, 1960, p. 3A.

[8] Interview with Marion Oldham, Former St. Louis CORE Chairman, November 20, 1967.

[9] *Post,* November 7, 1960, p. 26.

[10] St. Louis, Missouri, *The City Journal,* XLIV (June 6, 1961), p. 21.

[11] Nathan B. Young, ed., *Your St. Louis and Mine* (St. Louis, Mo.: N. B. Young, 1938), pp. 66–67.

[12] James Q. Wilson, *Negro Politics: The Search for Leadership* (Glencoe, Ill.: The Free Press, 1960), p. 263.

[13] Charles Merrill Smith, *How to Become a Bishop Without Being Religious* (New York: Doubleday, 1965), pp. 86–87.

[14] Wilson, *op. cit.,* p. 3.

[15] Richard Jacobs, *Post,* July 21, 1963, p. 1B.

[16] *Ibid.*

[17] *Ibid.*

[18] Steamfitters John L. (Doc) Lawler and Lawrence Callanan and some other labor leaders were indicted in 1953 by a federal grand jury for labor racketeering. They were charged with conspiring to extort $50,000 from a contractor. Callanan was sent to prison and is now out. The racketeering charges against Lawler were dismissed after several years.

[19] Jacobs, *op. cit.* (n. 14).

[20] Charles E. Silberman, *Crisis in Black and White* (New York: Random House, 1964), pp. 208–09. Also see Richard Jacobs, *Post,* July 23, 1963, p. 8C.

[21] Richard Jacobs, *Post,* July 22, 1963, p. 8C.

[22] Chuck Stone, *Black Political Power in America* (Indianapolis: Bobbs-Merrill, 1968), pp. 36–37, 39.

[23] See Lewis M. Killian and Charles U. Smith, "Negro Protest Leaders in a Southern Community," *Social Forces,* XXXVIII (March, 1960), pp. 253–57.

[24] Silberman, *op. cit.,* pp. 195–96.

[25] For a discussion as to how this situation affected Atlanta, see Jack L. Walker, "Protest and Negotiation: A Case Study of Negro Leadership in Atlanta, Georgia," *Midwest Journal of Political Science,* VII (1963), pp. 99–124.

CHAPTER 4

Small Ward: Foundation for Black Political Power

Black political activists who desire to see blacks serving on city elective policy-making bodies cannot simply say to the black electorate that since blacks comprise a given percentage of the voting age population, therefore, black people will elect that percentage of the members of the city council. It is not that simple, even if there are both a high measure of cohesion and a large number of politically socialized blacks herded into a city's black natural neighborhood. In order to accomplish this kind of goal, black political activists of the 1970's will have to do their homework, working hard to gain full understanding of a given political situation, as did those blacks in an earlier period who were able to elect a councilman or two here and there.

There is some evidence that, prior to the 1930's, some blacks in some cities did their homework and that their diligence helped them to engage in what they called "winning" political activity. It is true that much of what has been labeled as successful black political activity of the past actually amounted to black acquisition of only a few elective and appointive offices, plus some day-to-day survival benefits for some other blacks. In contrast, during the 1970's, black political activists will consider black political activity successful only if it effects meaningful black inputs in policy-making and the elimination of total white administration of those policies which fundamentally affect the lives of black people.

Although blacks will demand a more substantive effect on policies during the 1970's than their brothers of earlier years, their anticipated gains will not be realized unless and until they work hard to achieve an understanding of how to accomplish these gains. They must learn, for example, what factors allowed blacks in some cities to gain elective office earlier than blacks in some other cities and how these same elements or circumstances will affect today's black political activity. These factors (in-migration, housing patterns, strength of the dominant white political party, and the city's electoral structure) cannot be overlooked. Sufficient research and application of the mind will not only reveal to blacks how these elements affected past black political activity and their possible influence on future political activity, but a thorough examination of them will help enable blacks to plan effective strategies. Such an examination will also reveal a great deal about how the political game is played in a given city. Knowing the rules of the game in a particular city is essential in order to devise winning strategies.

It is most important that black people not believe that the only necessary ingredients for blacks to win elective office are effective organization, cohesion, and political socialization within the black natural neighborhood. True, these factors are important, but they in themselves are not sufficient to cause black people to acquire meaningful representation on elective policy-making bodies.

In St. Louis it appears that by 1920 there was a measure of cohesion within the black community and the Citizens Liberty League was organized to attempt to win elective and appointive offices for black people. Looking back, one can see that officers of the Liberty League had done their homework and were prepared to play the game according to existing political rules. The League's leaders persuaded white Republicans in 1920 that St. Louis' black vote could be delivered for A. M. Hyde as governor, if Republicans would help the League implement its platform. Among other planks it advocated election or appointment of blacks in several capacities: committeemen, committeewomen (if women were enfranchised), aldermen, state legislators, constables, U.S. Representative, firemen, additional clerks in city hall, and members of petit and grand juries. The League saw some of its dreams become concrete realities: a constable, a committeeman, firemen, a state representative, and jury service.[1]

Concrete evidence that League members had done their homework is seen in the decision that affected this active support in behalf of a gubernatorial candidate in 1920. Black people resented that there were no regular black uniformed police officers. High on the League's list of demands to be satisfied in exchange for its support was the demand that blacks would be hired as uniformed policemen in St. Louis.[2] This demand was most significant because the St. Louis police department was and continues to be controlled by a Board of Police Commissioners appointed by the Governor. Originally, the device was adopted to enable a pro-southern state administration to maintain police control in a unionist city. In later years, it gave a Democratic state administration patronage to dispose of in a normally Republican city.[3]

The League won its point. Not only were blacks hired as uniformed policemen, but allegedly they were personally trained by the president of the new Board of Police Commissioners, who had been appointed by the League-supported Governor.[4]

Was this another example of white paternalism? Or was it recognition by the elite of the reality of black political power? Did it represent both?

There is little doubt that the Republican elite did not highly appreciate the League's power to influence the political actions of black St. Louisans. An effective League could only lessen the elite's influence in the black community, especially since the League's leaders had proved themselves to be effective political organizers. One is tempted to classify them as adroit tacticians who had learned how to utilize organization for the benefit of black people. However, the Republican elite took a step to prevent losing its influence among black people. In the same year, 1920, white Republicans decided that they could keep blacks loyal to them and lessen the League's influence in the black community by supporting their own black candidate for the state legislature. They put up a black postal worker who did not make a single speech or engage in any so-called active political campaigning. He was elected.[5]

But it was not until 1922 that black people in St. Louis began to acquire a small measure of political control in a black ward. In that year, Robert T. Scott was elected Republican committeeman in the Sixth Ward, thus becoming the first black man to serve on the Republican City Central Committee. The Seventeenth Ward white committeewoman died in 1922 and Mrs. Elizabeth Gamble was appointed to fill the post, becoming the first black committeewoman. Scott's election was significant for local black people because the position of ward committeeman is the focal point of city political power.[6]

The Liberty League-Republican marriage was continually beset with trouble, and by 1932 the relationship became so rocky that divorce proceedings were instituted. A main source of incompatibility stemmed from the fact that loyalty to the Republicans had gained very little patronage for black people. Also, more than a decade of Republican unconcernedness for the black community, along with the Republican feeling of certainty that they had a firm hold on black votes, made it possible for Attorney George L. Vaughn, one of the original and more powerful Liberty League members, and Jordan W. Chambers to lead a large number of younger blacks (aged 21 to 35) into Democratic ranks. By 1937, 60 percent of the 50,000 St. Louis black voters were Democrats. Of the 19 acknowledged black Democratic leaders, only two were over 50. Whatever political astuteness they were in need of, resulting from a lack of experience, was more than compensated for by their zealous enthusiasm and positive outlook for the future. On the other hand, of the 43 recognized black Republican leaders, only three were under 40; 33 were over 55.[7]

Efforts to hold black people in Republican ranks in 1932 centered around such tired slogans as: "(1) no self-respecting black person could support Franklin D. Roosevelt, the candidate of a party which Jim Crowed and disfranchised blacks; (2) black people should stay with the party of Abraham Lincoln who issued the Emancipation Proclamation."[8]

Despite references to Lincoln and the Emancipation Proclamation, St. Louis Democrats received increasing black support from 1932 until 1940. Between 1940 and 1943, it appeared that blacks were shifting their political allegiance and the 1943 municipal election suggested that neither party controlled the black vote. However, blacks returned to the Democratic party to support Harry Truman in 1948,[9] and they have continued to vote overwhelmingly as Democrats in local as well as national elections since that time.[10]

Historically, black political leaders have not been very effectual in helping to accomplish beneficial economic, social, and political changes in behalf of black people. This is true primarily because in large cities black political influence has not increased proportionately to increases in the black populations. Therefore, those who are willing to try to see if black people can become a fully accepted part of this political system with political representation in proportion to black numerical strength must seek out and examine the causes of this historical fact. Efforts must also be made to devise strategies to see if the system will willingly accept blacks. Even if such strategies are devised and developed immediately, it may be too late since a growing number of black people—and not all of these are young—are coming to believe that this system will not work to the advantage of nor absorb black people in a meaningful manner. Such strategies must be developed for large cities, for it is here with the heavy concentration of blacks that any such strategies will have to be put to test. If they fail in large cities, it is highly doubtful that any type of scheme can be developed that will meaningfully incorporate black people into this system.

Those black people seeking causes for a low correlation between effective black political power and the number of black people living in a given city would do well to begin by determining why there were some black elected officials in some cities years before there were elected black officials in other cities where large numbers of blacks lived.

Black men were able to gain elective office in Chicago and St. Louis a little earlier than their brothers in some eastern, northern, and western cities. In Chicago a black man was elected to the city council in 1915 (the 1871 county commission position was not too politically significant in terms of power), and in 1920 a black man became ward committeeman. This was significant because the committeeman and not the alderman possessed power in Chicago wards.[11] In St. Louis a black man was elected constable in 1918 and a black man from the city went to the state legislative body in 1920. More meaningfully, St. Louis blacks nibbled at real political power when in 1922 a black man became ward committeeman. As in Chicago, St. Louis ward committeemen, instead of the alderman representing a ward, held the power. Despite aldermen being subservient to committeemen, St. Louis did not elect a black alderman until 1943. We will examine the structural reason for this shortly.

Early elected black public officials in Chicago and St. Louis were Republicans because the effective political power of those cities was held by white Republicans. A major factor that helped cause Chicago and St. Louis blacks to gain elective offices ahead of blacks in some other cities was that the Republican party organizations were strong in both cities, and historically, where parties played a prominent role in local elections, efforts were usually made to organize and control the vote in the black community for the benefit of the Republican party.[12]

The rate of in-migration and the density of the black population helped determine at what time in history black people were able to gain elective office. And in Chicago, New York, and St. Louis, blacks migrated early to all-black areas. Along with the two afore-mentioned elements, the presence or absence of a third element, structure of electoral districts, greatly helps determine whether or not there will be elected black public officials. If a city's political system, like those of Chicago and St. Louis, is based upon a number of relatively small wards with boundary lines generally drawn to conform as nearly as possible to natural neighborhoods of various ethnic or religious groups, it is easier for black people to elect city officials than when a political system is based upon large districts or an at-large system. The smaller the political unit the more diffi-cult it is to draw lines so that blacks will not be able to win elective office.[13]

There is another potential benefit for the black community when a city operates under a small-ward system. There is a greater dis-persal of power (spread among the various wards) which gives all citizens, and in particular black citizens in black-controlled wards, more points of access or avenues to influence city govern-ment—a policy which better ensures that natural neighborhoods, whether ethnic or religious, will receive better representation. If one had compared the political systems of Chicago and St. Louis prior to the 1930's with that of New York City, many similarities would have been found. However, although there were more black people living in New York than in either Chicago or St. Louis, no black man became a district leader and part of New York's Tammany Hall until 1935. It took another six years to get a second black district leader. This resulted, in some measure, because New York City's districts were relatively larger than Chicago's or St. Louis' wards. And the larger the electoral district the easier it is to gerrymander and prevent blacks from gaining elective office.[14]

An understanding of black people's quest for political power in urban America necessitates consideration of a fourth element—extent of partisanship. New York operates with large partisan districts while Los Angeles has large nonpartisan districts. Large districts in combination with nonpartisanship have hurt black people politically in Los Angeles. Rather than possessing the strong partisan flavor found in Chicago and St. Louis politics, Los Angeles is generally nonpartisan, with the resulting absence of strong ward leaders. It is necessary to be aware of the fact that it is easier for black people to move into the political arena in a given city where there is a strong party organization since parties historically seek to capture the black vote.[15]

Although nonpartisanship did nothing to facilitate black entry into Los Angeles politics, there is no evidence that this is the reason for nonpartisanship coming into existence in that state. In fact, nonpartisanship in California represents the successful efforts of Progressives to minimize political party influence in the electoral process.

By the turn of the century the Southern Pacific Railroad had successfully used its economic power to become politically influential in California politics, and the dominant Republican Party's Progressive wing sought to curb that influence. By 1909, the direct primary had replaced the party convention as the method to select candidates and the Progressives used it to capture control of the Republican party and move into the legislature. By 1913, the party circle was eliminated from the ballot, thus making it more toilsome to vote a straight party ticket. Cross-filling was introduced, and all city and county elective offices were made nonpartisan. Not only was there no strong party organization to facilitate black ingress into Los Angeles' political system, but the absence of patronage and material incentives—the very stuff that helps build and cement a party—made it unlikely that there would be a strong machinelike party system in Los Angeles in the future.[16] In fact, the Los Angeles County Committee was possibly the most active in California, but unlike the strong well-oiled party apparatuses in Chicago and St. Louis, it was debilitated, languid, and fragmentary.

In many other cities there was heavy black migration, partly as a result of economic opportunities created during the World War I period. The heavy black migration was not experienced by Los Angeles, however, until after World War II. As a result, there was no black city councilman in Los Angeles until 1963 when the council prevented Mayor Yorty's candidate from occupying a vacant seat by appointing a black man. Later that same year, the black appointee and two other black men became the first black men to be elected to the fifteen-member body.[17] It is rather ironic that Los Angeles' black people could not elect a black city councilman until the year they were also able to send a black man to the United States Congress. In 1963, Louisiana-born Augustus F. Hawkins was elected to Congress from Los Angeles' Twenty-first District. He had served in the California State Assembly ever since 1934.[18] Chicago, by contrast, first elected a black councilman in 1915, and a congressman in 1928. New York elected its first black district leader in 1935 and its first black congressman in 1944; and St. Louis elected its first black constable in 1918, first black committeeman in 1922, and first alderman in 1943, but did not elect a black congressman until 1968.

In addition to the lack of strong party organization and the presence of nonpartisan elections, population dispersion adversely affected black political ambitions in Los Angeles. Most central-city Los Angeles' blacks did not live in apartments and tenements as did their sisters and brothers in Chicago, New York, and St. Louis. Instead, they lived in an enormous number of small, single-family homes and duplexes spread over a wide area, producing a less dense population. This dispersion, along with the statutory requirement that the large heterogeneous councilmanic districts be reapportioned every four years, further disadvantaged blacks politically. A good deal of laborious effort was expended to insure that redistricting would not operate to the advantage of Los Angeles blacks. Since it is relatively easy to gerrymander large districts, this exertion was successful until the election of three black men in 1963.[19]

Apparently the black housing pattern in Los Angeles helped some black people acquire a false impression about the city which in some degree accounted for their being less assertative longer than blacks in some other cities:

> The existence of a less densely populated Negro community spread out over a considerable space, coupled with a general level of prosperity and an optimistic view of the future tends to reduce the number and intensity of Negro demands for change. Los

Angeles Negro leaders, for example, speak of the city and its problems with a tone and rhetoric that is in marked contrast to that employed by comparable Chicago leaders. Problems in Los Angeles are not felt so keenly nor is the status quo viewed with much despair, even though the denial of opportunities to Negroes may in fact be every bit as high. The city government takes little interest in race relations. . . .[20]

We believe that this less densely populated black community, along with the somewhat optimistic view of the future that Los Angeles blacks possessed, helped to reduce the number and intensity of black demands in the early 1960's in Los Angeles as compared to those of blacks in some other cities. However, we additionally believe that the discernible absence of concerted protest action among Los Angeles blacks in the early 1960's can also, in part, be accounted for by the nature of the declared goals sought, the diffusion of targets that were apropos, and the segmentation of the black community along class lines (including those middle-class blacks that black sociologist E. Franklin Frazier portrays in his *Black Bourgeoisie* as being in a world of make-believe).

These kinds of perceptions by various black communities, in Los Angeles and elsewhere, influenced the level of, or degree of, black protest. Regardless of the extent of this influence, we possibly would be in error if we failed to consider additional factors that may also have influenced the level and nature of black protest. For instance, the level of protest activity can be partially influenced by the perceptivity of formal and informal leaders, including officers of various community organizations (because of their own maintenance needs). When such leaders (and organizations) perceive the need for protest, they tend to reward those who lead protest action. Thus, in effect, they encourage a higher level of activity. When they do not sense the immediate need for such activity, they are reluctant to confer praise upon leaders of protest, thereby encouraging less protest activity.[21]

Whereas the perceptivity (as to goals, apropos targets, and the like) of blacks in Los Angeles in the early 1960's possibly helped confrontation politics to be dormant, it is highly possible that the gerrymander which made it possible to exclude blacks from the governing circles in Los Angeles was very costly. The Los Angeles

Times' Robert C. Kirsch believed that the exclusion made itself felt in various ways, especially since the only contact many blacks had with the "city government was through the Police Department, and then largely in situations that involved trouble."[22]

This factor of exclusion becomes most significant when considered along with expectations. Throughout the world many rural and small-town people move to urban areas expecting rapid improvement of their economic lot. Once migrants take up residence in the city, in most cases they quickly acquire tastes for many diverse consumer goods amply displayed. The greater the degree to which a society organizes itself around consumption and growth, the greater the likelihood that dangerous pressures will develop.[23] And since the mid-1950's, America has experienced consumption and expansion pressures. Vance Packard discusses this in *The Hidden Persuaders:* "In late 1955 the church publication *Christianity and Crisis* commented grimly on America's 'ever-expanding economy.' It observed that the pressure was on Americans to 'consume, consume, consume, whether we need or even desire the products almost forced upon us.' It added that the dynamics of an ever-expanding system require that we be 'persuaded to consume to meet the needs of the productive process.' "[24]

There were several causative factors as to why those blacks in Watts of Los Angeles released their pent-up resentments in 1965 to the extent that thirty-four were left dead.[25] Along with political exclusion, among other causes, it is highly possible that their released resentments represented bitterness against being deprived of the right to participate in the urban consumption orgy. And it would be extremely difficult, if not impossible, to prove that rural blacks, like other rural people who move into cities, do not acquire tastes for many of the diverse consumer goods as their expectations rise. If there is a semblance of truth in this assumption, it could partly explain why there were attacks upon stores in Watts, particularly on those which had lured the unsuspecting with "easy" consumer credit and then repossessed the treasured symbols of urban dignity. Los Angeles' blacks resented the terms which allowed them to participate in the consumption debauch.[26]

Political exclusion, the inability to participate in the consumption debauch, as well as the herding of people into specific city areas because of ethnicity all mark black peoples' subordinate role in

America. Herding black people into designated areas of a city and effectively segregating them from the white majority actually installs a form of political and social inequality bearing the mark of a subservient population within the larger political community. Nevertheless, whenever there is a racial crisis, the elite pays a price for forcing black people to live in so-called natural areas. When subject people are herded together, this makes possible the flow of information at an accelerated pace because of the narrowness of the channel and the homogeneity of the medium. Example: a rumor can sweep Harlem in a fraction of the time required for it to circulate through midtown Manhattan. Also, the herding of black people together made it possible for a movement like that of the Honorable Elijah Muhammed to grow, prosper, and survive.[27]

At the turn of the century, poor whites were also living in so-called natural neighborhoods. And during that period many potentially critical situations and possible revolts involving the working class in New York were apparently effectively handled to the satisfaction of the elite because of the elaborate personal and unreserved communication system developed by political party machinery. Apparently this kind of communicative apparatus allowed the party to exercise a high degree of social control at the local level. However, in the 1960's, even in those American cities where there was effective party machinery, there was no adequate communication system capable of dissuading herded black people from releasing resentment. And in Los Angeles, where there was an absence of a well-oiled machinelike party apparatus, there was even less communication between the herded blacks and the elite. Robert L. Kirsch believed that the exclusion made itself felt in many ways. His conviction is substantiated by the fact that once Watts went the one step beyond being just a potential crisis, the elite and city officials could not find local black leadership in Watts through whom they could communicate with Malcolm's "field niggers." This was true because for years potential black leaders had been excluded from the elite's policy decision-making machinery in Los Angeles, and the "field niggers" consequently had no confidence in or communication with in-name-only leaders.[28]

Despite the fact that most "good government" people abhor the concept of city government being based upon relatively small wards with lines generally drawn for racial, economic, and religious reasons, such a system has the potential to facilitate black people's entry into politics. St. Louis committeemen were elected by wards and black people elected a committeeman by 1922. Aldermen were elected on a citywide basis until the city charter was changed in 1943 to elect them by wards. In that very same year, Reverand Jasper C. Caston, Republican candidate for alderman in the Sixth Ward, became St. Louis' first black alderman. And in 1945 Walter Lowe, veteran ward worker, who was elected alderman over attorney David Grant, became the second black alderman. Therefore it can be seen that the small-ward system helped black St. Louisans gain elective office.

NOTES

[1] Herman H. Dreer, *Argus,* January 21, 1966, p. 3B.

[2] *Ibid.*

[3] Robert H. Salisbury, "St. Louis Politics: Relationships Among Interests, Parties, and Governmental Structure," *Western Political Quarterly,* XIII (June, 1960), pp. 500–01.

[4] Dreer, *op. cit.*

[5] *Ibid.*

[6] Howard F. Fisher, "The Negro in Saint Louis Politics, 1932–1948," (unpublished master's thesis, St. Louis University, 1951) p. 13.

[7] Nathan B. Young, ed., *Your St. Louis and Mine* (St. Louis, Mo.: N. B. Young, 1938), p. 38.

[8] Fisher, *op. cit.,* p. 21.

[9] *Ibid.,* pp. 74, 86.

[10] Salisbury, *op. cit.,* p. 502.

[11] James Q. Wilson, *Negro Politics: The Search for Leadership* (Glencoe, Ill.: The Free Press, 1960), pp. 23–26.

[12] Charles R. Adrian and Charles Press, *Governing Urban America* (New York: McGraw-Hill, 1968), p. 248.

[13] Wilson, *op. cit.,* pp. 23–26.

[14] *Ibid.,* pp. 25–28.

[15] James Q. Wilson, *The Amateur Democrat: Club Politics in Three Cities* (Chicago: The University of Chicago Press, Phoenix Edition, 1966), pp. 96–98.

[16] *Ibid.,* p. 101.

[17] Edward C. Banfield and James Q. Wilson, *City Politics* (Cambridge, Mass.: Harvard University Press, 1963), pp. 243–45.

[18] Mary Meyer, "Black Congressmen and How They Grew," *The Black Politician: A Journal of Current Political Thought,* I (April, 1970), pp. 3–11.

[19] Edward C. Banfield, *Big City Politics* (New York: Random House, 1965, p. 87; and Wilson's *Negro Politics, op. cit.* (n. 11), pp. 27–28, 108.

[20] Wilson, *Negro Politics, op. cit.* (n. 11) p. 108.

[21] As it pertains to Chicago and New York, this central theme is discussed in James Q. Wilson, "The Strategy of Protest: Problems of Negro Civic Action," *Journal of Conflict Resolution,* V (September, 1961), pp. 291–303.

[22] See Robert Kirch's Introduction to Jerry Cohen and William Murphy, *Burn, Baby, Burn!!: The Watts Riot* (New York: Avon Books, 1967), p. 15.

[23] John W. Dyckman, "Some Conditions of Civic Order in an Urbanized World," *Daedalus,* XCV (Summer, 1966), pp. 797–812.

[24] Vance Packard, *The Hidden Persuaders* (New York: David Mackay Co., 1957), p. 14.

[25] *Revolution in Civil Rights* (Washington, D.C.: Congressional Quarterly Service, June, 1968), p. 12.

[26] Dyckman, *op. cit.,* p. 803.

[27] *Ibid.,* 803–804.

[28] *Ibid.,* pp. 807–809.

CHAPTER 5

Black People: At-Large, Nonpartisan Elections

It has been somewhat difficult for black people in Los Angeles to move into the political arena because the city is formally nonpartisan and because there is an absence of strong ward leaders or a powerful party organization to seek to capture the black vote. Although Detroit city politics is also nonpartisan, and genuinely so, politics there has differed from that of nonpartisan Los Angeles because of the existence of an extensive labor movement of great power which has endeavored to operate in the same manner as a political organization. Like party apparatus, it endorses slates of candidates and makes attempts to organize workers in most precincts.

Labor, as a political organization in Michigan, worked with various groups of white liberals and the regular Democratic party at the state level to help Michigan enact Fair Employment Practice Commission legislation. The CIO United Auto Workers could afford to support such legislation because it was attractive to blacks and alienated few white workers. This coalition also helped to elect a governor, two United States senators, and many other statewide officials. However, those elections were plainly partisan. From the black perspective, the same coalition was ineffective in the nonpartisan city of Detroit. It could not dominate the city council nor defeat conservative four-time mayor, Albert E. Cobo.[1]

Black voters were an intimate part of this coalition, and they were so set against Cobo that they always voted heavily for his opponent. Nevertheless, the coalition could not defeat Cobo despite some white liberals believing, as did many black leaders, that Cobo's policies pertaining to public housing and real estate were antiblack, and that he appealed to whites who felt threatened by black residential expansion.[2]

Detroit's black people paid a dear price to be part of this coalition. Blacks could not influence the union to vigorously champion race issues when they moved from the national or state arena closer home to Detroit itself. With close-to-home issues it was necessary for the union to consider others, such as the Poles or Southern whites, who either were in the CIO or trod in the steps of its leadership politically. Therefore, being in alliance or confederation with the powerful Detroit CIO did not help black people with close-to-home issues like housing. "Lily white neighborhood 'improvement associations,' created to keep Negroes out of certain residential areas, often shared members with a CIO union."[3]

The price was dear, in part, because some black people believed that blacks could not afford to press too hard in behalf of black people collectively for fear of alienating other groups in the coalition. To have done so possibly would have raised the level of conflict between white ethnic groups and blacks, and internal fighting would have impaired the union's chances for success either in union bargaining or political campaigns. This point is significant because the union leadership was primarily concerned with the chances for success of the organization as a whole, and not with specific black concern for full citizenship.

The dear price can also, in part, be attributed to the fact that the union was "integrated." This is somewhat ironic since the union was first confronted with blacks when they were used as strike breakers in the 1930's. Later, blacks were incorporated into the union movement in a manner dissimilar to that used by many craft-oriented unions. Rather than segregating blacks into separate, all-black locals, the Detroit UAW admitted blacks in all locals. As a result, in the late 1950's and early 1960's, sizable numbers of blacks were found in most locals. In some as many as one-fourth to one-third of the membership was black. Thus, blacks could not control any single local and found it necessary to be content with such secondary positions as recording secretaries. Had there been a few all-black locals, there would have been a few black local presidents. Many blacks felt frustrated because they were subordinated to the point that blacks held very few official union positions.[4]

Not only were black auto workers subordinated and denied top positions in the union, but the union subordinated and influenced black people in Detroit in another manner. The UAW provided strong support for the Detroit NAACP, so much so that some of the NAACP's black leadership were concerned as to how the organization could maintain its image of independence. The UAW's support was so strong that it provided much white liberal leadership, and to some extent, impaired the effectiveness and reduced the size and importance of black leadership in the NAACP.[5] In political activity, the CIO concentrated heavily on Detroit's black areas and often experienced the results contemplated. It sought and received black votes for white congressional incumbents against black challengers in the late 1950's. But it did not help black people elect one of their own kind to the city's Common Council. It was 1957 before a black was included among the nine common councilmen.[6]

In other words, blacks being a part of the labor coalition did not prevent Detroit from blatantly ignoring its changing constituency by continuing to deny black people black councilmanic representation as the black percent of population in Detroit increased from 9 percent in 1940 to 16 percent in 1950. When the first black councilman was elected in 1957, blacks comprised at least one-fourth of the city's population (they comprised 29 percent by 1960). Therefore, in 1940, 9 percent of Detroit's population had zero representation on the Common Council. In 1950, 16 percent of the population had zero representation; and by 1960 (councilmen serve for four years), almost 30 percent of the population held only 11 percent of the representation on the council. When comparison is made between Detroit's "legislative fathers" and those in other cities, it can be seen that the situation was even more dismal and subordinating than it appeared. Detroit councilmen serve full time and come to learn enough about the city's business to be taken seriously. Therefore, they must be viewed as having more weight than the councilmen of most other American cities.[7]

The main reason the coalition could not effect the election of a black man to a council composed of men of "weight" until blacks became at least one-fourth of the population (apart from the fact that it did not possess a profound commitment and desire to do so) was Detroit's electoral system. As the electoral system pertained to the council it worked to the great disadvantage of black people because it made use of nonpartisan elections along with electing the nine councilmen-at-large from the city as a whole.

Nonpartisanship was one of the products of the reform movement. It was spawned, in part, because many people in the upper social and economic levels were disgusted with what they considered corruption, bad government, and the power wielded by political bosses early in the twentieth century. Their middle-class mentality helped them to come to believe that lower-class citizens were inadequately served and led astray by unscrupulous politicians. To them, all of this seemed possible because of the party organization, the root of the evil. According to Duane Lockard:

> Very few of the reformers had the perspicacity to see, as Lincoln Steffens did, that the root ran deeper—that bossism was a social phenomenon responsive to community conditions. Rather it was somewhat naively assumed that if the boss were denied his chance to use the party ticket to elect his crew, then the boss system would disappear. Thus it was proposed that city elections be held without benefit of party labels so that honest citizens would have a chance to win office without having to win the favor of the minions of the party machine.[8]

Supposedly, the elimination of party labels was to help remove the operation of city government from politics. William O. Winter believes this to be one of the accepted myths of the middle-class, good-government fraternity. However, according to Winter: "If nonpartisanship dominated the local scene, so also does politics. Nonpartisanship does not eliminate politics, but it does change the nature of political activity."[9] In fact, many styles of politics appear to take place under the facade of nonpartisanship.[10]

Edward C. Banfield and James Q. Wilson offer a similar hypothesis that allows one to reach the same conclusions.

> Officials in nonpartisan cities are elected on the basis, not of party affiliations or party loyalties, but of whatever sources of power or symbols of legitimacy may be dominant in the community; and their policies tend to express the interests and values associated with those symbols. In a large industrial city like Detroit, nonpartisan policy expresses big-business culture. In a small, resident-owned manufacturing city like Beloit, Wisconsin, it expresses "old family" culture.[11]

In reality Wilson's "power or symbols of legitimacy" or Winter's "coalition of dissident Republicans and Democrats, or . . . other groups and individuals outside the confines of the two major parties,"[12] which are dominant in a nonpartisan city, actually produce a number of unintended side effects.[13] One of these results because the nonpartisan ballot emphasizes the individual candidate over coherent group effort, and voters do not have the aid of familiar party labels to help select from the sometimes substantial list of names on the ballot. When there are no party labels to provide guidance, most voters encounter difficulty deciding which candidate stands for what so that they may mark their ballots intelligently. This is especially true in primaries where the number of candidates is sometimes large. Under these circumstances most voters cannot possibly be expected to know enough about the many at-large councilmanic candidates to choose them wisely. Some will face their quandary by voting for candidates who have a favorable position on the ballot, and many others will face it by choosing candidates with familiar-sounding names. In the latter type of case, these tend to be incumbents. Forty-five years after Detroit adopted its 1918 Charter, only twenty-two incumbent councilmen who sought re-election during that period suffered defeat.[14]

In addition to favoring incumbents, there is evidence that a familiar name helps one to be elected to the council in Detroit.

> Occasionally a challenger has a name that people recognize, or think they recognize, and this may turn the trick for him. A councilman named James Brickley, for example, is supposed to have benefited from confusion with the television news commentator David Brinkley. Several Murphys sit on the city and county courts, thanks, apparently, to the popularity of the late Frank Murphy, a mayor who became governor and then a justice of the United States Supreme Court.[15]

Another unintended consequence of nonpartisanship is the weakening of citizen influence on council members. Because of nonpartisanship and at-large elections, campaigning and other personal contacts with voters are minimized, since most individual candidates do not have the financial resources to meet the high cost associated with at-large campaigns. This is an important factor because many Americans like to see candidates in person. Since party campaign support is not at their disposal, at-large candidates are much more likely to be dependent on special-interest groups that have large bank rolls, or upon wealthy private individuals. After the election, the interest groups and wealthy individuals who have helped finance successful candidates exercise more than just ordinary democratic influence in the council.[16]

Because of the elimination of party labels which differentiate candidates from one another, information with respect to individual candidates to which voters are exposed before they enter the voting booth takes on a more important function than when party labels are used (partisan elections).[17] This is especially true in cities like Detroit, where nonpartisan electoral politics is effective in local elections. In such cities, there is an increase in the influence of the mass media on many voters. Without party labels and active party canvassing, many voters tend to become highly dependent on the press, radio, and television for information and "earnest persuasion." In partisan elections, ordinarily, mass communications have somewhat less influence on voter or voters' behavior than does face-to-face communication such as canvassing done by party workers. On the other hand, in nonpartisan elections, those upper-income elites who are able to influence and/or control the communication media are more likely to influence voting choices for many.[18] Therefore, blacks (browns and even poor whites) are disadvantaged in such a nonpartisan city, inasmuch as the instruments of communication are, in the usual course of things, disproportionately controlled or influenced by the elite and its supporters.

Considering party campaign support is not available to at-large councilmanic candidates in a genuine nonpartisan city, these candidates are more likely to be dependent on various segments of the establishment. Because in such cities there is greater voter reliance upon the communication media, which are generally disproportionately dominated or influenced by the power structure and its associates, those who have helped successful candidates in various ways tend to exercise more than just ordinary democratic influence in the councils of decision making. Therefore, whether they are motivated because of altruistic or self-seeking reasons, these businessmen, upper-class civic leaders, and reformer types object to city councils being selected on a small-ward system—in part, because the resources (communications media, social status, expertise, corporate wealth, etc.) over which they have sway sometimes are not too effective in influencing small-district councilmen. Also, these elite leaders feel that a politics of personal influence (immigrant ethos) and ethnic or religious neighborhood interests is wrong and inefficient (they prefer to eliminate the human element). They favor large districts or, preferably, nonpartisan at-large elections so that the resources they control will be more effective in helping to select the type of councilmen they desire.[19]

The available data clearly indicate that blacks (browns and poor whites) should resist at-large nonpartisan elections by any means necessary. Such elections tend to promote conservatives. Not that we necessarily equate a white conservative with an overt racist, or an insidious covert racist, but black (and brown) people must be on guard against conservative influence on a city council. Some students of urban politics believe that nonpartisanship is very advantageous to conservatives partly because, in the absence of active political parties, the so-called citywide frame of mind must be relied upon as a basis for campaign organization. Inasmuch as poor blacks (browns and poor whites) must utilize their energies attempting to acquire the basic necessities to sustain life, most of them generally have no energies left to devote to public-spirited issues. As a result, generally, citywide motives exist mostly among relatively well-educated, upper-income people who gravitate toward conservatism. Of course, conservatives do not totally monopolize organizational skills for public-spirited issues. In nonpartisan Detroit, the AFL-CIO Committee on Political Education (COPE) was not considered to be conservative and had a history of drafting platforms, endorsing candidates, using rank-and-file union members to work in precincts at election time. However, we have shown how the AFL-CIO, which experienced a high measure of success in partisan national and state elections, experienced total failure in nonpartisan Detroit when attempting to defeat Cobo.[20]

There is some available empirical evidence that seems to offer support for the assertion that one would expect conservative candidates to fare better in nonpartisan elections than in partisan elections: "In twenty-six California communities of over 50,000 inhabitants, it was found that 80 percent of the mayors and 68 percent of the city councilmen were registered Republicans although the great majority of the registered voters in these same communities were Democrats."[21] A further implication is that the larger the number of governmental positions in a given city filled according to nonpartisan electoral procedures, the more the upper-class elite will sway decision making in the community.[22]

Blacks (browns and poor whites) should therefore view with suspicion people who advocate utilization of a nonpartisan at-large elected city council in lieu of using small districts. If such persons happen to be businessmen, upper-class civic leaders, or reformer types, they must be viewed as people who invariably will have less influence under a small district plan than under an at-large system. When there are small districts, these elites are placed at a disadvantage (not subordinated) because then they are minority groups among other minority groups. Under small districts they may be forced to utilize more of their resources in attempting to effect something akin to John C. Calhoun's concurrent majority (see Chapter 13) or they may be forced to resort to personal-favor levels of politics to maintain their dominance; all in all, the small-district system is a more difficult one to control.

In those cities where small districts exist (as in Chicago, Cleveland, and St. Louis), black people would be justified to consider using any means necessary to resist if and when there are proposed schemes to change to nonpartisan at-large elections. Further, in cities like Detroit they should fight with a missionary zeal to change at-large systems to small ward-based ones. This is absolutely necessary. Accordingly, the power structure and its supporters must acquiesce to such demands if they desire not to be responsible for blocking the structural alterations that possibly could help delay igniting the fuse that could lead to the destruction of society.

Small districts have the potential to help in delaying ignition of the fuse. With the acceptance and implementation of the necessary structural changes, subordinated racial groups possibly could be provided with an incentive to feel themselves to be a small part of the system. But being a part of the system is possible only if the councilmen elected from small wards are the people's true choices and are not stymied in their efforts to work for the positive good of their constituents.

If the councilmen were to begin to experience what their constituents could call "victories for the people," then over a period of time many such victories could possibly cause subordinated racial

groups living in such wards to begin to feel a small sense of belong-
ing in the system (although one might ask, how much time does
America have?). Too, if political and economic results indicate that
the system has come to the point where it is willing and is rapidly
making necessary revolutionary structural changes to incorporate
subordinated minority groups into American cities, such minorities
may begin to feel that they comprise more than a small part of
the system. People who have reason to feel that they are an intimate
part of something which benefits and serves them, generally desire
to preserve and perpetuate it for their children rather than seeking
to destroy it.

Acceptance and implementation of the necessary structural
changes in America's cities would nevertheless require a revolutionary change in the elite's thoughts and actions. To protect its interests, the elite believes it must be in a position to influence city
government. Given this belief, is it at all possible for the elite to
cease utilizing various means to handpick "leaders" it desires to see
"represent" subordinated racial minorities? Under systems with
several small wards—which ensure more decentralization and a
greater dispersal of power—would the establishment find it extremely difficult (if at all possible) to allow the men elected to represent the desires and wishes of their black (and brown) constituents
and to make policy decisions without resorting to personal-favor
level politics?

Again, the evidence seems to indicate that because there is less
centralization under a small-ward system than under an at-large
system, poor blacks (browns and poor whites) will be better served
by such decentralization. The small-ward system, in which men
are elected because people believe they will represent the collective
good, gives poor and subordinated citizens more points of access
or avenues to influence city government. While we are positive
that this system holds the potential to grant natural neighborhoods
better representation with less control by the elite over black goals,
we are not quite so positive that the elite will allow it to work.

It is most important that blacks and other subordinated ethnic
minority groups have adequate and effective representation in city
government. In many cities, the question of race lies behind many
public policy decisions. If a new school or hospital is to be constructed, or if there is to be a major highway project or any new

construction not specifically designated for blacks, the public policy makers examine all proposals as to whether or not they will help prevent blacks (and other minority groups) from "invading" white neighborhoods. If the proposal in question creates conditions that do attract blacks, the policy makers concern themselves with whether or not the neighborhood will become integrated, then all black.[23] (Integration lasts only from that period when the first few black families move in until there is mass exodus by whites.) Therefore, when policies are being made based mainly upon race, black people must have representation at such policy-level meetings.

It is imperative that black (and brown) people have adequate representation on city councils. It will not be given to them gratis. They must take the necessary steps to ensure that representation. One such step is to point out the disadvantages of nonpartisanship to the extent that the mass of black (and brown) voters in general will become aware that nonpartisanship is inimical to black (and brown) interests. We have shown that because of it blacks may be forced to join unfruitful coalitions on the city level with dissident Republicans and Democrats, or with other groups and individuals outside the confines of the two major parties which may reduce and impair the effectiveness of black leadership. Rank-and-file black voters must be shown the negative effects of the absence of familiar party labels on informative or intelligent voting. They must also be made aware of how nonpartisanship necessitates many candidates to obligate themselves to wealthy individuals or special-interest groups that have a high measure of influence and control over the mass media so that they as candidates can finance the more expensive citywide at-large elections and receive the necessary publicity. Rank-and-file black voters must also be conscious of the fact that nonpartisan elections have a tendency to promote conservative candidates.

Additionally, the mass of black (and brown) voters must be informed that, historically, black candidates are disadvantaged by nonpartisanship because they are seldom promoted and endorsed by newspapers and prestigious civic organizations. Nor do they, as a rule, get the kind of publicity that would make their names well known. Ordinarily, when a black man is known politically to the public at all, it is likely to be mostly on account of his race.[24]

Thus, in those nonpartisan cities where the majority of the population is white, the black candidate must attempt to get white votes without benefit of a party label. In Detroit, a primary is held to select eighteen candidates from a field frequently of more than one hundred competitors. Each voter may cast as many as nine ballots, one for nine different candidates. The eighteen victorious candidates then compete in a runoff election from which nine will emerge to serve on the Common Council.[25]

Thus, in Detroit a black candidate must get a strong black vote without the aid of significant material inducements (jobs, favors, etc.) to offer. For this reason, he must be aggressive on most racial issues to get strong black support. But he is in a delicate position, for since it is a citywide election, he must somehow get the support of a newspaper or of some important citywide civic association if he hopes to have any chance of winning. This means that a "black" person who is light-skinned, Ivy League-educated, and "reasonable" on race issues stands the best chance because there is a greater likelihood that he will be acceptable to middle-class whites.[26] He will, in fact, not receive press and civic association support unless he is "reasonable" from the standpoint of conservative middle-class whites.[27]

By contrast, in partisan cities, being black can be beneficial. Parties generally attempt to run ethnically balanced tickets[28] or "slates" which are balanced with candidates who represent various elements within the party roughly in proportion to their voting strength. Under these conditions a black candidate potentially strengthens a ticket. Because of him, many blacks will vote for the ticket, and his presence on the ticket usually will not cause whites who are indifferent to, or mildly hostile to, blacks to vote against it.[29]

In some nonpartisan elections, slates are made up, promoted, and endorsed by local party or partylike organizations. There may even be attempts to balance the ticket. But such efforts usually serve very little purpose because most voters feel no special loyalty to an organization's slate since the organization cannot discipline the voters. And often in nonpartisan cities like Detroit and Los Angeles, black candidates do not get very many votes in white precincts.[30]

For the benefit of those blacks who desire to give electoral politics one more chance, we therefore go on record as condemning nonpartisanship and advocating partisanship and ticket balancing, despite the obvious disadvantages of these systems. Technically, eth-nic-group representation and party rewards are based upon the con-tributions specific ethnic groups make to the party ticket. However, history reveals that ethnicization of party organization is based upon a formula that permits the dominant group to entrench itself to the extent that there is a time lag before the ascendant group re-ceives meaningful influence and recognition. This is possible because the formula allows the dominant group ordinarily to retain power more than commensurate with its actual voting strength. Thus, even when there are attempts to balance tickets ethnically in partisan elections, blacks are disadvantaged since the existing party structure fashions rules that delay and often prevent blacks from using the road white ethnic groups used to acquire power and influence to benefit their people.[31]

One may classify ticket balancing as being akin to, or a form of, ethnic recognition politics. Ticket balancing, along with dis-tributing patronage rewards (especially appointments) on the basis of ethnicity, is an attempt to inject rationality into distribution of rewards predicated on psychological need. Recognition politics is inexpensive because, in part, it supposedly confers mass psychic gratification rather than mass power and involves specific elective or appointive office in lieu of general substantive public policies. Indeed, except for the specific politicians rewarded, the mass of blacks receive only the appearance of inclusion in the existing politi-cal organization.[32]

Recognition politics or attempts to balance a ticket are efforts on behalf of the political organization to provide evidence (largely spurious) that it honors blacks and takes into account their accumu-lated grievances. In reality, recognition politics is a type of limited payoff whereby professional politicians hope black masses will feel psychologically rewarded because some black has in some way been supported or recognized by the existing political structure.[33]

When the ticket balancing or recognition ploy is successful, it helps to sap the militancy out of the black community because appointments are often made with the expectation that many black voters will derive a high measure of satisfaction from the recognition and will not make substantive demands as well. Sometimes this works with appointees since they do not owe their positions to the black community and often are appointed with the implicit understanding that they will dissuade other blacks from pressing for substantive policy demands.[34]

On that account, recognition politics actually lessens the opportunity for the black masses to participate in policy making and reduces the concern for public policies designed to benefit black people. This point must be driven home to the black rank and file. They must thoroughly come to understand that white organizations are primarily concerned with the organization's goals, and with maintenance of the political organization. This means promoting policies designed to perpetuate the party and strengthen it if possible. Substantive race issues may cause strife and dissension within the party. Therefore, the leadership will deal with assertive blacks. As Edgar Litt has said: "Thus, there are numerous historical examples in which assertive ethnic leadership has been bought off by the dominant political group and, in return, has managed to suppress members of its own group who wished to act more aggressively within the party. Symbolic recognition and the judicious use of divisible benefits are cheaper coin than intense primary fights and challenges to the party ticket."[35]

Despite these obvious disadvantages that black people may expect under partisanship, blacks would fare better by becoming aware of the handicaps and coming to deal with them rather than choosing to support subordinating nonpartisanship.

NOTES

[1] James Q. Wilson, *Negro Politics: The Search for Leadership* (Glencoe, Ill.: The Free Press, 1960), pp. 28, 319.

[2] *Ibid.*

[3] *Ibid.*, pp. 28–30.

[4] *Ibid.*

[5] *Ibid.*, p. 30.

[6] *Ibid.*, p. 28.

[7] Edward C. Banfield, *Big City Politics* (New York: Random House, 1965), p. 54.

[8] Duane Lockard, *The Politics of State and Local Government* (London: Collier-Macmillan, 1969), pp. 214–15.

[9] William O. Winter, *The Urban Polity* (New York: Dodd, Mead, 1969), pp. 316–17.

[10] Fred I. Greenstein, "The Changing Pattern of Urban Party Politics," *The Annals of the American Academy of Political and Social Science,* CCCLIII (May, 1964), p. 10.

[11] Edward C. Banfield and James Q. Wilson, *City Politics* (Cambridge, Mass.: Harvard University Press, 1963), p. 164.

[12] Winter, *op. cit.*, p. 318.

[13] Greenstein, *op. cit.*, pp. 10–11.

[14] For discussions of this side effect, see Banfield; Banfield and Wilson; Greenstein; and Winter, *op. cit.*

[15] Banfield, *op. cit.* (n. 7), p. 303.

[16] *Ibid.;* also see Terry N. Clark, "Power and Community Structure; Who Governs, Where, and When?" *The Sociological Quarterly*, VIII (Summer, 1967), pp. 291–316.

[17] Clark, *op. cit.*, p. 303.

[18] Greenstein, *op. cit.* (n. 10), p. 11.

[19] Banfield and Wilson, *op. cit.* (n. 11), p. 97.

[20] Banfield, *op. cit.* (n. 7), p. 56.

[21] Clark, *op. cit.* (n. 16), p. 303. Also see Eugene Lee, *The Politics of Nonpartisanship* (Berkeley: University of California Press, 1960), pp. 56–57.

[22] *Ibid.*, p. 304.

[23] See Banfield and Wilson, *op. cit.* (n. 11), p. 44.

[24] *Ibid.*, p. 158.

[25] Wilson, *op. cit.* (n. 1), p. 28.

[26] Banfield and Wilson, *op. cit.* (n. 11), pp. 307–08.

[27] *Ibid.*, p. 308.

[28] Edgar Litt, *Beyond Pluralism: Ethnic Politics in America* (Dallas: Scott, Foresman, 1970), p. 46.

[29] Banfield and Wilson, *op. cit.* (n. 11), p. 158.

[30] *Ibid.*

[31] Litt, *op. cit.*, pp. 46–47.

[32] *Ibid.*, pp. 61–64.

[33] *Ibid.*

[34] *Ibid.*, p. 61. Also see Raymond E. Wolfinger, "Some Consequences of Ethnic Politics," in M. K. Jennings and L. H. Zeigler, eds., *The Electoral Process* (Englewood Cliffs, N.J.: Prentice-Hall, 1966), p. 52.

[35] Litt, *ibid.*, p. 64.

CHAPTER 6

Black People: Small-District, Nonpartisan, and Proportional Representation Electoral Schemes

Historically, white people have found ways to reduce black political influence when they so desire. Black people must be alerted that it is not just a matter of watching the elite to make sure they do not impose nonpartisanship upon blacks. They must be made aware that the elite may use other structural forms to make it easier for them to control city politics and subordinate blacks.

Lee Sloan describes how for twenty-three years a Michigan city with a population of approximately 85,000 elected its city commissioners in nonpartisan, but ward-based elections. Under this system one district, which was 90 percent black, elected its own version of a fiery ultramilitant black man. This black man effectively used his commission seat as a forum from which he criticized white leadership because of the inequitable manner in which it treated the city's black community. Most rank-and-file blacks identified with him in his struggles against the establishment.[1] Style was important to this black leader, as it was to Adam Powell,[2] and many blacks in this militant black commissioner's city appreciated him more for how he went about attempting to do business in behalf of black people than for the little he was able to accomplish.

The very style which made him so popular among many black people was so obnoxious to the city's influential whites that they considered him a nuisance and an irritant. They then devised a scheme to get rid of him and to make more difficult the election of any other blacks who were vexing to whites. The elite proposed a structural electoral change which was adopted in a 1962 citywide referendum.[3]

Under the system adopted in this Michigan city in 1962, a primary election is held in which voters in each district nominate two candidates who later oppose one another in the general election. However, in the general election voters living in the various districts are denied the right to a man of their own choosing. All voters are entitled to cast seven votes, one for a candidate from each of the city's seven districts. Therefore, the citywide electoral system represents, in fact, a form of political racism since it subordinates black people by denying the black community the opportunity to select a man to serve on the commission who represents its wishes and desires.[4]

The elite could have adopted a totally nonpartisan at-large system, which is more common in American cities, but if they had done so, their racist intentions would have been more obvious. Instead, this less commonly used, but politically racist nevertheless, system was chosen (in 1966 out of 3,010 American cities with populations over 5,000, only fifty-six used such a system). While this modified at-large system does not automatically exclude all blacks from the commission, it does mean that blacks only have an opportunity to be elected from those districts in which they constitute an overwhelming majority. It also means that some type of black man, but not one who is assertive on race, would possibly be elected from the one ward which was approximately 90 percent black and usually elected a black man.

However, in this same city there is another district approximately 60 percent black which had never elected a black man prior to the new system of 1962. With the advent of the new system it is highly unlikely that the 60 percent black district could ever elect a black commissioner of its own choosing because the black candidate must face a citywide electorate without benefit of a party label and with the need of newspaper and associational support in order to win.[5]

In this manner, white voters have the power to prevent the election of assertive blacks, and simultaneously are in position to co-opt unprogressive self-seeking blacks who have no interest in attempting to work in behalf of subordinated black people. When whites elect such a so-called black man, they then say that black people have representation. On the contrary, in the eyes of many blacks this gives them no representation at all.

Consequently, no black candidate can win unless, as with regular nonpartisan, at-large elections, he is unprogressive on race issues and thus is acceptable to middle-class whites. If a black candidate is acceptable to whites, he does not need strong support in his black district. There is evidence in fact that indicates firm support for a black candidate in his black district would be the political kiss of death. There is reason to believe that most white voters use the primary results to determine which black candidate is acceptable to them—the candidate receiving the least number of black votes.[6]

In the 1964 and 1966 general elections, voters living in the 90 percent black district were unable to elect candidates of their own choice. A nonassertive so-called black man, who did not carry the black district, won in both elections. In 1964, a white candidate who failed to be nominated in the primary by one vote in the 60 percent black district was elected in the citywide general election because of a write-in campaign. White people elected him to represent black people. He received less than 30 percent of the votes in his home district, the 60 percent black district, and less than 2 percent in the 90 percent black district in the general election. In both predominantly black districts the voters considered the white incumbent mayor a more desirable candidate for the council, but despite his being white, citywide white voters rejected black peoples' choice. Results of the 1964 and 1966 elections show that the citywide electorate denied the two preponderately black districts their preferred candidate four times out of four. In the five white districts, this came to pass only one time out of ten.[7]

It is easy to see why many black people in the Michigan city believe themselves to be disfranchised because of the new electoral system. They are actually subordinated inasmuch as they are now denied the "right" to choose their own representative since white voters choose for them. Many blacks are angry because whites have used "democratic" electoral procedures to take from blacks what they had under the old ward system, the right to select a black man of their own choosing. This ploy is considered by most blacks to be another form of white hypocrisy.

The new electoral system in the Michigan city under consideration is appropriately referred to as the "Black Beater," and blacks
have utilized much time and energy in devising strategies to overcome it. With adoption of the new electoral system the elite not
only got rid of an "irritating" black man (he went to Detroit and
became a leading nationalist or separatist), it also made it virtually
impossible for black people to elect a man who identifies with
the black community. Additionally, because the new electoral system works to the advantage of those candidates who are able to
finance citywide campaigns, and since it enhances the influence
of the news media, it makes control of city politics by the establishment easier than it was under the old ward system. The resultant
conservatism of the commission not only operates to the disadvantage of blacks, but also of the white working class.[8]

We have insisted that black people should use any means necessary to effect a partisan, small-ward system because this structural
arrangement possibly could help blacks experience more meaningful
representation and thus could possibly delay igniting the fuse that
could lead to the society's coming apart at the seams. Under nonpartisanship, blacks must abandon all hope of receiving representation in proportion to their numerical strength. However, we are
not saying that a partisan, small-ward system is the millennium.

When a city's electoral system calls for councilmanic representation to be based upon small wards, partisan elections are potentially
helpful to blacks if for no other reason than the fact that the resultant decentralization provides poor, subordinated black people
access to more avenues to influence public policies. This is not to
say that partisan elections cause the establishment of perfect government, free from the imperfections that allow subordination. Furthermore, there is some criticism of partisan elections which cause many
people to rely upon party labels at the same time as there is much
ideological fuzziness and confusion encountered when attempting
to distinguish between the two major parties. There is some purposeful effort to blur ideological distinctions so as to facilitate creating
broad majorities through compromise and bargaining.[9]

We are not so naive as to suggest that in the 1970's black people
will automatically vote for a candidate because of party loyalty
and familiar party labels. However much this has been true in the
past, future black politicians will inject race into campaigns, and

because of the black community's new consciousness, race can cause blacks to either support or oppose a party's nominees.

Furthermore, we have no desire to mislead our readers and cause them to come to believe that in America, party cohesion and discipline allow parties to dictate to the voters who generally support them. By worldwide standards, American parties are far from being cohesive and disciplined apparatuses. Therefore, in reality, party loyalty and control are relative terms.[10]

Partly because of the unpredictable coalitions brought together on account of the strategies that call for the creation of broad majorities, and in some measure because of a lack of ideological clarity in partisan elections, an electoral system used in some Western nations has long been espoused by, and is sometimes used in, large American cities. This system is called "proportional representation" (PR). Most people who support PR and who additionally oppose partisan elections believe that it is more likely to effect public policies that reflect, to a greater degree, the divisions of opinion among the voters in a given city. Of course, in some Western nations this asset is counterbalanced by the fact that the existence of PR sometimes brings forth so many parties that a government capable of action may be impossible to create. Also, where there is PR, parties seem to harden and intensify their differences, whereas under the American plurality system, parties seem to moderate and compromise their differences. According to a study by Rosenbaum, Spanier, and Burris: "Thus it appears that our electoral arrangements encourage moderate major parties and less party divisions at the cost of perhaps greater insensitivity and less attention to the finer shadings of opinion within the electorate."[11] It is because PR supposedly allows greater attention to be paid "to the finer shadings of opinion within the electorate" that those black people who desire to participate in electoral politics should examine it.

Reformers proposed proportional representation in the first decade of this century and it was subsequently put to the test in about twenty-five cities, but by 1963 it had been abandoned in all but one, Cambridge, Massachusetts. Diverse kinds of PR systems have been put into action. Cincinnati and New York used what is called the "Hare system," based on Thomas H. Hare's 1859 book, which appeared in London and helped popularize PR.[12]

Examination of the mechanics of PR as it operated in Cincinnati from 1925 until 1957 reveals that a voter placed a "1" before his first choice (candidates ran at-large), a "2" before his second choice, and so on to as many choices as he desired to express. After all ballots had been cast and they had reached the central counting place, the first choices of each candidate were separated by precinct. Invalid ballots were also separated in this manner. Then all of the valid first-choice ballots of each candidate were laid out on separate tables and stamped. The stamped serial numbers made it possible for ballots to be traced later if it became necessary. During these procedures parties were represented by watchers.[13]

After invalid ballots had been set aside, the total valid vote in the election was then determined. The next step was to determine the "quota," or the number of votes necessary to elect a candidate. The object in determining the quota was to secure the lowest possible figure without making it possible to elect more persons than there were offices to be filled.

> To compute the number of votes needed—the quota—the total number of valid ballots are counted. In the 1953 election this figure was 143,188. This figure is divided by the number of councilmen to be elected (9) plus 1, discarding all fractions, and 1 is added to the result, to achieve the quota necessary for election. In 1953 this formula worked out as follows:

$$\frac{143,188}{9+1} = \frac{143,188}{10} = 14,318 + 1 = 14,319$$

> Thus in 1953, 14,319 was the smallest number of votes that could elect a candidate to office.[14]

These mechanics prevented the waste of some votes by not allowing any candidate to receive more votes than he actually needed. They also helped increase the possibility that a voter's ballot would eventually be counted for some candidate that he desired to see win, even though he did not get his first choice. However, this was possible only for those voters who voted their preferences by marking "1," "2," "3," "4," and so on. It did not help the voter who possessed the mistaken notion that he could achieve his goal of electing a favorite candidate by casting a bullet vote (marking only a "1"). The voter who marked several choices was able to help elect another candidate of his choice because any candidate who received more than the quota during the first count, had what was called a "surplus." Those extra votes were transferred to the candidate whose name was marked second. If the voter's second choice, as well as his first choice, had already been declared elected, his third choice was used, and so on. Thus the person who marked only one or two choices (exhausted or ineffective ballots) could not help elect anyone.[15]

PR critics charged that the system was too complicated and confusing to be practical. There is some evidence to support their charges. During fifteen Cincinnati PR elections, the invalid vote averaged 5.34 percent of those cast. Some of those opposed to PR also estimated that at least 95 percent of the people did not understand how the votes were counted. The fact that the average count took from six to seven days possibly added to this confusion.[16]

Despite being somewhat complicated, confusing, and time-consuming, PR in Cincinnati was more beneficial to black people than either an at-large or district system could have been. In theory, PR makes it possible for various groups of voters who have a common view on political questions to have representation on the council in proportion to their voting strength. The ward system permits the selection of one member of the council from each ward. If there are two parties, one party may carry the ward by securing 51 percent of the vote, thus gaining 100 percent of the councilmanic representation from that ward.[17]

Black people must give this some thought since blacks generally can be the largest group in a ward long before they take control. For example, in St. Louis in 1959, six wards returned black aldermen, but only two, the 18th and 19th had black committeemen, the holders of real political power.[18] Black control of the committeeman is important because it is highly unlikely that an alderman will oppose the interest of his committeeman to speak in behalf of the black community. Thus, in the past, despite being the dominant group in a ward, it was impossible, in many cases, for black people to elect officials that would give them adequate influence on the council. Therefore, whenever the elite manages, by hook or crook, to influence enough wards by a small vote (51 percent), it can secure control of the council and deny blacks meaningful representation.

The above is more than a mere theoretical possibility:

> . . . In the election of 1931 in New York City, the Democrats polled 851,216 votes and the Republicans 339,020. With 70 percent of the vote cast, the Democrats elected 64 of the 65 aldermen,

or 95 percent. In 1921, Republican candidates for the council in Cincinnati received 68,000 votes, while the Democratic candidates received 61,000. With 53 percent of the votes supporting them, the Republicans secured 31 of the 32 councilmen, or 96 percent.[19]

The at-large electoral system also operates to the advantage of the establishment in a similar manner. Where the establishment controls the dominant party under at-large elections, it will secure representation out of proportion to its voting strength and dominate the city's policy-making body. Thus, in effect, all shades of public opinion will not be represented.[20]

It may be helpful here to look more closely at the case of Cincinnati, where PR operated from 1925 until 1957. For years Cincinnati had been controlled by a powerful Republican machine.[21] As a result, during the first quarter of the twentieth century Cincinnati, which had been called "corrupt and contented" by Lincoln Steffens, was favorite copy for the muckrakers, political reporters in general, and the political reformers. Around 1921 a small group of reformers began to organize what was called the "Birdless Ballot League" (the rooster and eagle were used as symbols of the two major parties). The League was interested in minimizing support for the political machine and therefore proposed, as its name suggested, one of the accepted myths of the middle-class, good-government fraternity: elimination of party labels through nonpartisanship. The Birdless Ballot League soon dissolved, however, and became part of the new City Charter Committee. The Charter Committee not only drafted a program of Charter revision which included nonpartisanship, but also a city-manager plan along with a small nine-man city council elected at-large by proportional representation.[22]

In 1924 the reform effort secured adoption of its major proposals and formed the Charter Party in order to safeguard the council-manager plan and PR. Although the Charter Party organization did not formally call itself a "political party," it became as well-oiled and organized as the best of the old-style political machines, which it hoped to eliminate.

> It not only has complete men's and women's ward and precinct organizations, but is actually built upon a broad base of block workers. It has publicity, literature and speaker's committees, poll watchers, telephone brigades, and all the other paraphernalia neces-

sary to get out the vote. Perhaps most important of all, it has
a permanent and effective organization for financing its efforts.
The party differs from traditional machines in that it is interested
in good government per se and makes no political promises in
return for volunteered efforts. That is, it is not based on patronage,
as are other political machines, but relies entirely on unpaid
citizens.[23]

Two black candidates ran for the council in the very first PR
election and were soundly defeated. They were independent candidates because the Republicans would not support a black man, and
there was a general belief that it would not have been very beneficial
to have had Charter backing, even if they could have gotten it.
It was felt that the vast majority of Cincinnati's black people (like
other black people throughout America) had not become politically
socialized to the point that race as an issue could transcend party
loyalty. In the predominantly black Eighteenth Ward, white Republican Fred Schneller received 2,374 votes out of the 3,619 votes
cast. Black candidate C. E. Hunter received only 192 votes in that
ward. Black candidate John S. Fielding received a mere 128 votes
in the Eighteenth Ward.[24]

In 1927 independent black candidate Frank A. B. Hall ran
eleventh on the first count but was dropped on the fifth transfer.
In 1929 he wanted to run with Republican backing, but instead
of receiving an endorsement, he experienced direct and overt Republican opposition. White Republican organization leader Fred
Schneller refused to put a black man on the Republican ticket
because he believed it "would hurt the balance." Despite this opposition Hall and another black man, George Conrad, ran as indepen-
dents. During the campaign, they received support from Chicago's
black Congressman, Oscar DePriest. DePriest told a Cincinnati audience of 2,000 that despite having received two warnings to stay
away, he had come to that city in order to urge black people to
work vigorously for the election of their own people. At the same
mass meeting a local black man, A. Lee Beaty, reminded the audience "that both local parties granted recognition to every group—
Catholic, Protestant, Jew, Irish, German, Labor—but not the
Negro."[25]

In 1929 Hall came in eighth with 6,781 first-place votes. However,
he was eliminated on the next-to-last count. Conrad received only
1,179 votes on the first count and thereby finished twentieth. Be-

cause of this significant independent black vote Hall's supporters issued a statement:

> We are serving notice upon the Republican organization that "the old order" in Hamilton County is gone and that the Negro district never again would be a transitory playground for unwholesome ambition and alien leadership.
>
> In the future the Republicans must look upon the Negro's secession from the ranks as a new order of things and a demand for real leadership which has been sucking the very vitals out of Negroes for the sole purpose of vote getting. The defection is permanent.[26]

Cincinnati's black community demonstrated its capacity for political solidarity to the extent that race could transcend loyalty to the Republican party. This was not lost upon the Republican organization. In order to continue "sucking the very vitals out of Negroes for the sole purpose of vote getting," in 1931 it placed Hall on its ticket. The *Times-Star* pointed out that this action was due black Cincinnatians because of their loyalty to the Republican party and because there were nine members on the council and approximately one-ninth of Cincinnati's population was black.[27]

With some Republican help the persistent Mr. Hall was elected to the council upon his third attempt in 1931. Thus PR had helped black people of Cincinnati get some representation on the council. However, PR in itself was not enough to ensure continued black representation. In 1933 Hall ran as an incumbent and also supposedly received the assistance of A. Lee Beaty, who had been made black Sixteenth Ward Republican committeeman. Despite receiving the largest first-place vote of his four attempts, his bid for reelection did not bear fruit. He was in need of 3,710 transfers but received only 1,353. Hall charged that the Republican campaign committee failed to give him sufficient help because pressure had been brought to bear upon it to defeat him. He additionally believed that $5,000 was raised to help ensure his defeat.[28]

What can black people today learn from Hall's defeat? Did it mean that because a black man who had been so determined and persistent that his actions forced the Republican organization to change its "balancing" policy had to be taught a lesson? During the 1970's those black people who challenge party organizations will have nothing to lose if they undertake their actions with the belief that the party elite will not be pleased with them. In fact, such a belief holds the potential to help persevering blacks: this is so because historically whites have attempted to teach assertive black men lessons. For those who say there is no lesson for black people to learn from Hall's defeat we add the fact that Cincinnati's Republican organization saw to it that its "Negro" candidate in 1935 got sizable transfers from other Republican candidates. He even received transfers "from Dr. Glenn Adams, who had support from certain groups with racist leanings."[29]

By 1936 the first of five attempts to repeal PR was undertaken. Whites who favored it used radio announcements and newspaper advertisements designed to garner black support for PR. They, in effect, told black people that during Cincinnati's first 123 years of existence no black man was elected to the council and because of PR two had served during the last eleven years. PR was retained by only 831 votes, but not because of help it received from the black community. Efforts to win black support failed. In one black ward it lost 4 to 1 and in the other it was defeated 3 to 1. In fact, results of the election suggest strongly that during the eleven years in which PR had been in existence black leadership in Cincinnati had failed to bring the black community to the point where it realized PR's potential.[30]

During the second campaign to repeal PR, in 1939, white Charterites again made special appeals to black people. The black community was told that it had to depend almost entirely upon black votes to elect a black councilman because not many whites would vote for a black man. Furthermore, black people were told that PR made it possible for blacks to be able to elect a councilman despite a lack of general white support, and that PR was the reason blacks had representation on the council.[31]

The Republican organization had fought against PR ever since its adoption. During the 1939 repealer, it sent Dr. R. P. McClain, the "Negro" whom it had helped in 1935, to tell black people not to support PR because it was the most "un-American and unpatriotic system inflicted upon a trusting public."[32] All black people did not believe that PR was "un-American and unpatriotic." Some were conscious of the fact that it was only after this electoral system was adopted that Cincinnati became "American" by including black representation on the city's policy-making body. Also, many black people were mindful that it was only after the adoption of PR that some blacks began separating themselves from the regular Republican organization, a move which forced the Republicans to endorse Frank Hall because they feared that black defections would increase.

We do not know whether Dr. McClain was following the dictates of the Republican elite or whether he was more concerned with Hitler and Mussolini than with retention of a structural form of government that gave black Cincinnatians an opportunity to secure representation on the council. The preelection consensus was that anti-PR forces would win in 1939 because the referendum was being proposed at a special June election. Conceivably, this traditional month of graduation, weddings, and vacationing would have been advantageous for the anti-PR Republican machine. Despite this presumed edge, the Republicans staged a careful "For Americans Only" campaign which subtly linked PR with Hitler and Mussolini. According to their erroneous belief, the use of the PR method for German elections under the Weimer Republic and Italian elections before 1922 was responsible for the governmental paralysis which gave Hitler and Mussolini their opportunities to seize power.[33] Since voters were not told that Germany and Italy used a party-list system quite different from the Hare system of PR used in Cincinnati, it may be accurate to assume that the machine included use of Dr. McClain (PR is "un-American and unpatriotic") in their campaign strategy.

Some of the evidence that all black people did not believe Dr. McClain became visible when long-time black Republican, W. L. Anderson, reminded black people that prior to PR the Republicans exploited the black vote and repaid black loyalty with a "bagatelle of patronage meager in salary and menial in character." A black circular asked black people "shall we be led by white overseers and Uncle Tom Negroes?" The Negro Committee of Labor's Non-Partisan League for PR also called upon black people to support PR. Despite a vigorous pro-PR campaign in the black community, PR did not receive a majority of the black vote, but the usual tremendous Republican anti-PR majorities were reduced. PR won by only 742 votes.[34]

In 1947, the third PR repealer coincided with the councilmanic election. Jesse Locker, a black Republican who served on the council from 1941 until 1953 when he was appointed ambassador to Liberia by President Eisenhower, found himself in a very precarious position. Locker was in a quandary because of strong Republican support to repeal PR, and because of the evidence that more and more black people were coming to the point of recognizing PR's potential.[35]

Caught between loyalty to the party and to his people, Locker attempted to take a neutral position. He issued a public statement in which he declared black people were divided on the merits of PR, therefore, he would have to study their wishes closely before he could commit himself against it. However, in the same statement he said that he favored submitting the issue of repeal to the voters no matter what his own opinion might be. Immediately the Cincinnati branch of the NAACP criticized Locker and declared that elimination of PR would make it practically impossible for minorities to send a representative of their choice to the council. The Cincinnati *Post* accused Locker of favoring repeal of PR because his record as a councilman indicated that he voted as told by Ninth Street (political power seat).[36]

No black politician desires to be branded as the handpicked lackey of the establishment. On the Monday prior to the August council meeting in which the law committee considered PR, Locker refused to vote to submit it to the voters. Following the meeting he issued a statement to the effect that Ninth Street did not dictate to him. His independence did not last very long, however. Two days later, he voted along with the other Republicans to submit PR to the voters in November.

All black people in America must learn the lesson that when the power structure supports a black man for office, it is not just performing some civic duty. It expects him to carry out its bidding. Under such conditions he will not be a free man, able to take independent action in behalf of the black community. In 1939, Cincinnati's elite was not quite sure how much, if any, black support Locker would lose after having been branded as controlled by Ninth Street. Therefore, the elite saw to it that he received stronger newspaper support than ever.

Much of the decision to provide stronger newspaper support for Locker could have been based upon the fact that a strong black man, Theodore Berry, entered the race as an independent amid rumors that he would receive support from the Charterites. To a great degree Ted Berry's election material and campaign were devoted to defending PR. In no sense of the word could we call Berry "provincial." He was not only aware as to the subordinated plight of his black brothers elsewhere in this country, but sought to pass such information on to his black sisters and brothers in Cincinnati. Berry asked black people to examine Detroit, a city with a much larger black population which, unlike Cincinnati, had never elected a black person to the Common Council. Berry considered that PR had made it possible for black Cincinnatians not only to elect a black councilman, but also to hold the balance of electoral power. He admonished black people that white politicians were aware of this fact and were seeking to destroy black people's bargaining power, and thus control the black vote. Berry, an astute black politician, recognized the necessity of political power in the hands of the black people and warned that if PR were to be eliminated the elite, especially white political bosses, would subordinate black businesses, employees, and unions to the extent that black Cincinnati would "suffer from poor housing, high rents, low wages, police abuse, vice, segregation, and discrimination."[37]

Locker received the fourth largest number of votes during the first count and the Republicans had garnered adequate support for him to receive enough transfers to be elected on the sixth count. Nevertheless, despite alleged covert Charter support, Berry suffered from the transfer handicap and was eliminated on the ninth count. Notwithstanding, he must have influenced some votes in the black wards. The 1936 PR repealer lost 4 to 1 and 3 to 1 in the two black wards. The 1939 PR repealer only saw the usual tremendous Republican anti-PR majorities reduced in black wards. But in 1947, with Berry campaigning for PR, one black ward voted to retain it and two others had bare anti-PR majorities.[38]

In 1949 Berry again ran, but this time under the Charter label. Because the majority of transfers to black candidates are party transfers, Charter backing was enough to elect him. The Republicans also helped reelect Locker. Despite the fact that an examination of the transfer votes showed that both candidates had been elected with large support from white voters, the election of two black men to the council caused consternation among many white Cincinnatians. Letters to the editor, editorials, and backyard gossip speculated to the effect that PR would die in Cincinnati because of the "new" overrepresentation of black people. The opponents of PR began using the argument that it was supposed to give each group representation in exact proportion to its population, not overrepresentation.[39]

Nevertheless, no repealer was initiated immediately after the 1949 election. Results of the 1951 election showed that in predominantly black wards and in wards that had some black population, Berry received approximately two votes for each one received by Locker. Not only was this an indication that there was diminished black support for Republicans, but it also indicated that black people preferred a Berry in lieu of a Locker.[40]

In 1953 Berry was reelected with a surplus on the first ballot and the cry was heard that since he came in with the largest vote, he should be mayor (only in 1925, 1933, and 1951 did the highest vote-getter fail to become mayor). However it was rumored that Berry was willing to sacrifice the mayorship for some things the black community demanded, such as a citywide Fair Employment Practices Commission and other measures for which he had been fighting since his election to the council. He did not become mayor, but he received the important and strategic post of chairman of the finance committee. He then continued to fight for his pet measures, most of which he did not get.[41]

In 1955 the Republicans failed to place a black man on their slate for the first time since 1929.[42] In that election Berry was elected Vice-Mayor after running second in a field of twenty-one candidates.[43]

The above account indicates that black Cincinnatians were able to use PR effectively to achieve a measure of political recognition. Their success, along with the thought that black people would continue to use PR effectively until Berry became mayor, motivated racist bigots to work for the repeal of the structural system. During the 1957 repealer white citizens were asked whether or not they desired to see Berry as Mayor. They were also questioned as to whether or not they wanted Berry as a next door neighbor. In order to reinforce this idea, enough rumors were initiated and circulated to have Berry buying a home in almost every white neighborhood in Cincinnati. On September 30, 1957, more than a majority of white Cincinnatians indicated that they had enough of PR and killed it by a vote of 65,593 to 54,004.[44] Thus, white people were able to use legal "democratic" electoral machinery to abolish an electoral system that black people had learned to use to their advantage.

Despite the possibilities for black people that lie in the small-ward and PR systems, and even if the elite could bring itself to allow adoption and implementation of the necessary structural changes to bring these systems into play, all we have said pertaining to a delay in igniting the societal fuse may be wishful thinking. Even with the desired changes, black political and civic organizations would find it necessary to deal with and sometimes become a part of various white groups to accomplish some citywide projects.

This is a problem because of the nature of black-white relationships. Cooperation with white groups holds high potential to frustrate black ambitions. For this very reason, more and more black people are coming to think along the lines of black political scientist Mack H. Jones. According to Jones, subordinated black people will find it extremely difficult to develop strategies to benefit the black community, unencumbered by undue deference to the sensitivities of the oppressors who control the various white groups with which black people must deal. Relationships of that kind have the tendency to blur the distinction between the self-interests of the subordinator and the subordinated. Jones states: "Such blurring is readily understood inasmuch as both the oppressed and the oppressor share the same culture, work in the same organizations, and claim citizenship in and therefore profess loyalty to the same government. The fact that this is easily understood, however, does not lessen the deleterious impact of this blurring of self-interest in the struggle for liberation."[45]

When blacks are associated with white groups, instead of analyzing their plight from the perspective of a colonial, or oppressed and subordinated people, and devising strategies in that light, they generally begin from the perspective of citizens who are part of the system. Such a perspective ultimately limits their devising and implementing strategies that would help liberate black people. What they usually accomplish, therefore, are marginal changes and adjustments, since the elite is committed to the preservation of the existing normative and institutional arrangements.[46]

This line of thinking does not necessarily hold that black people

cannot operate simultaneously within white organizations and promote black interests. Nevertheless, it holds that the relationship between black people and whites is an adversary one, that the activities
of white organizations are likely to be placed in contrast to black
interests. [The Mack Joneses demand that priority be given to developing independent black structures that cut across all dimensions
of black lives so as to enhance the capability of acting independently
of white control.] It is conceivable that ward-level organizations
can be developed and used effectively as independent black structures if they are not too provincial in outlook. Those who believe
as Mack Jones does have developed a worldwide perspective which
includes oppressed and subordinated black people everywhere since
none are really independent. Everywhere black people are subordinated and oppressed in varying degrees by people of European
origin.[47] This line of thinking has the potential to spread rapidly.
It also reveals that some of the ideas of EL-HAJJ Malik EL-Shabazz
(the late Honorable Malcolm X)[48] continue to live in some black
people.

NOTES

[1] Lee Sloan, "The 'Black Beater,'" in Edward C. Banfield, ed., *Urban
Government: A Reader in Administration* (New York: The Free Press,
1969), pp. 422–25.

[2] See James Q. Wilson, "Two Negro Politicians: An Interpretation," *Midwest Journal of Political Science*, IV (1960), pp. 346–69.

[3] Sloan, *op. cit.*

[4] *Ibid.*

[5] *Ibid.*

[6] *Ibid.*

[7] *Ibid.*

[8] *Ibid.*

[9] For ideas pertaining to partisan elections, see William A. Rosenbaum,
John W. Spanier, and William Burris, *Analyzing American Politics: A New
Perspective* (Belmont, Calif.: Wadsworth, 1971), pp. 220–21.

[10] *Ibid.*

[11] *Ibid.*, p. 221.

[12] Edward C. Banfield and James Q. Wilson, *City Politics* (Cambridge,
Mass.: Harvard University Press, 1963), pp. 96–97.

[13] Ralph A. Straetz, *PR Politics in Cincinnati: Thirty-Two Years of City
Government Through Proportional Representation* (New York: New York
University Press, 1958), pp. 269–70.

[14] *Ibid.*

[15] *Ibid.*, pp. 271–73.

[16] *Ibid.*, pp. 274–83.

[17] Charles M. Kneier, *City Government in the United States* (New York: Harper & Brothers, 1947), p. 265.

[18] James Q. Wilson, *Negro Politics: The Search for Leadership* (New York: The Free Press, 1965), pp. 24, 319.

[19] Kneier, *op. cit.*, p. 265.

[20] *Ibid.*, p. 266.

[21] Charles A. Adrian, *Governing Urban America: Structure, Politics, and Administration* (New York: McGraw-Hill, 1955), p. 81.

[22] Straetz, *op. cit.* (n. 13), pp. xv–xvii.

[23] Adrian, *op. cit.*, p. 81.

[24] Straetz, *op. cit.* (n. 13), p. 109.

[25] *Ibid.*

[26] *Ibid.*, p. 110.

[27] *Ibid.*, pp. 110–11.

[28] *Ibid.*, pp. 111–12.

[29] *Ibid.*, p. 112.

[30] *Ibid.*, pp. 112–13.

[31] *Ibid.*, pp. 113–14.

[32] *Ibid.*, p. 114.

[33] George H. Hallett, Jr., "The P. R. Lines Hold," *National Municipal Review*, XXVIII (July, 1939), pp. 556–57.

[34] Straetz, *op. cit.* (n. 13), p. 114.

[35] *Ibid.*, p. 117.

[36] *Ibid.*

[37] Straetz, *op. cit.* (n. 13), pp. 117–19.

[38] *Ibid.*, p. 119.

[39] *Ibid.*, p. 120.

[40] *Ibid.*, pp. 120–21.

[41] *Ibid.*, p. 123.

[42] *Ibid.*

[43] Wilson, *Negro Politics, op. cit.* (n. 18), p. 31.

[44] Straetz, *op. cit.* (n. 13), p. xi.

[45] Mack M. Jones, "A Note From a Black Political Scientist," *The Black Politician*, II (April, 1971), p. 24.

[46] *Ibid.*

[47] *Ibid.*, pp. 24–25.

[48] See Louis E. Lomax, *To Kill a Black Man* (Los Angeles: Holloway House, 1968), pp. 146–58; 201–28.

CHAPTER 7

Jefferson Bank's Resistance to Change

Despite small or large wards, and partisan or nonpartisanship, black political activists may use some ad hoc protest organizations that come into existence to fight for black economic and social advancement as effective apparatuses in helping blacks to overcome political powerlessness. However, not every incipient powerless-people's organization can organize and surface viable enough to participate in activities that will help advance black people politically. If the organization is composed of people who have long been quiescent and have not heretofore made demands that a city's power structure considers threatening, certain elements must be present before it can become effective enough to cause the establishment to listen to it.

There must be the necessary cohesion for organized political action. Then the organization must somehow obtain adequate resources. Among the resources needed are skilled professionals, including lawyers, many of whom will only work if there is adequate compensation. Of course, there are other needs for which an organization must obtain the necessary financial resources: office space, telephone service, supplies, mimeographing, and the like. If an organization obtains adequate resources, it has the potential to survive and become viable enough to be used to help blacks overcome powerlessness.[1]

In some cases organizations may lack resources, and professionals, including lawyers, may volunteer their services. However, this may not prove to be adequate since the organization may suffer from sporadic and undependable performances from the volunteers since they may not be able to devote the necessary time or lack adequate motivation or both. If such proves to be the case, the incipient organization will, no doubt, flounder and not become viable.[2]

In this chapter, we shall examine a case in which a civil rights organization, deficient in resources, especially financial resources, became viable. The organization, St. Louis' chapter of CORE, for the most part was not led by paid professionals or by volunteer professionals who did not donate enough of their time. Its leadership consisted of people representing many walks of life: men and women who held full-time jobs (professional and unskilled), full-time high school and college students, as well as some unemployed people. These people, along with a few black men and women who were associated with various city political organizations and who had become associated with CORE, were able to put it all together.

Among the many reasons CORE was able to become viable despite deficient resources was the fact that among its leadership were three attorneys who made their skills available, and the fact that other attorneys came to the organization's aid once it became involved with the judicial process. Later chapters will show how the organization and some of its politically oriented members were enhanced because of the results of the judicial proceedings. This enhancement put them in better positions to help the collective black community initiate steps designed to overcome black powerlessness.

St. Louis' black community had been quiescent prior to 1963, in the sense that it had made no demands that the city's power structure considered very threatening. It was clearly evident that because of St. Louis' discriminatory economy there had been virtually no improvement in employment and in meaningful job opportunities available to black people. These negative factors helped incite the young Turks of the Clay-CORE group (see Chapter 3) and provided motivation with the necessary sustained intensity to fight and suffer for economic advancement in behalf of black people for more than three consecutive years. Although the young Turks and CORE initiated the fight, their plans did not call for demolition of the system, but its fulfillment. Grant that they did lay some plans, there appears to be room to question just how thoroughly they had prepared themselves to attack the bank that most of black St. Louis came to call its "enemy."

When a sizable group of people come to believe that conditions are so unacceptable that there must be a change, they should first identify who or what is responsible for what they consider obnoxious. Such an identification will enable them to direct pressure in the desired direction.[3] Once the so-called enemy has been identified, those seeking change may find it advantageous to learn what their enemy's relationship is with those who make policy decisions in that particular community. If it is discovered that what has been identified as the opposition is a part of the establishment, or that the seat of power has an affinity for that opposition, such information should help those seeking change to better lay plans. In all probability, it is impossible to learn as much as any group would like to know about its identified opposition. On the other hand, it will possibly prove to be more fruitful to base plans on whatever incomplete information may be obtained than on no information.[4]

Acquiring such intelligence requires hard work and resourcefulness. It entails consulting references such as *Moody's Industrial Manual, Poor's Registry of Executives and Directors,* and other sources to locate the seat of power. Many of these materials, including old newspapers and census data, may be found in local libraries. Organizations directing the drive for desired changes will find it advantageous also to read society pages and send some of their members who are not known in the community to talk with socialites, business and labor leaders, and active politicians.[5]

Until 1963, St. Louis' black community had not precisely identified its enemy. Many in the middle class had been fighting what they called "segregation," and most of the younger less affluent blacks had been engaging an ill-defined enemy called the "white power structure." However, both groups learned whom they were fighting against after there developed a near ceaseless and exhausting struggle between CORE and an apparently insignificant financial institution: "At first it seemed to be a dispute between a small organization and a minor financial institution. But the affair of the St. Louis Committee for Racial Equality (CORE) and the Jefferson Bank and Trust Company affected the entire community and its vaunted racial harmony and progress."[6]

The brand of active opposition employed by the elite in this struggle in St. Louis caused those CORE members who were observant to be rewarded. As a result of observing and suffering establishment maneuverings, they acquired the type of knowledge which

helped to reveal the magnitude and pervasive influence of the establishment, thus allowing them to shed some of their fictitious beliefs
relative to the seat of power. The acrimonious struggle with the
Jefferson Bank and Trust Company revealed that there was a complex combination of economic and political forces that did not adhere to traditional political party lines. Black people already knew
that the power structure was not representative of the city's population because only whites were a part of it. However, since the
stand opposed to racist employment practices at Jefferson Bank
forced many things to come out from under the rug, it was possible
for black leaders to acquire a better understanding of the enemy:

> . . . When you know who your enemy is, he can no longer
> keep you divided, and fighting, one brother against the other!
> Because when you recognize who your enemy is, he can no longer
> use trickery, promises, lies, hypocrisy, and his evil acts to keep
> you deaf, dumb and blinded!
> When you recognize who your enemy is, he can no longer
> brainwash you, he can no longer pull wool over your eyes so
> that you are living in pure hell on this earth while he lives in
> pure heaven right on this same earth! . . .[7]

Being in a position to identify precisely the racist forces that
were instrumental in preventing black people from moving forward
economically helped to produce an unanticipated positive result for
CORE. Accurate identification of the "active opposition" made it
possible to fight better elite attempts to sow seeds of divisiveness.
Such efforts usually cause some misguided blacks to attempt to
induce white people to believe that they are "different from those
others." Whenever the establishment successfully employs that kind
of tactic, a black community usually becomes divided "one brother
against the other." When this occurs, those black people who are
more interested in their personal furtherances than in advancement
for the black masses, whether they realize it or not, usually are
engaging in activities that are a disservice for an entire city—black
and white. Their only utility is to help sustain white peoples' low
opinion of black people, thus lending aid to keeping their own
people down. This only delays the day of settlement. The late
Malcolm X was well aware that this could cause problems: "This
is still one of the black man's big troubles today. So many of those
so-called 'upper-class' Negroes are so busy trying to impress on

the white man that they are 'different from those others' that
they can't see they are only helping the white man to keep his
low opinion of all Negroes."[8]

But during and immediately after the 1963 Jefferson Bank confrontation, only a few black St. Louisans appeared to attempt to
impress white people that they were "different from those others."
CORE's publicly released research on the bank's racist hiring policies was so damning that many "black white men" possibly were
not willing to try and prove that they were "different from those
others," and lend, in effect, support to the bank.

There is evidence that CORE and the young Turks had acquired
some intelligence pertaining to their selected target when they continued the militancy initiated by young Arthur Shaw in 1960 (see
Chapter 3). They had acquired information that caused them to
believe that in 1963 the St. Louis banking industry employed 5,160
people and that only slightly more than 5 percent, 269 people, were
black. Moreover, according to their intelligence, 93 percent of the
black banking employees were employed in service capacities as
custodians, elevator operators, maids, and messengers.[9] Thus, up
until 1963, the St. Louis banking industry was guilty of helping
to maintain economic racism by hiring black people only in unde-
sirable or dead-end jobs despite their potential to perform at higher
levels.[10]

The Jefferson Bank and Trust Company, CORE's target, employed at least ten blacks in other than service positions in the
early 1950's. However, by 1958, only two blacks were working
in the bank, and one of them was a service employee. Twice during
that year, CORE attempted to persuade the bank to hire additional
blacks. The bank employed "liberal" rhetoric: CORE was assured
that the bank did not have a discriminatory policy and that it expected to hire additional blacks soon. No black people were hired
and two years later CORE representatives returned to the bank
only to receive more promises.[11]

They returned again in 1961 and 1962. There is a point where
promises, if they are to be meaningful, must be translated into
action. And after more than four years of promises and unsuccessful
negotiations, CORE's anticipation that some black people would
become white-collar employees at Jefferson Bank had not come
to pass. Therefore, CORE felt it imperative to adopt tactics other
than the type of negotiations which had not yielded positive results

for it since 1958. Many came to believe that, in reality, negotiations had failed because bank officials had only been holding "conversations" with CORE leaders, in which the latter stated their grievances and demands, and then were simply informed of the bank's decisions.[12] Such negotiations closely resembled those described by Charles Silberman when he said "whites are accustomed to holding conversations with Negroes in which they sound out the latters' views or acquaint them with decisions they have taken."[13]

Prior to 1963, CORE did not initiate its bargaining with Jefferson Bank from a position of strength as a cohesive labor union does when it bargains for its members with a company that desires to avoid a strike. It would be a sound theoretical argument to reason that the bank found it extremely difficult to place itself in a position to bargain with CORE. First, the CORE representatives were not handpicked, accommodating compromisers. Secondly, what, in a tangible sense did it have that the bank wanted or needed, to serve as an inducement for the bank to bargain in good faith and not simply inform CORE of its decisions?[14]

CORE's specific goal, more and better jobs, was so much a part of the often stated American principle of equality that it could not compromise on the issue. Therefore, it had actually offered the bank a negative inducement, possibly hoping it valued its reputation to the extent that it would choose to hire four persons of color rather than become involved in a community controversy which would align it with racism. CORE learned it was in error when the bank's obstinacy helped cause the civil rights organization to demand in August of 1963 that St. Louis banks hire a specific number of blacks within a given time limit. The size of a bank's work force was to be used as a guide in determining the number of blacks to be hired. Two small banks, Easton-Taylor and Mound City Trust, rid themselves of some of their economic racism and ceased to pay mere lip service to the idea of employing blacks when each hired two blacks within CORE's two-week time limit during the summer of 1963.[15]

However, there was no acquiescence on the part of Jefferson Bank. Its actions repudiated its public proclamation of "soon." On August 14, 1963, Robert B. Curtis, a young black lawyer and chairman of CORE, sent a letter informing the bank that large numbers of black people used the bank and that because of its discriminatory hiring policies CORE's membership had authorized the organization to initiate direct action against the bank. However, CORE would withhold action if the bank were to hire four blacks as white-collar workers within two weeks.[16] John H. McConnell, executive vice-president of the bank, reiterated the same phrases and promises that had been voiced by the bank since 1958. Only this time, after Curtis' letter had been received, he said the bank had no vacancies and did not anticipate adding any new employees.[17]

Thirteen days later, Wayne L. Millsap, attorney for Jefferson Bank and Trust Company, answered Curtis' letter. Not only did the bank refuse to hire four black people, but Millsap additionally employed the old trick of putting black people on the defensive by raising the question of qualifications. His answer indicated that the bank had not received applications from four "qualified" blacks. In addition, his reply to Curtis' letter did nothing to help dispel the notion held by most black people that laws in this country are for white people when he proceeded to bring the law on his side in his fourth reason for not hiring black people: "The demands of your organization are in violation of the Fair Employment Practices Act which has been adopted by the City of St. Louis and the State of Missouri in that you are asking the bank to discriminate in its employment practices in favor of Negroes."[18]

Despite the fact that broken promises by the Jefferson Bank were among the many factors creating discontent in the black community, the bank remained obstinate. The fifth point presented in reply to CORE's letter as to why the bank refused to comply with CORE's request is indicative of this obstinacy, referring to: ". . . the unwarranted charge by your organization that the Jefferson Bank and Trust Company has been discriminating in its employment practices, when in fact this bank has always given full consideration to the employment of qualified Negroes." The statement "when in fact this bank has always given full consideration . . ." seems highly questionable considering the bank would not accept applications from blacks and had not hired a black person in seven years.[19]

Black people generally believe that when white people desire to postpone or take no action at all, they create a commission of some type. Such strategy is usually based on the assumption that the protest group will not maintain its cohesion long enough to be around when a commission makes its recommendations.[20] The sixth point of the bank's letter leaned in that direction: "The St. Louis Commission on Equal Opportunities has been recently established and should be given an opportunity to deal with the problem of job opportunities for Negroes. The bank and all reasonable employers in St. Louis will be strongly influenced by the recommendations of the Commission." Regarding commissions Robert Curtis, chairman of CORE, stated that "Mayor Tucker's Committee on Human Relations is only a 'buffer' between Negroes and Employers. . . . The history of committees is to delay action. . . ."[21]

The final paragraph of the two-page letter from attorney Millsap on behalf of the Jefferson Bank attempted to intimidate blacks by warning them that they would hurt their cause, supposedly, because black people would lose the white man's support if they persisted in direct action, or in any action not approved by whites.

> The Jefferson Bank and Trust Company cannot accept the demands you have put upon it and cannot approve the action you suggest taking against it on Friday, August 30th. I therefore urge you, in the interest of the entire Negro community, to reconsider the position your organization has taken concerning the demonstration you have planned at the bank on Friday, August 30th. The demonstration you propose may impede the progress which is being made toward obtaining equal job opportunities for Negroes in the St. Louis area.

St. Louis was faced with a potentially dangerous situation and according to the *Missouri Teamster*, the "Jefferson Bank and its politically ambitious legal counsel, Wayne Millsap, handled it badly."[22] The stage was set, with central-city blacks receiving help from white students living in University City and other county municipalities. This combination, it was hoped, would help cause "the old king pins of our power structure . . . to learn sadly, if they have not already, that the days of the white boss are gone."[23]

Prior to August of 1963, on the surface at least, it appeared that white St. Louis generally accepted the idea of the new black assertiveness. However, this idea was erroneous. According to the *Missouri Teamster*:

> St. Louisans generally applauded the Negro Revolution as long as it kept its distance.
>   They were relieved that the School board demonstration in

downtown St. Louis last summer was a singing of hymns and
peaceful speeches. The white press hailed the March on Washington for its "dignity" (more hymns, more speeches).

But the Jefferson Bank brought the whole movement too close
to home. Suddenly you could feel the hard-bitten inner power
structure of our fair city at work.[24]

Aware that the bank was seeking a restraining order, CORE
met to discuss its possible consequences. Charles Oldham, an attorney
and the former white National President of CORE, admonished the
group that if such an order were obtained they did not know what
action it would prohibit, and that CORE should comply with it.
After a lively discussion, by a vote of eighteen to thirteen, it was
decided to proceed with direct action. Where there was a measure
of disagreement among CORE members pertaining to direct action,
it was observed that the press showed no such inclination.

The Post-Dispatch on August 28 had editorialized, apropos
of the March on Washington, that "a great minority of citizens
is appealing to the American people for a right to the American
way of life. . . . A long time ago, America took hazards and revolutionary steps to secure these rights. . . ." But on August 29, when
members of that same great minority proposed to take "hazardous
and revolutionary" steps to secure these rights the Post-Dispatch
warned against "unjustified direct action." While employers were
reminded by the Post of their duty to provide evidence of non-
discriminatory policy "as a token that the era of procrastination
is over. . . ."

The Globe-Democrat said, "The efforts of this infinitesimally
small but boisterous segment of the St. Louis community will
disgust and revolt all of those who—like this newspaper—have
been trying so long to open new opportunities to Negroes and
improve the status of the race." This long campaign to open
new opportunities is a bit difficult to document in the pages of
the Globe and never included any advice to the Jefferson Bank
to hire Negro workers. But now, advice was given: "We hope
that the Jefferson Bank does not give in to blackmail and
intimidation."[25]

It did not "give in." Seven banks, including Jefferson Bank, met
with the city's Council on Human Relations the day before direct
action was to be set in operation and made more promises in the
form of a ten-point program. By this late hour, the ten-point pro-

gram only meant more promises to be broken and empty verbalism to the black community. The following day, St. Louis City Circuit Court Judge Michael Scott complied with the bank's request and issued an order which contained the names of fourteen individuals, restraining them from interfering with the "proper" and "normal" business of Jefferson Bank.[26]

CORE publicized its anticipated demonstration to inform the community of the honesty of its purpose and seriousness of its intent. Around 4 p.m., approximately two hours after the restraining order had been issued, protesters began picketing the bank. The sheriff (one of the city's "county" officers) proceeded to serve the restraining order. However, because of personal reasons, community dissatisfaction and restlessness, coupled with a tinge of missionary zeal to right an existing injustice, some demonstrators decided to ignore the order. They were willing to go to jail and proceeded to enter the bank and sing as others blocked the door. It is highly possible that those who entered the bank were partially motivated by the expectations created two days earlier by the "March on Washington for Jobs and Freedom" since it was too early for them to learn what the march really represented.

The national racial climate at the time of the March on Washington in August, 1963, forms an important part of the background for the St. Louis struggle. According to the *Autobiography of Malcolm X*, by August of 1963, black people in America had acquired a national bitterness which was militant, unorganized, and leaderless. Many of the embittered were young blacks who were sick and tired of the white man's foot on black people. They were defiant to the extent that they were not obsessively concerned with consequences for any actions they might take. These youngsters, along with other rank-and-file blacks, began kicking around A. Philip Randolph's proposal of more than twenty years earlier for a march on Washington. They could conceive of black people reaching Washington by any way possible—old rickety cars, buses, hitchhiking, even walking. In their minds, once in Washington, thousands of bitter, unorganized, leaderless, but militant black people would utilize various direct action tactics to impress upon the National Legislative and Executive branches that there must be meaningful action to directly benefit black people.[27]

Awareness that such a march would possibly transpire caused

the national elite to develop "nervous worry." There was the realization that some minor or insignificant, unpredictable incident could trigger thousands of blacks into uncontrollable action right in the nation's capital. According to Malcolm, the White House then requested that leaders of the major civil rights groups stop planning the march. But they could not because they had not begun it. Therefore, they had no control over it. Malcolm believed that in order to defuse the black powder keg, national civil rights organizations were given $800,000 and promised more to become involved in the proposed march. After this, "march-nervous" whites announced that they were going too; and the use of massive publicity caused many of E. Franklin Frazier's black bourgeoisie, who earlier had deplored the idea of a march, to join with such enthusiasm that the status seekers among them used it as a symbol after the march: "Were you there?" became a popular refrain. Malcolm and others could refer to it as a "farce" because: "All placards carried by marchers were approved in advance by the committee in charge of the demonstration; no acts of civil disobedience were allowed; and portions of a speech by John Lewis, then Chairman of the Student Non-Violent Coordinating Committee, were deleted by march leaders as inflammatory and out of keeping with the mood of the day."[28]

Given the national racial climate at this time, St. Louis CORE's decision to take direct action was no uncommon occurrence. By the end of 1963, some type of demonstration had taken place in more than 800 cities and towns as the initial response to the gigantic August 28 "March on Washington for Jobs and Freedom," causing it to serve as some type of symbol indicating a move toward unity in America. However, just as millions in America began to think that there would be some black advancement, the racial climate in this county began to undergo change.

> The very fact that millions, black and white, believed in this monumental farce is another example of how much this country goes in for the surface glossing over, the escape ruse, surfaces, instead of truly dealing with its deep-rooted problems.
> What that march on Washington did do was lull Negroes for a while. But inevitably, the black masses started realizing they had been smoothly hoaxed again by the white man. And, inevitably, the black man's anger rekindled, deeper than ever, and

there began bursting out in different cities, in the "long, hot summer" of 1964, unprecedented racial crises.[29]

At the same time blacks were being lulled—and a point of great importance—many Northern whites, especially those of low income, increasingly became hostile to black efforts to secure meaningful employment (and better housing and schools). The rising opposition is seen in Jefferson Bank's decision just two days after the "grand march." The pickets' entrance into the bank prompted the bank's attorney, Wayne Millsap, to go to Judge Michael Scott's home in order to obtain authorization for arrests to be made. When Millsap learned that the demonstration had terminated, he ceased to push for arrests, but stated that on the following Tuesday he would seek citations for contempt of court. Subsequently, Al Williams, a NAACP field secretary who had participated in the demonstration extolled the participants for their courage. He also referred to the fact that there had been no arrests: "We defied an injunction of the court and no arrests were made. I choose to believe the reason why no one was arrested is that the people who got the injunction knew it was unfair."[30]

The NAACP field secretary could not foresee that more was in store to intimidate CORE nor that "Defying an injunction" would reveal the pervasiveness of racism in St. Louis. All black St. Louisans living between 1963 and 1967 were about to witness what the late Minister Malcolm X learned as a gambler: "It's like the Negro in America seeing the white man win all the time. He's a professional gambler; he has all the cards and the odds stacked on his side, and he always dealt to our people from the bottom of the deck."[31]

After the demonstration at Jefferson Bank, there appeared to be reason to question whether biased television and newspaper reporting would be among the odds against black people seeking economic justice.

A customarily courageous television newscaster on a local station concluded his program with an apology for covering the demonstrations. This incredible performance could only have resulted from the pressure of advertisers on his harried superiors.

A daily newspaper headlined that Negro pickets "abuse police." In fact St. Louis police handled the demonstrations with dignity.

> But to heap scorn upon the pickets with such exaggerated head-
> lines seemed to be an attempt to curry favor with the local business
> community. . . .
>   You could see the white power structure pulling out all of
> the devices that worked for years as a club over the head of
> Negro leadership . . . [32]

Although no one was arrested and Millsap withdrew his request
for arrests after 6 p.m. Friday, second thoughts were shaping behind
the scene. CORE's direct action was assailed by both dailies, Mayor
Raymond Tucker, and the governor of Missouri, John M. Dalton.
Governor Dalton promised to confer with city fathers and the Board
of Police Commissioners concerning the alleged acts of lawlessness.
Saturday, the day after the demonstration, several top figures met
at the Board of Police Commissioners, and that night, Judge Scott
authorized arrests for nine who were designated in the original restraining order. He instructed the sheriff to make immediate arrests
and placed bail at $10,000 each. By 1:30 a.m. Sunday morning,
Marion Oldham and Herman Thompson, two public school teachers,
were in confinement. Unable to obtain so high a bail at such an
unattractive hour, they, out of necessity, remained in the city jail.
The remaining seven persons, on their own accord, delivered themselves to the sheriff Sunday at more decent hours.[33]

In effect, in this situation the power structure had reached on
the shelf and put into use a device used in 1904 to intimidate black
people: incarceration. However, in 1963 excessive bail was added
to the pressure of incarceration. In 1904 the all-black Liberty Party
had held its National Convention in St. Louis and nominated
William T. Scott of East St. Louis, Illinois for President of the
United States. Subsequently, William Scott was confronted with
an old unpaid fine of $99.80. Because of costs and his incarceration
he found it necessary to resign as a candidate.[34] Thus, bank demonstrators in 1963 were subjected to a device that had worked in
the past to intimidate black people. William T. Scott readily acquiesced to white demands. But the results of the intimidation were
not so clear-cut between 1963 and 1967.

The "jail the leaders device" employed by the bank knocked
CORE's predemonstration planning out of kilter. CORE had no
desire to see nine of its influential members incarcerated simultaneously. From the bank's point of view it was sound strategy,

especially since three of the nine were attorneys (Robert Curtis, Raymond Howard, and Charles Oldham). The midnight arrest of two public school teachers, one being a black woman, so incensed the black community that job equality ceased to hold the center of the stage by itself. Black people generally believed that the action taken by the authorities was not only unusual, but unreasonable. And when Robert L. Witherspoon, one of the defendants' black attorneys, stated that CORE leaders had been denied due process when they were improperly served with papers for the restraining order, the $10,000 bail loomed larger than excessive. Members of the Ministers' and Laymen's Association for Equal Opportunity (MALEO), a predominantly black group, were so angered that the organization decided to picket Jefferson Bank in support of CORE.[35]

At CORE's Sunday meeting, after the demonstration, Mayor Tucker was denounced. The meeting was moved to Grace Presbyterian Church because of the overflow crowd. Even at the larger church, many people had to stand. William Clay, the prominent black politician in St. Louis (see Chapter 3), was greeted with cheers as he entered the church. He proceeded to classify the mayor as a phony liberal and denounced the governor's remarks pertaining to respect for the courts. Clay pointed out that eight months earlier, Governor Dalton had signed a resolution at the Southern Governors' Conference denouncing the federal court system.[36] Later, we will show how Clay's anger proved to be politically detrimental for Mayor Tucker and for Dalton's candidate to succeed him as governor.

While the arrests were totally rejected by the black community, the bank received editorial support from the *Globe*.

> Wanton violation of property and business rights, of law and order, cannot be tolerated. It demands punishment quickly and effectively.
> The Jefferson Bank . . . showed courage and judgment in flatly refusing this week to accede to CORE pressure for . . . Negro jobs in two weeks.
> . . . And other banks have made it clear that they will cooperate with the St. Louis Council on Human Relations. When jobs are available they will be granted applicants, without regard to race, on the basis of ability.[37]

The injunction issued to protect the "property and business rights" of Jefferson Bank was possibly in accord with the concept that property ownership has rights. But it might also be argued that owners of property have obligations to the society that made this ownership possible. A positive response to this would suggest that no one, including bank directors, has a right to do with his property as he pleases if his wishes are inimical to society. In this dispute, one could consider that the right to earn a living is even more basic a right than the right to own property. Would it not have been proper in August of 1963 for white St. Louisans to have asked whether or not Jefferson Bank was preventing black men from performing their natural duties and obligations to provide for their families and themselves? Furthermore, the St. Louis banking industry generally, and Jefferson Bank in particular, for years made contributions to ensuring that black people would receive low incomes by employing blacks only for low-level jobs. This guaranteed a low level of living for blacks, including poor food, bad housing, and poor health.

The *Globe*'s August 31 editorial raised an additional question. If the bank were willing to hire blacks in cooperation with the St. Louis Council on Human Relations, one could ask why, after this editorial appeared in the *Globe*, the bank's commercial customers received letters in September signed by the president of the bank saying it: ". . . will never hire anyone as a result of coercion or as a matter of expedience."[38] Also, one could question the employment of five white employees hired by Jefferson Bank between September 9 and October 14. Four of the five were hired in a three-day period, September 9 to 11.[39]

On the other hand, the *Post* published a letter to the editor in which the writer apparently realized the discrepancy between the American profession of faith in a fair and equitable judicial system and the actual situation as it pertained to Jefferson Bank demonstrators.

> The sole purpose of requiring bail is to insure the appearance of the accused in court at the appointed time. This being the case, it seems to us that the $10,000 bail set for the CORE leaders arrested in connection with the Jefferson Bank demonstrations was both an insult and excessive.
>
> It is our opinion that release on their own recognizance would

have been more appropriate than setting such a bail. In all the confusion about this difficult situation, one thing is clear—the accused will be more than accessible to the authorities. We suspect they will be found on picket lines in front of the bank demanding jobs now.[40]

Once the trial began on September 3, 1963, a defense attorney requested that CORE leaders be informed of the charges pending against them, but this request was denied. A second attempt was made to have specific charges enumerated based on the fact that five defendants had not had an opportunity to be advised by legal counsel. Judge Scott again overruled the motion. The defense lawyers were again overruled when requesting time to prepare their defense although they were unaware of the specific charges against their clients. They then read Judge Scott a statute appertaining to contempt of court and reasonable time to prepare to defend against charges. The "reasonable time" they were granted was one-half hour. After the "reasonable time" expired, the defense was overruled in its request for continuance. However, time was granted until 10 a.m. the next day to file a writ of prohibition. The very next day, Judge Scott acquiesced to the plea for a continuance, and CORE lawyers were given five days to prepare their cases.

Because of Wayne Millsap's request, it was necessary for the defendants to give their depositions on Saturday, September 7. Their testimonies were taken under pleadings charging civil contempt. Twenty-one days after they had been ordered arrested, and twelve days after having given depositions, the defendants were officially notified that they were charged with criminal and not civil contempt. This was only four days before the trial was to commence after a second continuance.

The distinction proved to be most significant. A civil contempt proceeding arises when there is failure to carry out the court's orders for the benefit of the other party to a civil action. To effect compliance the court ordinarily imposes a penalty, and when it is a jail term it generally lasts only until there is compliance. In other words, the individual has the key to the jail in his pocket since he usually can purge the contempt and be released at any time by agreeing to acquiesce. On the other hand, a criminal contempt proceeding occurs when the court believes the act or action impaired its authority because it was perceived to have been directed against the court itself. In effect, the individual allegedly breached the public order by challenging the authority of the court. Therefore, the court (alone) punishes the individual or individuals.

Now CORE leaders were no longer charged with violating a court order designed to protect the rights of the bank, but with willful disobedience and open disrespect directed against the court itself. The full story as to what transpired between September 3 and September 18 to change the offense from civil to criminal contempt is obscured by secrecy and official statements that apparently established the legality of the action.[41]

The September 19 notification of criminal contempt of court was not the beginning of CORE's legal troubles. Their lawyers became exasperated the previous day when Judge Scott appointed Millsap as "special prosecutor" for the Court. In addition to being the son-in-law of the bank's president, he had represented the bank when CORE lawyers believed they were fighting civil contempt. Since Millsap was one of the bank's regular attorneys, there existed a belief that the "special prosecutor" had a personal and financial interest in the case.[42]

The differences between civil and criminal contempt became more important to CORE after October 4, 1963. Although the injunction was not violated as the bank was being picketed in September, on October 4, fifteen demonstrators were arrested for violating it. Not only were they detained at the police station, but they were not given an opportunity to see legal counsel. Juveniles were not held, but seven adults were charged with violating the original restraining order and received "special treatment." Judge Scott held a preliminary hearing for them commencing shortly after their arrests and lasting until 3 a.m., October 5. Their trial was scheduled for October 7. Attorneys for the second group of defendants proclaimed that no citation had been filed, nor had any charges been made against the seven, causing them to be unaware of what to defend against. They were overruled, but there were additional efforts by CORE lawyers to have the second group of demonstrators tried under the rules of civil contempt.[43] An exchange between Robert L. Witherspoon, a CORE attorney, and the bank's lawyer is indicative of the problem concerning charges:

> MR. WITHERSPOON: I would like to see or have a copy of the citation. I looked in the court file and I failed to find a citation

issued by this court setting forth the day and time and place and the charges against these defendants. I saw the attachment, but it stated no date as to when these defendants committed an offense in any way, and there were no charges in there that they had committed an offense.

MR. MILLSAP: . . . In the proceeding against the nine other individuals . . . we clearly proceeded as a matter of criminal contempt . . . with reference to these defendants . . . we have not taken this course . . .

MR. MILLSAP: In view of the statements which have just been made by Mr. Witherspoon . . . I am prepared to proceed in that manner, for criminal contempt. I have all the papers here with reference to anything in connection with the criminal contempt charges against these individuals . . .

MR. WITHERSPOON: If he has them in his brief case, Your Honor, we think he ought to file them.

THE COURT: All right, gentlemen. Motion will be overruled.

MR. WITHERSPOON: I would like to know which way he's going to proceed now.

MR. MILLSAP: The record speaks for itself.[44]

Was the civil contempt charge replaced with criminal contempt because of the possible imprisonment under criminal contempt which some white people believed would teach black people a lesson? Was the change made because, under civil contempt, CORE leaders possibly would have been released once it could be established that they had ceased to violate the court order? Even to this day it would be a prodigious task to convince so much as a small minority in the black community that CORE leaders were tried for other than punitive political reasons. Subsequent events promoted additional alienation as black St. Louisans were soon to be reminded that it was almost impossible to be treated impartially, in a black-white confrontation, by a judicial system that most white people accept without question.

NOTES

[1] Ideas pertaining to powerlessness and organizations are discussed in Michael Lipsky, "Protest as a Political Resource," *American Political Science Review,* LXII (December, 1968), 1150–51.

[2] *Ibid.*

[3] Martin Oppenheimer and George Lakey, *A Manual For Direct Action* (Chicago: Quadrangle Books, 1964), p. 106.

[4] *Ibid.*, pp. 15–16.

[5] *Ibid.*

[6] Virginia Brodine, "The Strange Case of Jefferson Bank vs. CORE," *Focus/Midwest*, XI (November, 1963), p. 12.

[7] Alex Haley ed., *The Autobiography of Malcolm X* (New York: Grove Press, 1964), p. 251.

[8] *Ibid.*, p. 106.

[9] *Post*, August 26, 1963, p. 3A.

[10] For a discussion of economic benefits derived from racism see *Racism in America and How to Combat It*, The United States Commission on Civil Rights, Clearinghouse Publication, Urban Series No. 1 (Washington, D.C.: U.S. Government Printing Office, January 1, 1970), p. 20.

[11] Brodine, *op. cit.* (n. 6), p. 12.

[12] *Ibid.*, p. 13.

[13] Charles E. Silberman, *Crises in Black and White* (New York: Vintage Books, 1964), p. 198.

[14] Ideas pertaining to bargaining relationships, tangible and intangible compensations, and negative inducements are discussed in James Q. Wilson, "The Strategy of Protest: Problems of Negro Civic Action," *Journal of Conflict Resolution*, V (September, 1961), pp. 291–303.

[15] Brodine, *op. cit.* (n. 6), p. 12.

[16] Letter of Robert B. Curtis, chairman of CORE, to Harold Booker, assistant auditor, Jefferson Bank and Trust Company, August 14, 1963.

[17] Brodine, *op. cit.* (n. 6), p. 12.

[18] Letter from Wayne L. Millsap, attorney for Jefferson Bank and Trust Company, to Robert B. Curtis, chairman of CORE, August 27, 1963.

[19] Brief for the Appellants, *Ford* v. *Boeger*, 18011 and 18033, 1964, U.S. Court of Appeals, Eighth Circuit.

[20] Lipsky, *op. cit.* (n. 1), pp. 1156–57.

[21] *St. Louis Globe-Democrat*, August 31-September 1, 1963, p. 4A. Henceforward in footnotes the *St. Louis Globe-Democrat* will be referred to as *Globe*.

[22] Jake McCarthy, *Missouri Teamster*, October 18, 1963, p. 8.

[23] *Ibid.*

[24] *Ibid.*

[25] Brodine, *op. cit.* (n. 6), p. 13.

[26] *Ibid.*

[27] Haley, *op. cit.* (n. 7), pp. 278–81.

[28] Richard Worsnop, "Black Pride," in *Editorial Research Reports on the Urban Environment* (Washington, D.C., Congressional Quarterly, 1969), p. 131.

[29] Haley, *op. cit.* (n. 7), p. 281.

[30] *Post*, August 31, 1963, p. 1A.

[31] Haley, *op. cit.* (n. 7), p. 16.

[32] McCarthy, *op. cit.* (n. 22).

[33] Brief for the Appellants, *op. cit.* (n. 19), p. 6.

[34] Nathan B. Young, *Your St. Louis and Mine* (St. Louis, Mo.: N. B. Young, 1938), p. 65.

[35] *Post*, September 3, 1963, pp. 1A, 3A.

[36] *Ibid.*

[37] *Globe* (editorial), August 31, 1963, p. 2F.

[38] *Post*, September 27, 1963, p. 3A.
[39] *Post*, October 29, 1963, p. 3A.
[40] *Post*, September 6, 1963, p. 2B, letter to the editor from Daniel Kohl and Gorman Mattison.
[41] Brodine, *op. cit.* (n. 6), p. 14.
[42] Brief for the Appellants, *op. cit.* (n. 19), p. 8.
[43] *Ibid.*, pp. 8–9.
[44] *Ibid.*, p. 9.

CHAPTER 8

Elitist Justice Contributes
to Black Unity

It has been suggested that the black community sheltered a suspicion that black people generally did not receive impartial justice in St. Louis. St. Louis blacks over the past half-century had become involved in city politics increasingly to the extent that they developed the realization that economic power conditioned political power. They were aware that how the city government actually worked depended in part on the combination of political factions, and in part, on the combination of economic factions. Although they desired to believe that the judicial system was not so much a part of the power elite that black people would be denied impartial and impersonal justice, certain actions taken—midnight arrests, $10,000 bail, heavy sentences for demonstrators ranging up to one year, a black demonstrator's arrest for failure to make TV payments—were soon to indicate to the black community the pervasiveness of the power structure's influence. In particular, the action taken against Taylor Jones, an East St. Louis, Illinois, resident, who was arrested with the second group of demonstrators against Jefferson Bank, gave the black community reason to increase its suspicion and to include the judiciary in that suspicion.

It was made clear that there was some type of relationship between St. Louis' financial world and the court when a warrant was sworn out on October 8, 1963, charging Taylor Jones with deceptive practices because payments on a rented television set were not up to date. Utilization of this "device," a practice not commonly used to collect payment for rented TV's in the St. Louis area, was indicative of the pervasiveness of the power structure's influence. Jones was due in Judge Scott's court at 10 a.m., October

11, for demonstrating; but he was arrested earlier that morning in East St. Louis, Illinois, for default on TV rental and was not allowed to post bond until one-half hour after he was to appear in the St. Louis Court. He arrived in St. Louis and learned that his $5,000 bond had been forfeited and that Judge Scott had ordered him arrested. Scott would not rule on a motion to set aside the forfeiture of bond, but recessed court until 3 p.m. The recess was used to arrest Jones and his bond was increased to $10,000. Unable to make bond, Jones was sent to jail apparently because he "did not voluntarily surrender himself to the court."[1]

Black political scientist Matthew Holden, Jr. has a good explanation as to why black people are subject to experiences similar to those of Jones. According to Holden:

> . . . the political scientist may find his central clue in Adam Smith's dictum that the very object of government is to give security to wealth and to defend the rich from the poor. Class and property interests are not a sole and adequate explanation but they constitute a reasonable beginning. Owners and managers of commerce and industry need constant protection against arson and robbery, hi-jacking and shoplifting, embezzlement and industrial espionage, and they have a relatively great ability to secure that protection. They also have non-entrepreneurial needs that link them with the high-salaried middle class. By an exercise of market power, this sector can segregate itself residentially, but there is no way to purchase actual control of city streets and limit the movement of persons therein. Accordingly, public agencies of order become a vital part of this group's defense establishment.[2]

The public agencies of order went into action again on October 7 when a third group of demonstrators was arrested and charged with peace disturbance and trespassing. None of them were CORE members, nor were their names listed in the original restraining order pertaining to CORE and Jefferson Bank. While they were in police custody, an attorney for the bank filed an affidavit against them. "The verification . . . was sworn to three days before the facts stated therein were alleged to have occurred."[3] By now it was obvious to the defendants' attorneys and the black community that the full weight of the power structure, through the many trained legal minds at its disposal, would press hard to thwart efforts designed to improve employment opportunities for black people. Furthermore, no one could say where they would stop. The pretense of consulting and using legal machinery was now perceived by black St. Louisans as a mere piece of political chicanery by which the discontent of the black masses could be held in check.

The Ministers' and Laymen's Association for Equal Opportunity (MALEO) decided to support CORE more actively. On October 11, it announced that ministers in at least eighty-five churches would request their members to participate in a two-day semieconomic boycott of what it considered the bank's adamant position.

> As ministers of some of the oldest and some of the most respected congregations in the City of St. Louis, it seems to us that Negroes need to express themselves about the Jefferson Bank situation and all that it stands for with a great silent and articulated protest.
>
> We should have two days in which we will make no purchases at all other than food and medicine . . . and very little of these. . . .
>
> Jefferson Bank seems to hold itself or it appears to be regarded as the symbol of the attitude of white people in St. Louis toward the Negro and particularly the employment of Negroes.
>
> This fight is no longer CORE's fight. It is now the fight of every Negro and every person in this community who stands for human rights.
>
> Let us not confuse the issue. The issue is jobs. . . .[4]

Thirteen physicians and several medical technicians joined in the picket line and carried placards stating: "Responsible People Want Justice," "Doctors Demand Democracy," and "We Cannot Condone Recklessness or Stubbornness." They believed that their participation would help the power structure come to realize the pervasiveness of concern in the black community. It was hoped that such a realization would effect some type of solution acceptable to both sides.[5] Indeed, on October 9, CORE made a conciliatory gesture, in the form of a telegram, proposing to talk about the situation. The bank declined the overture and made it clear that it had no desire to deal with the new black leaders.[6] In rejecting CORE's endeavor to talk, John H. McConnell, the bank's executive vice-president, said that the demonstrators had acted like animals and the bank would never bargain or negotiate with anyone associated with CORE.[7] Old-line black leaders, no doubt, would not have been referred to as "animals."

It is clear that bank officials misinterpreted what the arrests meant to the black community. Dillon J. Ross, Jefferson Bank's president, denounced those black and white ministers who had joined the picket line because he felt they should have condemned the demonstrators as "sinful and shameful." He suggested the black doctors walking the picket line "search their consciences because no group resists interference with its own affairs as strongly as the medical profession."[8] This clearly shows how bank officials misunderstood St. Louis' black people. The ministers considered the protest justifiable. And in their minds, the physicians were not interfering in someone else's dispute. They were black and it was a collective black effort.

Efforts in behalf of CORE by MALEO, black physicians and medical technicians, and other groups and individuals in the total St. Louis community were to no avail. As CORE and the supporting groups continued their demonstrations throughout the trials, the general public was informed by newspapers that they were unruly, disorderly, and lawless, despite the nonviolent nature of the demonstrations.[9] On October 24 and 25, Judge Scott not only found all nineteen who had demonstrated at Jefferson Bank guilty of criminal contempt, but he denied bond, pending an appeal. He also ordered immediate incarceration without giving the demonstrators any time to put their personal affairs in order. Their sentences ranged from sixty days to one year in jail, and included fines from $500 to $1,000.[10]

The imposition of stiff fines and harsh, extended sentences are ingredients that dishearten many people. The defendants possibly could have become even more depressed since they had failed to instill within St. Louis' banking industry more concern for human economic survival than for property rights. However, on the positive side, it was clear to the demonstrators that there was nothing accidental about thirty-five to forty-five blacks being hired in downtown banks during the period between their initial demonstration and their receiving harsh sentences and stiff fines.[11]

By now Judge Scott and attorney Millsap were so detested that their combined efforts (in behalf of the elite) to keep blacks in their place caused unity in the black community. "Millsap and

Judge Scott . . . made the greatest contribution to Negro unity in St. Louis in twenty years."[12] Because of these two men, the central city would never be the same. In their minds, CORE lawyers could not separate the two.

> We cannot know how Judge Scott arrived at his verdict. We do know, however, that the findings were not specific. They were copied verbatim from the specifications in the Notice of Contempt prepared by Wayne Millsap. It is hard to imagine how a judge could find that all petitioners committed contempt in exactly the same manner after two weeks of trial and more than 1,000 pages of testimony. This anomaly is nothing less than fantastic. Petitioners were never informed as to their specific words or conduct found to have been in violation of the restraining order. The question still persists—what standards did the trial court use in determining Guilt? The failure of the record to disclose how the findings (which were in reality conclusions of fact and law) were made, indicates gross lack of procedural safeguards for petitioners' constitutional rights.[13]

From the first day CORE demonstrated at Jefferson Bank, its efforts were attacked. During the early stages, there were newspaper accounts of statements by the governor of Missouri, the mayor of St. Louis, St. Louis' president of the Board of Aldermen, a white state senator who represented a large black constituency, and a black state senator—all of whom were influential political leaders. The jailed demonstrators did not consider any of those public figures' remarks helpful to their cause. The local newspapers, television, and most radio stations assailed the pickets. From August 28, 1963 until mid-January, 1964, the city's only morning daily published no less than fourteen editorials and seventeen smear articles stigmatizing the demonstrators. The October articles were apparently designed to influence the judge and prejudice the general public. There is no evidence that Judge Scott took any steps to curb such publicity, which possibly violated a Missouri Supreme court rule, especially since Wayne Millsap had made statements to the press and on television.[14]

> Newspaper publications by a lawyer as to pending or anticipated litigation may interfere with a fair trial in the courts and otherwise prejudice the due administration of justice. Generally

they are to be condemned. If the extreme circumstances of a particular case justify a statement to the public, it is unprofessional to make it anonymously. An ex parte reference to the facts should not go beyond quotation from the records and papers on file in the Court; but even in extreme cases, it is better to avoid an ex parte statement.[15]

On October 15, 1963, a front-page *Globe* headline stated that a "Bank Demonstration Leader Is Convicted Morals Offender." It is possible that through this publicity James Peake, a white paraplegic demonstrator, was erroneously portrayed. Peake, a former Southern Illinois University undergraduate, launched his civil rights career when, in 1962, he joined activists in Cairo, Illinois. During the Cairo struggle for black economic advancement and equal public accommodations, he was arrested at least eight times. In July, 1962, he was charged with indecent or lewd behavior, but pleaded not guilty. A jury of only seven found him guilty and he was fined fourteen dollars. His friends claimed the charge was brought unfairly as harassment for his civil rights activity. They support their charge by pointing out how Peake was released by police at 2 a.m. at a point nearly a mile from his home. He had to wheel himself home.

The one-year sentence received by Peake led black people to believe that adverse publicity influenced his sentence. His one-year jail sentence was not legally declared to be cruel and unusual punishment, but the actual situation revealed that his wheel chair was too large for the four feet by eight feet cell, placing him completely at the disposal of other prisoners with total reliance upon them whether he desired to go to bed or use toilet facilities.[16] This inhumane sentence for a white man caused most black people to believe that his punishment was designed to teach other white people not to attempt to help black people remove the economic straitjacket holding them down.[17]

It is possible that Peake received the longest sentence, and because of his physical condition, the most cruel because:

> The white participant is singled out for special treatment by local opponents of the civil rights movement. As a white he is seen as a traitor, which is worse than being a Negro. His presence in the struggle serves to undermine the delicate structure of thinking and excuses which most white[s] . . . have created for them-

selves to account for segregation and discrimination. His presence by itself tells them their system is a lie. It is a shock. Therefore, it infuriates. It has to be accounted for: the white participant is seen as an outside agitator, a Communist, perhaps a light skinned Negro, and if a woman, a prostitute. For no real white person (read: no one from "our way of life") could walk with a sign, could "want a Negro to marry his sister. . . ."[18]

It is not unusual for the power structure to ignore discontent as long as possible, then declare it is a conspiracy. Thus, many St. Louisans began to read that the Reds were at it again. Before Judge Scott announced his decision in the three cases, there appeared in the *Globe* ten articles (most of the articles pertained to national CORE) evidently designed to cause the white community to believe that the local chapter of CORE was communist-influenced. It appears that the *Globe* influenced the public through implication and association by using the term "Red," along with sweeping generalities. Such a device, when successful, will prevent a community from concentrating on the core of a controversy.

The communist-conspiracy implication was so farfetched that it was ludicrous. No real evidence was brought to support it. However, it was easier to manufacture a scapegoat than to attack the fundamental problem and attempt to eliminate the root causes that were leading to unemployment and underemployment of black people in St. Louis. The charge was ludicrous because black St. Louisans did not need outside "Red" agitators to motivate them when they had been economically oppressed since Laclede and Chouteau outpost days.

Whenever a local elite can blame difficulties on "troublemakers" and "outside elements," it is in a position to minimize the root causes and sometimes even deny they exist. It simplifies matters for the establishment when its supporters learn that the (alleged) malefactor has been identified. With such an identification, the power structure is in a position to proceed to oppress and punish those who have dissented from its established procedures and practices. Oppression and punishment are a necessity because of the elite's commitment to preserve the existing normative and institutional arrangements. This not so uncommon pattern of blaming troublemakers and outside elements is usually followed when problems are so complicated and serious as to be potentially threatening enough to tear an entire metropolitan community asunder. In such a case the elite usually seeks a quick solution: invariably, not only quick, but simple. Furthermore, when they pertain to race, simplistic projections are easier to offer and more likely to be accepted by the general white community than a solution that would require undergoing the painful experience of introspectively reviewing one's own personal and institutional racism as it operates in that total community. The point is that the elite seeks the quickest answer, and takes the first simple one.

Significantly, most of the *Globe*'s conspiracy articles appeared on page one. Furthermore, in addition to this type of publicity, and before the heavy sentences were handed down, the two dailies and two black weeklies published a large advertisement paid for by the bank. This advertisement sought to gain sympathy for the bank and discredit the defendants by giving the bank's "Facts on Jefferson Bank and Fair Employment." CORE's attorneys believed that this type of publicity prejudiced the defendants' constitutional rights and, for support, cited a statement by the Honorable William O. Douglas in the *Rocky Mountain Law Review:*

> Newspapers, radio and television are in the hands of men who have their own political philosophy and their own ideas as to what justice is and how it should be administered. Some newspapers dominate a community. When ownership of the paper is combined with ownership of the radio and television station, the community may become saturated with one point of view. We have had publishers who were tyrants and sought to impose their will on the courts as well as on the people. . . . Even federal judges who have life tenure may feel the lash of editorials demanding that cases be decided this way or that.
> . . . At times the papers can help to arouse passions in a community so that no trial can be a fair one.[19]

Not only did the jailed demonstrators have to contend with newspaper articles pertaining to CORE and communism, Peake and morals, and newspaper accounts of statements made by the governor, mayor, president of the Board of Aldermen, two state senators, and Millsap, but also three of the demonstrators were attacked by the St. Louis Bar Association. Despite the numerous murders, rapes, robberies, and other types of felonies committed annually (at this time St. Louis recorded in excess of 10,000 major crimes each year), the St. Louis Bar Association, represented by John Shepard, elected to condemn three demonstrators who were attorneys, for their alleged contempt of law and their supposed lawlessness. Shepard issued his press release despite the fact that the complaints which had been filed against attorneys Curtis, Howard, and Oldham, along with the defendants' appeals, were undetermined.[20]

The black community became genuinely concerned when it was realized that a major part of St. Louis' communication media was helping to mold white public opinion against CORE's fight for economic justice. CORE's legal counsel was aware of how extremely difficult it is, even for judges who have life tenure, to ignore public opinion and editorials appearing in powerful newspapers. Therefore, it was of very grave importance to them that the defendants found themselves in criminal proceedings before a judge who depended upon election for his position. To them, he was a man who wore several hats. He was an elective officer, and thus political. He issued the original restraining order, served as trial judge, and was the sentencing judge—all wrapped up in one enigmatic, official personality. These facts caused the defendants to question, in appeals, whether or not newspaper publicity had caused the trials to bear little resemblance to what the Supreme Court has usually defined as a "fair trial".[21]

A letter to the editor which appeared in the *Post* reflected much of the sentiment in the black community on this point: ". . . I have witnessed some Northern justice, and I wonder where I would rather be, St. Louis or Alabama. I find justice is much harder here. I have read about the unfavorable treatment that those people get down South. How about this in St. Louis? The lack of bond, the stiff fine and jail punishment."[22]

It is not uncommon in Missouri for persons convicted of criminal contempt of court to be punished with a one-hundred dollar fine or a smaller amount, and three months or less jail sentences. The sentences ranging from sixty days to one year and fines from five-hundred to one-thousand dollars decreed at Scott's discretion[23] infuriated the black weekly, the *Defender:*

> The sentences handed down by Circuit Judge Michael J. Scott in the Jefferson Bank and Trust Company demonstration were unwarranted, to say the least.

From the beginning, it has been apparent that the court and
Wayne Millsap, the Bank's attorney, were hell-bent to "make
an example" of Negro leaders who dared to spearhead a drive
for equal employment opportunity. Almost all defense motions
were denied, and all statements that may have been useful on
the defendant's behalf were ordered stricken.[24]

In the face of what the black community considered as unwarranted sentences and gross inequalities of justice, it is significant
that the *Defender* emphasized black people doing whatever was
necessary to let racist whites know "once and for all" that black
people were fed up with being "slapped in the face" by white
people. The *Defender*'s hope for impartial justice had been displaced
by what was probably a more realistic, and certainly a more cold-
blooded, demand for action.

It would be the end of everything we hope to gain insofar
as job opportunities are concerned, if this gross miscarriage of
justice is allowed to stand unprotested by the Negro people of
this city. Now is the time for us to join together, and fill the
streets, and even the jails, if it becomes necessary. Our Negro
leaders who are being persecuted must not be made to feel that
they suffer in vain. Negroes who do business with merchants
and other businesses that have money on deposit in the Jefferson
Bank should demand that those businesses withdraw their funds
immediately from that establishment, or face a total boycott by
the Negro community. The New Age Federal Savings and Loan
Association should be requested by the Negro community to withdraw whatever capital it has on deposit with the Jefferson Bank.
City officials should be asked in no uncertain terms to take our
taxpayer's dollars out of the bank.
And we should as one united group, do whatever may be
necessary to let the bigots know once and for all that we are
fed up with being slapped in the face by them at anytime that
suits their fancy.[25]

For one of the few times since they came into existence, three
black weeklies were together on an issue. The *Argus* even used
its "Chit Chat" column to denounce one scale of justice for black
people and a different scale for white people. Ernest Calloway,
a black labor leader, earlier had been critical of CORE and its
direct-action tactics. But after its leaders received harsh and repres-

sive punishment, he publicly pointed out that the matter over tactics was now irrelevant. He believed that because the white power structure had shown a massive disposition to injure and exploit black people for its own purposes, the black community was obligated to firmly support the "sincere young people and set a living example for generations to come."[26] According to one account: "Negro St. Louis was angry. This was not a 'sore spot in an otherwise favorable racial picture.' This was one law for the white and another for the Negro; this was the 'white power structure' using its power to put the Negro in his place."[27]

The city and county branches of the NAACP were highly critical of the fines and sentences and proclaimed they were purposeful efforts to support the Southern style of justice in St. Louis. Their joint statement pointed out how black people expected due process of law and equitable justice from the court, and that they did not "expect to reap acts of vengeance under the guise of justice."[28]

The *Globe*, in its October 25, 1963 editorial pertaining to Jefferson Bank, apparently realized the potential for a loss of confidence among citizens within the community. But it appears that the *Globe* only considered white racism and gave no thought to the fact that black people could collectively become angry.

> . . . We are in agreement with . . . [the Negro] . . . "There is no chance of our struggle failing . . . we don't need to violate any laws to get our rights."
> The . . . [Negro] is right. Time is on the side of the Negro. But irresponsible actions and the deliberate violation of laws to gain preferential treatment, if continued, would leave a deposit of bitterness in the community which the strongest civil rights bill would not erase.[29]

Whether one accepts or rejects the idea of preferential hiring, that premise possibly did not cause the above paragraph to be written. It is highly possible that it was written because the *Globe* accepted the word of one whom it called a "Negro leader," when in fact the man had misjudged the temper of the new black community. The *Globe*'s Negro leader was denounced by the *Defender*: "We repeat our contention that . . . [the Negro] quoted by the *Globe* is a puppet of the downtown power structure, having been lauded by the biased morning daily newspaper, as 'one of the real

Negro leaders.' If he is, you can have him. We'll take Gov. Wallace. At least, he talks out of only one side of his mouth."[30]

After Judge Scott sentenced the defendants, the *Globe* planted additional seeds of mistrust and suspicion in the black community with its "tribute to the character and courage of the Judge himself."

> Yesterday's decision by Circuit Judge Michael J. Scott and the sentences imposed upon nine persons who willfully violated his court order are a vindication of law in this community—which was indeed on trial—and a tribute to the character and courage of the Judge himself.
>
> Had the decision been otherwise, had the sentences handed down been mere wrist-slappings, encouragement would have been given to every irresponsible element in St. Louis to take the law into its own hands when its own cause was involved.[31]

The defendants continued to regard their actions as necessary and just; and the "vindication of law" produced, at the most, only outward conformity because the sentences were considered to be unguided by reason and unmindful of justice. And on Sunday, October 27, a rally was held at which more than $5,000 was raised for the demonstrators' legal defense fund. More than 400 people left the rally and went to the jail to sing and pray, as had at least 200 supporters of the demonstrators each night since the demonstrators had been sent to jail.[32]

Each night thereafter supporters went to the jail. Rain and cold weather did not disturb them, but they would always become silent on those nights when some so-called Negroes would park their automobiles on the adjacent parking lot and walk in front of them and proceed across the street to Kiel Auditorium to see a basketball game.

An additional element in the community became involved. On Sunday, October 27, Bishop George L. Cadigan, of the Episcopal Diocese of Missouri, issued a pastoral letter which was read in many churches. He told the white community that it could not remain uninvolved and that: "Up to this time too many of us have been as spectators, witnessing in the abstract one of the greatest social revolutions. We have felt comfortably secure in what was taking place in Montgomery, or Oxford. . . . But now it is increasingly in our midst."[33]

Although the Bishop's letter viewed the violation of the injunction as a "departure from responsible leadership," he apparently understood (to that extent that a white man can understand) why it was not obeyed and how Jefferson Bank had helped further divide an already badly divided city. According to the Bishop's letter: "At this point in time, the cleavage between Negro and whites is very marked, indeed. The understandable hostility of the Negroes is matched only by the increasing bitterness of the whites. It is not inconceivable that disorder and violence are on our threshold."

On October 28, approximately 350 Catholic laymen, priests, and nuns showed their concern by holding a benediction service at the Church of St. John the Apostle and then walked to the Civil Courts Building for candlelight prayers. They also heard John E. Dunsford, Associate Professor of Law at St. Louis University, refer to the demonstrators' violation of the injunction and the position taken by the bank. He said that: "Those who smugly agree that lawlessness cannot be tolerated are tilting at windmills. Of course it cannot, but neither can the silent strangulation of Negro manhood with the rope of racism."[34]

The traditional tactic of generating sympathy for and propagating favorable publicity in behalf of one who has performed according to the white power structure's desires was employed. The *Globe* extolled Judge Scott and informed its readers how he had overcome personal handicaps when he lost both legs as a preschool child. It then showed the "Kind of Judge He Is."

> His reputation as a fair-minded judge, as a just and unprejudiced man has been long and well established.
> The purpose in recalling these things now is that Judge Scott's handling of the CORE has been questioned by some misguided souls who should know better.
> Nothing could hurt the cause of civil liberties and equal opportunities more in the St. Louis area than for anyone to get the impression that he is not one of the best friends the people of any minority group have in this community.[35]

However, if he were a "fair-minded judge," "a just and unprejudiced man," and one of its "best friends," the black community did not believe it. Furthermore, black people were of the opinion that if his excessive bail and extended sentences were the acts of a friend, then they could ill afford to have enemies. The *Argus* helps to reveal how deep and enduring the hatred and suspicion were that Judge Scott helped to create in the black community. The white community generally considered the *Argus* a responsible "Negro" newspaper. But Scott helped generate so much distrust in black people for the judicial system that more than three years after the Jefferson Bank demonstrations, an *Argus* editorial read: "Well does the Negro know that some white judges are prejudiced against Negroes. Judge Scott is not God. He is definitely human, and definitely exposed to the St. Louis tradition of discriminating against Negroes."[36]

On October 24, 1963 after the original defendants received their sentences, their attorneys requested bond pending appeal. The request was denied apparently because appeal is not allowed in criminal contempt cases. However, on the first day of November, all nineteen defendants were granted bail by the St. Louis Court of Appeals, among other reasons, because the defendants' attorneys argued that the demonstrators had been denied due process of law.[37]

The January 15, 1964, results from the St. Louis Court of Appeals were mixed and mostly disappointing to the black community.

> . . . From what has been herein held that the petitioners Curtis, Clay, Seay, Richards, Perkins, Ford, Iran Grand, Goins, Tournour, Jones, Lee, Gleen, Michela Grand, Pollack, and Peake are not illegally restrained, and as to these petitioners our writs should be quashed and these petitioners remanded to the custody of the respondents. As to the petitioners Howard, Thompson, Marion Oldham, and Charles Oldham, we hold they are illegally restrained in that the evidence does not support the finding that they were guilty beyond a reasonable doubt, of any of the specifications found in the judgment entered as to each of them. Accordingly they are to be discharged. . . .[38]

Additional legal maneuvers (in behalf of those not discharged) saw the Supreme Court of Missouri in an unreported decision deny the defendants a writ of habeas corpus without a hearing. More disappointment set in when the United States District Court for the Eastern District of Missouri refused to entertain the application for writs of habeas corpus because the appellants had not applied for certiorari to the Supreme Court of the United States. It also denied bond. However, on appeal, the Eighth Circuit Court of Appeals disagreed with the Eastern Division District Court and ordered it to determine whether federally protected rights had been denied, and whether an evidentiary hearing was necessary. The appellate court admitted the appellants to bail. The Federal District Court then resolved the question independently when it did not grant CORE attorneys an opportunity to come before it and present arguments. The Court decreed that an evidentiary hearing was not required.[39]

It is an understatement to say that the demonstrators experienced a measure of disillusionment after having spent fifty-five days in jail. Also, in lieu of "having been taught a lesson in obedience by the white power structure," most of them lost faith in the judicial process. Some of them stated:

> We never thought we'd be in so long. The lawyers were very encouraging. Then there [was] terrible disillusionment when our chances for release were shattered. . . .
> I was outraged and surprised by the Court decision which sent us to jail. I had faith in the judicial system but it has been shattered.[40]

On the other hand, incarceration possibly caused some of the demonstrators to become more determined to fight for racial equality, as revealed by one remark: "And if the courts and jail have given me anything it's been a determination to fight for what I think is right."[41]

The city jail is under the control of the Department of Public Welfare. This fact becomes somewhat interesting when considering that CORE was also concerned with jail conditions. However, during the period that the Jefferson Bank demonstrators were being jailed, the organization was not specifically fighting for improved conditions at city jail. But complaints informally registered by jailed demonstrators while discussing their feelings after having been in jail for fifty-five days became more significant when in 1965 Arthur Kennedy, slightly older than the young Turks, but associated with them, was appointed as Director of Public Welfare.[42]

It might be mentioned that a few months prior to Kennedy's appointment, members of CORE devoted many hours to his unsuccessful campaign for an elective office. These efforts indicate that, although some CORE members had lost faith in the judicial system, they had not moved so far to the left that they had given up on the existing political system.

The jailed demonstrators received another taste of judicial oppression, although out on bond, when President Lyndon Johnson came to the St. Louis Bi-Centennial Celebration February 14, 1964. CORE was denounced after announcing it would picket the celebration, not as an act against the President, but because it:

> . . . wanted to save the President from being used as a pawn by the St. Louis community figures whose objectives were to create an artificial feeling of racial progress in our city. . . .
>
> CORE felt that the city fathers were grossly insensitive in the midst of such widespread suffering. Our demonstration on February 14, sought to petition the President's aid, forcing the city fathers to honestly begin the fight against poverty and racism, which President Johnson as a national leader, had championed.
>
> We attempted to get all of this information to the public by means of press releases. Our message was completely distorted by all of the news media. We were forced to attempt to place a quarter page ($700.00) advertisement in the St. Louis Post Dispatch. The Post Dispatch refused to carry our ad.[43]

Apparently there were suggestions prior to the Bi-Centennial demonstration that, if CORE members were to demonstrate, the act would be detrimental for those out of jail on bond for picketing at Jefferson Bank. On February 11, nine of those out on bail were called in by Judge Rodney Weiss and told that they were to return to his office on February 14, at 1 p.m., then go home and remain inside until President Johnson had left St. Louis. A black state legislator and attorney, Hugh J. White, possessed affidavits signed by seven people confirming the acts of Judge Weiss and White made the Judge's threats public, whereupon the Judge said it was a lie. On February 14, Weiss apparently had a change of heart and did not completely deny CORE members the right to picket and petition as guaranteed by the United States Constitution, but said they could demonstrate if pickets remained six to eight feet apart and did not sing.[44]

Failure of the traditional devices of intimidation and threats, the manifestations of judicial repression, forced the power structure to utilize an additional device which caused a schism within the black community. A CORE release explained:

> Seventeen "prominent" members of the Negro community called a press conference and said that "any demonstration at the President was ill-timed, ill-advised and pointless."
>
> The editorials in the two daily newspapers denounced CORE while at the same time the St. Louis Argus took up their fight to describe CORE as an irresponsible group for picketing the President.[45]

Denied access to the communication media to propagate its ideas, CORE felt it was necessary to demonstrate. Approximately one-hundred demonstrators adhered to Weiss' instructions, remained six feet apart and silent; nevertheless, all were arrested. After a questioning session at police headquarters that lasted until after the President had left the hotel, they were released without being booked and charged.[46]

Evidently, the arrests were carried out without any question either as to the morality of these means or as to what the black masses would learn from the experience. Furthermore, the action was indicative of how far the power structure would go to reach an ulterior end. Part of its goal apparently was to prevent St. Louis from acquiring a reputation as a city where the President of the United States is picketed. But the action had a different meaning to CORE.

> The lesson to be learned here is that the financial interest represented on the Bi-Centennial Committee used all of the traditional methods of a police state to preserve the mistaken image of progress and racial peace in the city of St. Louis. The use of the courts for intimidation, the use of political prisoners as hostages, a well managed public relations campaign in the news media, and finally, mass arrests, are clear examples of a carefully coordinated display of naked power.
>
> However, the burning issues of poverty and racial discrimination remain unrelieved. Until the issues are honestly faced and solved, our voice of protest will not be silenced.[47]

It would seem highly appropriate that St. Louis take a long hard look at its judicial system. Some St. Louisans may consider the midnight arrests, $10,000 bail, sentences for protestors ranging up to one year, Jones's arrest for failure to make TV payments, and the arrest of those who picketed President Johnson (including the police state tactics used by Judge Weiss), as maintaining law and order. On the contrary, such treatment caused enduring suspicion and distrust of the judicial system. In most of the 1967 riot cities black people had lost confidence in the local judicial system, which operated so as to increase tensions rather than relieve them.[48] In the next chapter it will be pointed out how the judicial system, as it worked in the Jefferson Bank case, pushed St. Louis to the point where many St. Louisans believed violence and destruction were imminent.

NOTES

[1] Virginia Brodine, "The Strange Case of Jefferson Bank vs. CORE," *Focus/Midwest*, XI (November, 1963), pp. 13–14. About ten days later the Court did set aside the forfeiture. Because of the forfeiture Jones was unable to get the required bond of $10,000.

[2] Matthew Holden, Jr., "Politics, Public Order, and Pluralism," in James R. Klonoski and Robert I. Mendelsohn, eds., *The Politics of Local Justice* (Boston: Little, Brown, 1970), p. 240.

[3] Brodine, *op. cit.*, p. 11.

[4] *Post*, October 11, 1963, p. 1A.

[5] *Ibid.*, p. 3A.

[6] Brief for the Appellants, *Ford v. Boeger*, 18011 and 18033, 1964, U.S. Court of Appeals, Eighth Circuit, p. 10.

[7] *Post*, October 12, 1963, p. 1A.

[8] *Post*, October 13, 1963, p. 26A.

[9] Brief for the Appellants, *op. cit.*, pp. 11–12.

[10] Brodine, *op. cit.* (n. 1), p. 14.

[11] *Ibid.*, p. 15.

[12] *Ibid.*, p. 24.

[13] Brief for the Appellants, *op. cit.* (n. 6), pp. 56–57.

[14] *Ibid.*, p. 75.

[15] State of Missouri, *Missouri Supreme Court Rules*, No. 4:20.

[16] *Globe*, October 15, 1963, pp. 1A, 7A.

[17] Brief for the Appellants, *op. cit.* (n. 6), pp. 12, 76.

[18] Martin Oppenheimer and George Lakey, *A Manual for Direct Action* (Chicago: Quadrangle Books, 1964), pp. 92–93.

[19] Brief for the Appellants, *op. cit.* (n. 6), pp. 74–76.

[20] *Ibid.*

[21] *Ibid.*

[22] *Post*, October 27, 1963, p. 2F; letter to the editor from Ray Bolden.

[23] Brodine, *op. cit.* (n. 1), p. 15.

[24] *St. Louis Defender* (editorial), October 29, 1963, p. 6. Henceforward the *St. Louis Defender* will be referred to as *Defender*.

[25] *Ibid.*

[26] Brodine, *op. cit.* (n. 1), p. 24.

[27] *Ibid.,* p. 15.

[28] *Post,* October 27, 1963, pp. 1A, 8A.

[29] *Globe* (editorial), October 25, 1963, p. 8A.

[30] *Defender* (editorial), October 29, 1963.

[31] *Globe* (editorial), October 25, 1963, p. 8A.

[32] *Post,* October 28, 1963, p. 1A.

[33] *Ibid.*

[34] *Post,* October 29, 1963, p. 14A.

[35] *Globe* (editorial), October 28, 1963, p. 14A.

[36] *Argus* (editorial), March 10, 1967, p. 2B.

[37] Brief for the Appellants, *op. cit.* (n. 6), pp. 12–14.

[38] *Curtis v. Tozier,* 374 S. W. 2nd., 606 (1964).

[39] Brief for the Appellants, *op. cit.* (n. 6), pp. 12–14.

[40] The Newsletter of the St. Louis Committee of Racial Equality, #2, March, 1964.

[41] The Newsletter of the St. Louis Committee of Racial Equality, #3, March, 1964.

[42] Among the informal complaints of the demonstrators were: "What bothered me most about jail was that it was still segregated even though the warden had announced that this policy would be changed. . . ." "Tensions develop at a very fast rate. Fights develop easily. There were three stabbings while we were there. We 13 demonstrators stayed clear of all this. There are no facilities for exercise. . . . A fight can start over anything. What TV programs to watch, for instance." See CORE Newsletter #2, March, 1964, p. 2.

[43] "Police State Tactics," a two-page February 15, 1964, St. Louis CORE release, p. 1.

[44] *Ibid.*

[45] *Ibid.*

[46] *Ibid.*

[47] *Ibid.*

[48] National Advisory Commission on Civil Disorders. *Report of the National Advisory Commission on Civil Disorders.* A response to Executive Order 11365, issued by President Lyndon B. Johnson on July 29, 1967 (Washington: U.S. Government Printing Office, 1968), p. 337.

CHAPTER 9

The Aftermath of Jefferson Bank

If the *Defender* was correct on October 29, 1963, when it interpreted Judge Scott's stiff fines and harsh sentences as an attempt to make an example of the black man and at the same time keep him in his place,[1] then the judge failed to accomplish his goal. What Scott and the elite actually did was to shock one of the demonstrators from a state of lessened awareness to a degree of new consciousness.

When the Jefferson Bank refused to hire four black people and resorted to active opposition, the bank management did not foresee that the prolonged dispute which ensued would open the way for the rise of a new and different type of black leader in St. Louis. The bank encounter had deepened black people's doubts and disillusionment, causing a concomitant decline in black faith in legalism as a weapon to advance black people economically.

No society, unless its government is prepared to maintain a police state, can afford for a sizable minority of its citizens to become disillusioned and lose faith in it. If this does happen, as it did in St. Louis, it should not come as a great surprise (even in a police state) when those disenchanted citizens are incited to action. Therefore, St. Louis should not have been surprised when, approximately fourteen months after CORE initiated direct action against Jefferson Bank, some of its members began to feel that they could accomplish more if they, being dedicated to direct action, established a separate organization. The move to set up a separate group transpired, in part, because of the historical difficulty of any group to remain organized on a continuing basis for protest activity.

With lessened faith in legalism as a tool to advance black people economically, CORE announced in March of 1964, that it would broaden its efforts and fight other industries as well as banking. There was general agreement among the membership that this was a necessary step. Despite this, the disillusioned members realized that there was the unresolved legal battle with Jefferson Bank, and believed that its active opposition would cause CORE to expend a disproportionate amount of its energies on legalities in that dispute and less on other industries.[2]

As a result, Percy Green, one of the most active CORE demonstrators, and approximately two dozen others, founded a new organization, ACTION (Action Committee to Increase Opportunities for Negroes).[3] Thus, Jefferson Bank's racist subordinating employment practices helped produce a new black leader in St. Louis. This new leader, Percy Green, was willing to negotiate but perceived direct action as a way to confront the power structure with a conflict situation with which it must somehow come to terms.[4] As a result of this belief, Green and his followers employed techniques heretofore not utilized by civil rights groups in St. Louis.

A close look at the man behind the formation of this new organization might cause one to deduce that ACTION was a true outgrowth of protest. It was organized by Green, who had been an active CORE member several years prior to Jefferson Bank. His position as Chairman of CORE's Employment Committee allowed him to gain a wealth of experience and knowledge pertaining to protest activity.[5] Green's exact motives for leading two dozen CORE members out of that group and into his organization are not known. However, the *Post* reported that a month prior to the formation of ACTION, Green had been defeated when he ran for the chairmanship of CORE.[6] On the other hand, Green's general dissatisfaction with the civil rights movement in St. Louis, his experiences with Jefferson Bank, and his loss of faith in legalities—all of these were influential too in causing him to attempt the formation of a new group.[7] Green may also have been driven to form ACTION in part because he believed that he had lost his employment with McDonnell Aircraft Corporation (now McDonnell-Douglas) as a research and development technician because the company practiced racial discrimination. Green duly registered a complaint with the President's Committee on Equal Opportunity in 1964.[8]

If we do not know the precise reasons for it, Green was certainly instrumental in ACTION's being born. However, as one factor among others, it is highly possible that because of his Jefferson Bank and McDonnell Aircraft experiences he had been pushed that one extra step to the point where his anger and hostility were able to free him from the internal restraint that cages the potentially defiant "bad nigger" that is harbored inside every black man. According to black psychiatrists William H. Grier and Price M. Cobbs:

> One of the constant themes in black folklore is the "bad nigger." It seems that every community has had one or is afraid of having one. They were feared as much by blacks as by whites. In the slave legends there are tales of docile field hands suddenly going berserk. . . .
>
> Today black boys are admonished not to be a "bad nigger." No description need be offered; every black child knows what is meant. They are angry and hostile. They strike fear into everyone with their uncompromising rejection of restraint or inhibition. They may seem at one moment meek and compromised—and in the next a terrifying killer. Because of his experience in this country, every black man harbors a potential bad nigger inside him. He must ignore this inner man. The bad nigger is bad because he has been required to renounce his manhood to save his life. The more one approaches the American ideal of respectability the more this hostility must be repressed. The bad nigger is a defiant nigger, a reminder of what manhood could be.[9]

When Percy Green organized ACTION in November, 1964, his voice began to clearly project jobs for black men as the major goal. He did not possess a college degree as did most NAACP leaders, self-appointed black leaders, and those CORE leaders who went to jail in 1963. He considered himself part of, and a representative for, the "folk thought" of the black masses. The elevation of Green from a follower and active participant to an indefatigable operant leader provided St. Louis blacks with a new type of leadership that could express grievances of the black masses with a greater degree of accuracy.

"Bad nigger" Green was hated and despised by many middle-class blacks and whites. They called him a "militant." Nevertheless, many blacks (and some whites), believed that when Green left CORE there was a legitimate and positive place for him and his organization in St. Louis. Possibly they held this belief because up until 1965, almost all civil rights activities were led by middle-class blacks and white people who for one reason or another had some association with the black community.

Green believed that many middle-class black people who held privileged economic positions were not always able accurately to interpret the needs and thoughts of the black masses. In his mind, one of the characteristics of the black protest and struggle in St. Louis was that self-appointed or white handpicked black leaders from among the black bourgeoisie frequently did not accurately convey thoughts of the black masses. Green's beliefs seem to be adequately substantiated. As a result, the gap between the St. Louis black bourgeoisie and the masses was probably another factor that made it possible for Green to organize ACTION.

Whether Jefferson Bank and/or McDonnell were primarily responsible for a "bad nigger" coming to life in St. Louis was not as significant as the fact that he came into being. His presence provided a positive benefit for the black community. Percy Green was a man who was willing, regardless of potential consequences, to expose and fight institutional racist economic policies that had been perpetuated because of the economic and psychological benefits derived by whites.

One could argue that the appearance of a defiant "bad nigger" in St. Louis was also beneficial to those whites who desired to see this society live longer (regardless of whether they recognized this fact). This was true because the very essence of institutional racist subordination is its indirect nature, which permits it to set forth itself in innumerable ways and to execute its purposes in countless ways that make it hard to recognize for most white people. As a result, the overwhelming majority of white St. Louisans did not recognize, accept, or understand how, in part, they were responsible for Jefferson Bank's refusal to employ black people in white-collar positions. After all, the vast majority of whites used other banks and had no contract with Jefferson Bank; and they had very little, if any, direct contact with the black people who were fighting the bank. Separation of the races in St. Louis was (and is) so complete that there was seldom an opportunity for the latter.

While some of the whites might not have held racist attitudes to the extent that they participated in or condoned actions like those of the bank and the industries attacked by Green, actions which had the practical effect of disadvantaging black people, they were still behavioral racists. And, since most white St. Louisans did not directly subordinate black people, they did not want to believe that blacks were forced into ancillary and subservient positions because of whites. This attitude, along with the need to deny racism, helped them (and whites all over America) in the development of an extensive catalogue of euphemisms which obscured feelings and conduct toward black people. Thus it was easy for white St. Louis to accept Jefferson Bank's executive vice-president's statement when, under the guise of standards, he said that the bank had not received applications from four "qualified" black people. As a result, white people could rationalize that blacks had not been denied employment at the bank because of their color, but because "they were not qualified." Such a rationalization helped those whites who were not guilty of individual overt racist acts to believe that they were not racists.

This use of the device "they are not qualified" reflects the type of systematic racism that is built into this society and helps make institutional racism the most serious problem of racism to be dealt with. This type of racism makes it possible for institutions to operate in such a way that blacks would not receive equal economic opportunities, even if no individual racist controls or participates in that institution. Thus, because of the pervasiveness of racism and the fact that it is built into the society, all white institutions are racist or more accurately, white supremacist, and all operate to perpetuate white privileges since racism is an integral part of this country's history and culture (reflected in behavior towards Indians as well as blacks). Some institutions are more strategically located within the system and more effectively racist than others. But in one writer's view: "Whatever the variation, institutions, by definition, seek to perpetuate themselves; in the process, they perpetuate racism as well."[10]

The institutions which eternalize racism are not easy to get to so as to deal with them. There is also a difficulty because of the overwhelming pervasiveness of racism—the whole American system is saturated with it. Social inertia alone makes it almost impossible even to begin to overcome racism. It is so permeating that it is also ruinous to white people. Recognizing this fact, in the spring of 1968 People Against Racism (PAR), a new organization of whites based in Detroit, became active. Most of the original members of PAR had read the report of the Kerner Commission, which officially exposed white racism in America. National Director Frank Joyce and his members realized from its inception that PAR would be a minority movement in America since so few whites in America recognized the validity of PAR's basic premise. PAR believes that it is in the interest of white people to confront the roots of racism in white communities since white racism transports the seeds of destruction not only of black people, but of whites as well.

As a result, PAR commends black liberation and other minority movements for self-determination, and offers direct support in those efforts only when requested. Not only does PAR recognize that whites should no longer attempt to lead blacks, but it is additionally not organized to center its efforts in black ghettos. PAR believes that the struggle against white racism has to be waged in the white community, against the white power structure and white institutions.

> . . . White people must begin to see that the present racist system is . . . destructive to them. . . . It is robbing white America of its humanity and preventing a healthy society. . . . "Racist institutions are responsible for white people having no knowledge or distorted knowledge of the histories and cultures of people of color, and little or no knowledge and understanding of black peoples' struggle for liberation. Thus white institutions have created a world of fantasy for white people. Unable to realistically and humanly coexist with people of color, white America pursues policies of repression and destruction at home and abroad." . . .
>
> . . . The only way absolute social disaster can be prevented is for whites to confront the roots of racism in their own communities. Whites, no less than blacks, must struggle for the power to control the institutions which create and perpetuate a disastrously distorted system. Anti-racist whites must first recognize their own powerlessness, particularly as individuals, to take on institutions. They must, therefore, organize themselves and others. They must build a base. They must begin the task of bringing revolutionary change to the white institutions that control and define the identity and destiny of white America.[11]

Percy Green's presence was possibly beneficial to a few whites, if in any way his activities helped any white St. Louisans come to realize that business and industry in St. Louis utilized employment policies inimical to black people and destructive to them. These employment policies promoted institutional racist subordination of the type which is accomplished by very few acts of overt individual racism and carried out by a small number of people, but which is supplemented by the general white population, most of whom may not be aware of their contributions. Green's value to whites becomes more apparent when one realizes that it was highly unlikely that those few white St. Louisans who desired some type of equitable solution to the city's monumental racism problem could accomplish anything positive until and unless they could recognize that there was a problem and what the problem was specifically. Otherwise, they would never attempt to organize a base from which to launch the struggle for the power to control or influence the institutions which created and perpetuated racist hiring policies. When Green began to attack certain institutions (Southwestern Bell Telephone and Laclede Gas) and exposed how institutional racism had denied employment opportunities to blacks, white people who could not previously recognize the pervasiveness of racism could now see the full extent of it, and the full destructiveness of it. They could have, if they so desired, attempted to counter the pervasive mentality in St. Louis, which demanded repression and teaching blacks a lesson for getting out of their place and interfering with the operation of a white bank.

No one will ever know how many white people came to recognize the racism dramatized by Green, and to realize how it was (and is) robbing white America of its humanity and preventing the existence of a healthy society. Green's actions possibly did not affect too many whites because some whites who sincerely detest racism in principle and openly oppose individual acts of overt racism, at times find themselves opposing obvious antiracist actions. This occurs because some antiracist actions threaten to reduce certain economic and almost subconsciously perceived psychological benefits that some whites have been gaining from living in a society in which they are considered members of a superior group. Identity as a member of a superior group depends more upon who members are not, than upon who they are.

The modern implications . . . lie not so much in how whites
defined . . . themselves. By categorizing other races as inferior,
whites automatically defined themselves as superior. PAR concludes that the significant result is that white Americans as a
society—do not know who they are, "because they have constructed an identity that depends primarily on who they are not."
White American society, to put it another way, suffers mental
illness, a psychosis manifested by delusions of superiority based
on the inferiority of others. The psychological need to identify
others as inferior—and it is a need, since whites' self-identity
depends on it—becomes a compulsion to "keep them in their
place" because any change in their inferior status threatens the
whites' self-concept of superiority.[12]

For these reasons, even if Green's actions did open the eyes of
a few whites, it was difficult for him and his organization to attain
the goal of more meaningful employment for black people. Resistance to eradicating racism is far more widespread than most people
realize because so many whites receive significant psychological
as well as material benefits, if only dimly perceived, from the subordination of black people.

At the beginning of the decade of the 1960's, Table 9.1 shows
that 10,040 St. Louis families, or 5.2 percent of the city's total
families, received annual incomes of less than $1,000; and 5,182
or 51.6 percent of these families were black. There were 15,106
families, or 7.8 percent of the total families, receiving from between
$1,000 to $1,999 annually; and 6,785 or 44.9 percent of these were
black families. An additional 16,536 families, or 8.6 percent of the
total families, received from between $2,000 to $2,999 annually;
and 6,941 or 41.9 percent were black families. In addition, 19,738
or 10.2 percent of the total families, received annual incomes from
between $3,000 to $3,999; and 7,009 or 35.5 percent were black
families. As a result 25,917 or 54.1 percent of the city's black families
received annual incomes of less than $4,000, whereas 34,503 or 24.6
percent of the white families received less than $4,000. The city's
white family median income was $5,899 as compared to $3,718
for black families.

The above data indicate the extent to which the St. Louis economy subordinated black people. However, the data in themselves
do not reveal the true extent to which black people were subordi-

TABLE 9.1
Black and White Family Income In St. Louis, 1960

Amount of Income	Income Popu-lation	% of City's Popu-lation	Black Popu-lation	Black % of Income Popu-lation	White Popu-lation	White % of Income Popu-lation
Under $1,000	10,040	5.2	5,182	51.6	4,858	48.4
$1,000–1,999	15,106	7.8	6,785	44.9	8,321	55.1
$2,000–2,999	16,536	8.6	6,941	41.9	9,595	58.1
$3,000–3,999	19,738	10.2	7,009	35.5	12,729	64.5
$4,000–4,999	24,761	12.9	6,800	27.4	17,961	72.6
$5,000–5,999	27,442	14.2	5,208	19.3	22,234	80.7
$6,000–6,999	20,724	10.8	3,216	15.5	17,508	74.5
$7,000–7,999	16,266	8.4	2,148	13.2	14,118	86.8
$8,000–8,999	12,238	6.3	1,510	12.3	10,728	87.7
$9,000–9,999	8,289	4.3	1,011	12.2	7,278	87.8
Above $10,000	20,733	10.8	2,075	10.0	18,658	90.0

SOURCE: U.S. Bureau of the Census. U.S. Censuses of Population and Housing: 1960 Census Tracts Final Report PHC (1)—131; Table P-1, p. 15 and Table P-4 Characteristics of the Nonwhite Population, for Census Tracts with 400 or More Such Persons: 1960, p. 131.

nated. Where 54 percent of the city's black families received the same income as only 24 percent of the city's whites, black income did not buy as much as the income of the whites. Institutional racist economic policies not only ensure that black people will receive lower wages, but helps ensure that blacks will pay higher prices and higher rents. At the same time they receive less desirable credit terms and have poorer living conditions than do whites. The type of racism which was (and is) systematically practiced by white realtors (including past restrictive covenants), renting agents, landlords, and homeowners caused St. Louis' black people to be hemmed in the heart of the city where most housing was poor. Racist housing patterns helped make it possible to conceal that the differentials in wages, prices, credit terms, and other policies were the result not of geographic differences, but of racism.

Such comparisons implicitly assume the Negro's $3,000 buys as much as the white (man's) $3,000.

It does not.

American cities have two housing markets: the citywide market and the circumscribed Negro market. Because supply is restricted, Negroes "receive less housing value for their dollars spent than do whites. . . . Census statistics indicate that . . . non-white renters and homeowners obtain fewer standard-quality dwellings and frequently less space than do whites paying the same amounts." A Chicago welfare department study found "housing defects significantly greater for Negro than for white families, despite the fact that rents for Negro families are 28 percent per month higher than for whites in private dwellings."

Landlords are sometimes judged greedy extortionists for charging Negro tenants higher rents than whites. But they are operating in a market of restricted supply; high Negro rents reflect supply-and-demand relationships, not conspiratorial landlord greed. . . . [Nevertheless, because] 15 percent of the consumption expenditures of urban Negro families is for shelter, [their] real income is significantly reduced by relatively high rents.

Poor urban Negroes also pay more than whites for identical consumer durables bought on credit. (Negroes pay more than whites for residential financing too.) The difference may . . . [arise from the] white [s'] reluctance to sell to Negroes . . . [from] Negro immobility, or . . . [from] the sellers' assumption that poor Negroes are poorer risks than poor whites. Whatever the cause, real income suffers.

Poor Negro families average a half-person larger than poor white families. Consequently, per capita real income of poor Negroes is even farther below [the] per capita real income of poor whites with the same money income.

If, then, $3,000 in Negro money buys only as much as $2,800 or even $2,500 in white money and is distributed over more people, one should keep in mind appropriate reservations when comparing percentage of whites with percentages of Negroes below some income level. . . .[13]

In St. Louis, the black population per household was 3.53 and the population in the smaller white household, 2.74. Thus, with these differentials, a "bad nigger" willing to assert himself was a positive benefit for the black community and for those few whites who were interested in a decent and just society.

Many black St. Louisans were aware that in that city, as in other American cities, the results of economic racism indicate that black people are unwanted. However, there has been no mass overt extermination of blacks because this society's values prohibit the use of overt genocide. On the other hand, this society's morality (including St. Louis') condones black people being systematically herded into hemmed-in colonies in major American cities to suffer because of a lack of a fair slice of the economic pie.

Aware of how the economic pie was cut for black people, AC-TION, under Green's leadership, became active in behalf of black economic progress. It also became controversial. During April and May of 1965, it found itself disagreeing with the well-established, middle-class-dominated, local branch of the NAACP. The NAACP "announced progress . . . with the Southwestern Bell Telephone Company after (NAACP) committee members met with telephone company officials recently."[14] Green disagreed with this statement and attacked the company's policies as racist when he charged that Southwestern Bell, despite repeated negotiations, refused to hire blacks as telephone installers, linemen, and repairmen, and would not upgrade blacks who were already working for the company. He accused the company of not training installers because it anticipated a problem when black men would go into white homes. A black woman who had worked for the telephone company for twenty years supported Green's allegation pertaining to upgrading with a statement to the *Argus*. She said:

> I am certainly shocked that the NAACP should issue a statement which in effect praises the telephone company. There is much work to be done by Southwestern Bell before it gets any pats on the back.
> But when we, who work for the telephone company, have been trying for years to get routine promotions . . . and without success . . . and then the NAACP comes along and pats the company on the back, why, it does nothing but hinder our progress.
> It looks to us like the telephone company is using the NAACP as a wedge to cause friction.[15]

As ACTION dramatized its complaints by picketing Southwestern Bell, the dispute continued in the black community. AC-TION drew attention to its telephone company demonstrations when it employed a technique not previously used by civil rights organizations in St. Louis. Insect repellent was sprayed in the telephone company's lobby and on the front of the building. A month later ACTION used paint in its demonstrations with Union Electric.[16] The telephone company dispute became inflamed, in all likelihood, because the company would not negotiate with Green in good faith. This was evident when Buddy Lonesome devoted his *Argus* column "Hellbox" to the dispute. Lonesome appeared particularly disturbed not so much because of the telephone company personnel officer's "obvious southern twang." He was concerned because apparently the company had no desire to negotiate with Green, and preferred to deal with handpicked "responsible Negroes."

> The present chain of events which finds the local branch of the NAACP and the new group "ACTION" at odds over hiring policies at Southwestern Bell Telephone Company, also brings to issue the current definition of the word "responsibility." This reporter had reason to listen to the personnel director at the telephone company, Donnell Hurst, via a secret tape recording made by Percy Green, Chairman of ACTION. It was quite an experience. To hear the obviously southern twang of this executive insinuate that the telephone company, and he personally, only dealt with "responsible" Negro organizations or groups, was a revelation.
>
> The way this man said it, and without prejudging the accuracy of his comment, or the position of the telephone company—it would surely seem an insult to have the Hurst brand of "responsible." For irresponsibility of certain groups or organizations . . . isn't the basic point of issue really the accuracy or veracity of their statements? There is rapidly becoming prevalent, through increased usage, the term "accommodating." I'm mighty afraid that there are many white persons, possibly of sincere good will, who would tend to believe that an organization or person who seems to "accommodate" them is responsible.[17]

It appears that Lonesome's primary concern in this article was analogous to that voiced by St. Louis blacks as early as 1937 when they complained that the establishment selected the blacks it desired to recognize and negotiate with because they advocated what white people believed was good for black people, and not those blacks who possibly reflected thoughts of the black community. As Charles Silberman has said: "Manifestly the white power structure finds black people who think like the black masses distasteful."[18] This pet trick of selecting black leaders, if not necessarily a conscious conspiracy against black people, was an attempt on the part of the establishment to maintain and perpetuate itself. But regardless of intent, it served to help subordinate black people.

The ACTION-NAACP dispute pertaining to the telephone company negotiations had the potential to help educate the elite as to why, in part, much of black St. Louis was angry, for it helped to point out:

> What is crucial is that whites must learn to curb their ingrained habits of authority and paternalism if there is to be genuine communication between the races. For their own well-being, and even more for the well-being of the community, businessmen and civic leaders must realize that when they talk only to the eight or ten most prosperous or most socially polished Negroes in town, they are not really talking to the Negroes at all, and that as a result they can be badly misled as to the temper and desires of the Negro community.[19]

Unsuccessful negotiations with the telephone company did not demoralize ACTION. Its incessant efforts to obtain jobs for black men led it to demand that Laclede Gas Company hire black men as meter readers. In this case Green's followers used chains to bar the door of the gas company's building. On May 13, 1965, a *Post* article pertaining to the demonstration in which the chains were used read in part: ". . . two men were arrested and handcuffed to a parking meter yesterday as other civil rights demonstrators taunted police and halted rush-hour traffic in front of the Laclede Gas. . . ."[20] The article continued and identified one man as being twenty-five-years old and the other as being thirty-two-years old.

In referring to the very same demonstration, the *Globe* disregarded completely black people's equality to whites and proceeded to write an editorial that insulted and humiliated all black people as it proceeded to classify a protest against economic institutional subordination as a "protest against something or other." According to the *Globe*, demonstrating ACTION members were "strange creatures," two of whom were described as "clowns" and "boys." The *Globe* had not, presumably, learned how to distinguish between black "boys" and black men of twenty-five and thirty-two.

> Wednesday afternoon in the 1000 block of Olive Street a little swarm of strange creatures congealed and took to insulting police,

chanting, cursing, lying down in the traffic—generally succeeding in making themselves obnoxious to all who observed them, in protest against something or other at the Laclede Gas Company whose doors they chained and padlocked.

They inconvenienced hundreds of innocent people and two of the clowns were arrested. They had been before for similar stunts. On June 10 they come before Judge George Cady on charges of general peace disturbances and blocking traffic.

As these characters have promised us a "long, hot summer," we think it only fair the judge—if they are found guilty—should reciprocate and promise the two boys at least one "long, hot summer" in the City Workhouse.[21]

The *Globe*'s editorial was a perfect example of one of the many ways in which racism manifests itself in this society. And the *Globe*'s form of oppressive racist subordination angers all black men. A black man resents being called "boy" by another black man, and it becomes more than resentment when a white man calls him "boy."

> The worst indignity of all is being patronized by whites who "know how to handle Negroes." The housekeeper . . . was obviously pleased with the way the Negro porter had cleaned the room. "You're a good boy, Jimmy," she told him by way of compliment; and Jimmy said "Thank you, Ma'am." Jimmy was forty-eight years old. Perhaps he had become so used to being treated like a boy that he took the insult as a compliment. Or perhaps he had merely learned for his own well-being [to] hide his anger behind a mask of servility. In any case, he knew that no supervisor would say, "you're a good boy, Jack," if the white orderly did a good job of mopping up after a patient. "There is a form of oppression which is more painful and more scathing than physical injury or economic privation," . . .
>
> Negroes are given humiliation, insult, and embarrassment as a daily diet, and without regard to individual merit. They are convinced, as a result that most whites never see them as individuals. . . .[22]

As ACTION continued to press for job equality with varied tactics which caused the *Globe* to insult black people and call for repression ("and promise the two boys at least one 'long, hot summer' in the City Workhouse"), there remained the possibility that the 1963 jailed demonstrators would have to serve their sentences, in addition to the time they had already spent in jail. After more than three years of legal efforts in behalf of the demonstrators, they finally stood convicted of violating Judge Scott's original injunction. In February of 1967, the United States Supreme Court decided against reviewing their appeal.[23] When the court of last resort let their sentences stand, those in the black community who argued that black people should use legal means to obtain their goals found that argument less convincing. Even many "conservative" blacks came to realize that the legal system helped institutionalize the white power structure.[24]

The black community was convinced that its leaders had received lopsided justice, not only because among the original nine defendants, three—William L. Clay, Robert B. Curtis, and Norman Seay—had not gone into the bank as demonstrators, and continued to declare that they were not guilty, but also because: ". . . it is not necessary to believe that Curtis, Clay, and Seay were innocent to recognize that all of the original defendants were treated brutally. College students protesting the war in Viet Nam, or labor union members picketing a secondary employer, are not subjected to midnight arrests, excessive bail, and enormous sentences."[25]

After the United States Supreme Court denied review in February of 1967, the defendants returned to serve their jail sentences. The *Argus* articulated its opinion of the sentences and Judge Scott to the black community:

EIGHT MARTYRS FOR ECONOMIC JUSTICE FOR THE NEGROES OF ST. LOUIS HAVE GONE BACK TO JAIL. It is commendable that many sympathizers demonstrated as a protest against the demonstrators having to return to jail. The sentences were all excessive, both as to time to be spent in jail and as to fine assessed in money. Judge Michael J. Scott acted like a despot. He exhibited the kind of action that is inconsistent with democracy.[26]

Where the *Argus* considered the sentences "excessive" and "inconsistent," a constitutional lawyer, Jules B. Gerard, (Washington University), submitted that they were "outrageous." He reasoned that the cases cited by the court to support its decisions were drastically unlike this case. Two cases pertained to communist bail-jumpers who were trying to leave the United States. Another was concerned with a witness who declined to cooperate with a federal

grand jury by refusing to answer its questions. The fourth dealt
with manufacturing perjured testimony.[27] The court did not cite
a more representative case or one similar to the then very recent
Louisville, Kentucky, case, in which open housing demonstrators
violated an injunction and were sentenced to thirty hours and thirty
dollars. It was not a pleasant task for black St. Louisans to compare
a Southern city's thirty hours and thirty dollars to St. Louis' sentences ranging up to one year in jail and $1,000 fines.

By February of 1967, it is possible that the *Post* realized how
effectively the Jefferson Bank case had created an atmosphere of
tension and hatred in the city. It also appears that it realized blacks
did not receive impartial justice and that additional vengeance and
repression would not contribute to peace and tranquility. According to the *Post:*

> . . . the Jefferson Bank case has now run its legal course, and
> has taken four years to do it. Most St. Louisans by now have
> probably forgotten the details of the case, and it would be well
> if the community could finally forget the bitterness it once
> engendered.
> . . . Courts cannot overlook contempt, now or in the past.
> Those days in 1963 were days of tension. There was, however,
> no violence at Jefferson Bank and no property was damaged.
> And in the days and months after the demonstration, St. Louis
> banks and business generally took a sound civic look at civil rights
> issues and began constructive efforts at interracial employment.
> Thus the tension was absorbed by an improved public understand-
> ing on all sides—a condition in which St. Louis can take more
> pride than most cities.
> So the point of order has been made, and the point of civic
> progress has been extended. Today the situation leaves no room
> at all for any spirit of vindictiveness. St. Louis may hope that
> the bank can be relegated to history in the context of four years
> of better community relations.[28]

The *Globe,* too, possibly realized that the black community was
angry. But its February 15 editorial revealed the extent to which
it supported judicial oppression and how it in no way desired to
see Judge Scott blamed for his role in helping to inflame black
people. The editorial also revealed how it desired to see black people
and those whites who had betrayed the elite by fighting institutional

racism, humble themselves if they were "aware of their transgressions against law and order" and were "truly repentant of their crimes." In true white supremist style the *Globe* would have praised Scott for "tempering justice with mercy" if he had decided paternalistically to "remit all or part of their sentences." Very few black people read the *Globe*, and most of those who read its February 15, 1967, editorial pertaining to Jefferson Bank concluded that if Judge Scott had not been guilty beyond any doubt, the *Globe* would not have found it necessary to attempt to defend him, beginning in October, 1963.[29] In 1967, it defended him by saying:

> . . . all of the appeals having been exhausted Judge Scott is now free to remand the prisoners to jail to serve the balance of their sentences, or to make any other disposition of the cases which seems wise to him.
>
> If the prisoners are unrepenting and are remanded back to serve the balance of their sentences, no blame can be attached to Judge Scott. . . .
>
> On the other hand, if Judge Scott feels that they are aware of their transgressions against law and order and are truly repentant of their crimes, and in consideration of this and the high degree of community stability which was maintained in St. Louis, decides to remit all or part of their sentences, he would be greatly praised for tempering justice with mercy.[30]

One could deduce from the February 14 and 15 editorials in the *Post* and the *Globe* respectively that St. Louis had realized its past mistakes as a matter of time working a change. But that is too easy. Nor did any form of moral persuasion effect a change in the city. Somewhere along the line the power structure had recognized (Percy Green had helped to effect this awareness) that the black community was so inflamed that only a near miracle would prevent the worst kind of violence from erupting.

Now the matter had come to a head. Black people would not accept what they considered hypocritical expressions of public concern about the deterioration in race relations. They demanded action— release of all prisoners. When the *Globe* voiced approval of the "high degree of community stability," and decided that Judge Scott "would be greatly praised for tempering justice with mercy," there is little doubt that it realized how its previous articles had helped both to unify the black community and to make it easier for an aggressive consciousness to predominate in it—and now the city was trembling on the edge of violence.

While the demonstrators were in jail, their attorneys requested commutation or parole for the balance of their punishment. Possibly because the court was influenced by the sentiment generated in the white community by the February 14 and 15 editorials, along with the general belief that there would be violence should the prisoners remain in jail, hearings on these applications were held. They were so arranged that they were held first for those defendants where there was greatest evidence of possible guilt. Judge Scott was not content to accept the customary apology for contempt of court. He found it desirable to read to the defendants a humiliating and degrading discourse. They were, in effect, reminded that they had not stayed in their places (blacks had gotten out of place and white demonstrators had betrayed the elite) and had ignored "laws enacted for your protection." Judge Scott failed to mention how those same laws protected and helped to perpetuate the very institutional racism which had brought the city to the brink of violence. We assume that he believed (as did those members of the elite who approved of his statement before it could be read) that the laws were good enough to protect white institutions; therefore it was axiomatic that they were good for black people. The only thing wrong with this type of thinking was that the very new black consciousness that Judge Scott himself had helped to bring into existence in St. Louis caused black people no longer to accept the assumption that laws which were good for white institutions were beneficial to black people, when in effect, they helped to subordinate black people. According to Judge Scott's humiliating and degrading discourse:

> Your offense against the majesty of the law and authority of the court was a very serious offense. The existence of a free and democratic society is dependent upon voluntary obedience to lawful authority. You might well be one of the first to suffer if every man or organized group were allowed to take the law into his own hands.
>
> You chose to ignore the laws enacted for your protection and take the law into your own hands. You willfully and deliberately violated the order of this court. Your conduct must be condemned and deplored.

Your statements in open court have convinced the court that you are . . . truly and deeply repentant of your offense. In consideration of your repentance and your solemn promise to this court to obey the laws, it being within the power of the court to temper justice with mercy (you are released on parole).[31]

On March 17, clemency was granted to three of the first demonstrators to apologize to the judge.[32] William L. Clay, Robert B. Curtis, and Taylor Jones were angered and entertained the idea that Judge Scott's insulting reprimand was designed to humiliate them before they were released. They found his statement so objectionable that their new consciousness caused them to dismiss their lawyers and withdraw their motions requesting clemency.[33] Several hundred people attended a rally in their behalf and heard Dr. Benjamin F. Davis say that Judge Scott had "made these people crawl on their bellies and completely cast aside dignity of the human spirit."[34]

Each night, beginning on March 12, 1967, ACTION members picketed Judge Scott's home until after Clay, Curtis, and Jones were finally released from jail. The initial demonstration was designed to urge the judge to grant clemency.[35] However, before the power structure reached a decision, the city became tense as indicated by an *Argus*, page-one headline: "Citizens Now Seething Over the Jailing of Eight Demonstrators." The first paragraph of the article began by saying: ". . . there is a time bomb ticking in this city and something like 30,000 people know it and over a million don't even know what is happening. . . ."[36]

Five days after the *Argus* mentioned the "time bomb ticking" three ACTION members engaged in activity which was potentially more destructive than that of the August, 1963, demonstrators. The three were arrested and charged with attempting to chain the doors of Jefferson Bank.[37] It is clear that the *Post* recognized how potentially dangerous the Jefferson Bank confrontation had become. It said: ". . . the situation is enough to cause concern in the community. This city has avoided the racial troubles inflicted elsewhere, but summer is approaching and conservative Negro leaders are worried about the mood of people in one third of the city. There are always extremist groups ready to exploit charges of injustice."[38]

Clay, Curtis, and Jones, no doubt, were even more determined when the black community came together and organized the

Greater St. Louis Community Council and paid for a large newspaper advertisement requesting their release "as a matter of simple
justice." Their determination was possibly reinforced after Stokely
Carmichael was invited to speak to a group gathered on Jefferson
Bank's parking lot. Carmichael encouraged the large crowd to make
heroes of those in jail and received a loud and long applause when
he referred to Scott as a "honky" Judge.[39]

It was now apparent that the trio had widespread support. The
black community realized that the demonstrators had possibly violated the injunction, and anticipated and would have accepted some
type of punishment which it considered commensurate with their
"crimes" and which was meted out impartially. But the black community came to believe that the first major effort to obtain more
and better jobs for black people in St. Louis was met with a denial
of impartial justice because of racism.

NOTES

[1] *Defender* (editorial), October 29, 1963, p. 6.
[2] Interview with Percy Green, Chairman of ACTION, January 12, 1968.
[3] *Post,* January 10, 1965, p. 3A.
[4] Interview with Green, *op. cit.*
[5] *Ibid.*
[6] *Post,* January 10, 1965, p. 3A.
[7] Interview with Green, *op. cit.*
[8] *Post,* September 1, 1964, p. 6A.
[9] William H. Grier and Price M. Cobbs, *Black Rage* (New York: Basic Books, 1968), pp. 54–55.
[10] Erbin Crowell, Jr., "Anti-Racism: The New Movement," in *Civil Rights Digest,* II (Winter, 1969), pp. 25–30.
[11] *Ibid.,* pp. 27–28.
[12] *Ibid.,* p. 26.
[13] Alan Batchelder, "Poverty: The Special Case of the Negro," *American Economic Review,* Papers and Proceedings, LV (May, 1965), pp. 531–32.
[14] *Argus,* April 30, 1965, p. 4A.
[15] *Argus,* April 30, 1965, pp. 1A, 4A.
[16] *Post,* May 25, 1965, p. 6A; and *Post,* June 16, 1965, p. 2D.
[17] Buddy Lonesome, *Argus,* May 7, 1965, p. 3B.
[18] Charles E. Silberman, *Crisis in Black and White* (New York: Random House, 1964), p. 195.
[19] *Ibid.,* pp. 197–98.
[20] *Post,* May 13, 1965, p. 1.
[21] *Globe* (editorial), May 14, 1965, p. 8A.
[22] Silberman, *op. cit.,* pp. 52–53.

[23] *Curtis et al.* v. *Boeger, Warden*, 386 U.S. 914, 978. Motion for leave to file second petition for rehearing denied, 387 U.S. 949 (1967).

[24] Jules B. Gerard, "Jefferson Bank Dispute Rocks St. Louis," *Focus/Midwest*, V (1967), p. 14.

[25] *Ibid.*

[26] *Argus* (editorial), March 17, 1967, p. 2B.

[27] Gerard, *op. cit.*, p. 14.

[28] *Post* (editorial), February 14, 1967, p. 2C.

[29] Interview with Robert B. Curtis, past CORE chairman, January 23, 1968.

[30] *Globe* (editorial), February 15, 1967, p. 10A.

[31] Gerard, *op. cit.* (n. 24), p. 13.

[32] *Post*, March 18, 1967, p. 3A.

[33] *Post*, April 2, 1967, p. 10C.

[34] *Post*, April 10, 1967, p. 4B.

[35] *Post*, March 13, 1967, p. 8C.

[36] *Argus*, March 17, 1967, p. 1.

[37] *Post*, March 22, 1967, p. 3A.

[38] *Post* (editorial), April 26, 1967, p. 2C.

[39] Gerard, *op. cit.* (n. 24), pp. 14–15.

CHAPTER 10

Letters from Jail

The anger of William L. Clay, Robert B. Curtis, and Taylor Jones, because of Judge Scott's condescending reprimand, no doubt reinforced their consciousness. All three wrote letters from jail indicating that they were angry, and that the various subordinating experiences had helped to clarify their ideas and strengthened their determination. Clay and Curtis had each served 105 of their 270-day sentences, and each paid $1,150 in fines and court costs. Jones had served 120 days of his one-year sentence, and paid $605 in fines and court costs. When they were finally released from incarceration, the patronizing manner in which this release occurred helped to ensure that it would be highly unlikely that they would ever abandon their new awareness and determination. Their official release contained no admission of guilt in the Jefferson Bank incident and no apology for Judge Scott. However, Judge Scott said in releasing them that he was giving some weight to their earlier request for clemency. Jones's letter from jail revealed that not only was he angry and determined, but also that he had lost respect for Judge Scott and the judicial system.

> . . . Judge "King" Scott in his pious and callous diatribe against three defendants who sought clemency. "King" Scott likes to refer to the "majesty of the law and the dignity and authority of this (his) court."
>
> This pitiful relic of reaction must be taught that the first principle of human association is the "majesty of human dignity and freedom" and that no amount of judicial tyranny by political conspirators of his ilk can snuff out its flame.
>
> I categorically refuse to submit myself to the degradation of his "justice." . . .
>
> I do not plead for mercy. I DEMAND . . . justice. . . .

"King" Scott can hide behind the sham of the "majesty and dignity" of his court if he wishes but someday, in heaven or hell, he must answer for the injustice he has wrought. If he is not aware that he has been the vehicle for a miscarriage of justice then I pity him and the people of this community because, in that case, he is either a fool or the most incompetent judge ever elected to office, in whose hands the people have placed the power of life and death.[1]

Taylor Jones's March 31, 1967, letter from jail is indicative of how the power structure and Judge Scott had driven him to the wall. It is interesting to note Jones's thinking when in his letter he states that: "I would prefer to serve the sentence one-hundred times over rather than apologize to a racist judge who allows himself to be dictated to by a fascist coalition of bankers, politicians, policemen, newspapers and, yes, sadly enough, a few Uncle Toms."[2]

As the community became tense, there was increasing use of the terms "racist" and "racism." Those words might have been stirring in the black community, but possibly helped white people to look in the other direction. It would be difficult for a white man to admit that he is a racist, even if he desired to cleanse his soul or believed that the truth must be faced before it was too late in St. Louis. Jones's letter makes it clear he believed that equality before the law and due process of law were in reality power structure discretions. His use of the word "fascist" refers to the fact that fascism repudiated the concept of equality, and its scheme made possible the changing of rules to suit changing purposes.

It has been shown (Chapter 7) that, in August of 1963, fair play and nothing akin to fascism was expected when after the August 30, 1963 demonstration, the NAACP field secretary praised the demonstrators and informed them that there had been no arrests because "the people who got the injunction knew it was unfair." However, his assessment later proved to be erroneous. He had no idea that the power structure would use what black people came to call "repressive" legal devices. It is also highly possible that the bank, too, erred. Those responsible for the demonstrators receiving long sentences possibly failed to realize that black men such as Clay, Curtis, and Jones) would resent such tactics and no longer respect white power and cease to fear it. Those few who admired and respected Stokely Carmichael and Rap Brown were ambivalent in 1967 when the demonstrators returned to jail. Although they had no desire to see black people intimidated and jailed, they knew that the bank's tactic of "jail the leaders" would help make the black community fertile for seeds planted by Carmichael and Brown to grow and develop. We do not know his exact motive, but Jones, the former peaceful demonstrator, stated in his letter: ". . . I regret that I have placed so much faith in and caused others to believe in and practice, 'non-violent, peaceful demonstrations.' The Black Community and its friends must reassess their tactics and find more forceful ways to insure equitable solutions to its problems."[3]

Jones asserted himself and remained in jail. In nineteenth-century America, to be an aggressive white man was a source of pride, but assertive black men were "kept in their place" and lynched as "sassy niggers." Thus, for generations, general segregation was more detrimental for black men than for black women and helped prevent most black men from becoming strong father figures. This factor, along with the current generation's high rates of divorce, separation, and desertion, makes it impossible for all but a minority of black children to live the first eighteen years of their lives with both parents.[4]

William L. Clay, too, exhibited awareness of the need for strong black male figures, and this made it evident that Judge Scott would encounter difficulty "keeping him in his place." Rather than apologize and submit to what Clay considered an overt act of intimidation, humiliation, and degradation, he chose to remain in jail. His April 27, 1967, letter from jail indicated that suffering had helped him become conscious of the need for a black man to set an example for black children. He hoped that his not bowing to institutional racism would indelibly impress on the minds of young black people that it was no longer necessary to destroy their personalities and aspirations by accommodating and submitting to racism. He said:

> Judge Scott proclaims that he wants to show mercy. But his conditions for freedom are humiliating and degrading. I will never bend my knees, bow my head or apologize to a racist judge. Freedom without dignity is really not freedom. I am certain that at this very minute, in jail, I am more free than many on the outside who have succumbed to pressure, intimidation and threats.
>
> I am much too proud to beg. When I am freed, I will walk out of jail, not crawl. It is important in the Negroes' struggle

for equality that Negro men exemplify courage and integrity. Your children must have living examples to which they can point.[5]

Bill Clay believed that black people in St. Louis were victims of a double standard of justice and received heavier penalties than whites who were charged with the same offense. According to him:

> . . . in the state of Missouri, Negroes are subjected to double standards of justice by our courts. Negroes are generally given much sterner punishment than whites for the same crimes. Our case is an excellent example. Several weeks ago McArthy of the Machinist Union broke the lock on the Union Hall in direct violation of a court order. The Judge said that McArthy had a "moral responsibility" to his membership. He was found NOT GUILTY of contempt. Last year, two Laclede Gas workers in the same court which convicted us, pleaded guilty to using explosives in destroying gas mains thus endangering the lives of gas customers. Their fines were (fifty) $50.00 dollars each.[6]

Clay's letter from jail indicated he believed that the court which fined white men fifty dollars for endangering human life evidently assumed that he had no "moral responsibility" to the black community. This became a significant point to Clay, for in his mind no property had been destroyed nor any lives endangered by his alleged offense. This, no doubt, reinforced his beliefs that the St. Louis power structure was "oppressive" and "vindictive" and intended to make examples out of Jefferson Bank demonstrators.

> The question is not whether Bill Clay, Bob Curtis, and Taylor Jones will be free, but whether the Negro community will be kept in chains. As long as we are in jail, no Negro has the right to effectively protest the oppression of a vindictive white community without fear of the same treatment. . . .
> . . . Judge Scott has set a precedent with the sentences in this case. But most important he has made an example of us that has not been lost upon the Negro community. That example reduced to its crudest form is this: "If a black man attacks the very foundations of the system of racism he will be crushed at any cost with whatever weapon is at hand, but preferably with the law."[7]

Robert B. Curtis, too, wrote to his community from jail. His March 17, 1967, letter depicted a personal awareness that efforts to obtain jobs that would help restore black people's self-respect caused the demonstrators to be jailed primarily to satisfy an economic system based on racial exploitation.

> Today we languish in jail in order to satisfy a system based on racial exploitation, disfranchisement and murder. But with the passage of time sophistication will grow among persons committed to racial justice, and as Judge Scott's name becomes famous as the man who threw the book at civil rights demonstrators, the people as a whole may assert their belief that moral right and devices of law are not the same thing at all.[8]

Where most black St. Louisans complained about the results of Judge Scott's decisions, Curtis complained additionally about the process by which the decisions were made. This may indicate that he possessed some affinity for the New Left, for it cares more about how a decision gets made than about what the decision is.[9] However, he cannot be placed totally in that camp because he did care about results. He did not lose faith in the total political system, but he did condemn the judicial process because he believed that the defendants did not receive a fair trial. His letter also included some uncomplimentary remarks pertaining to the governor of Missouri and the press, because he believed that they were a part of a conspiracy of silence.

> If anyone ever tells you that Mississippi represents the nadir of American hypocrisy, injustice and oppression—tell them to come to St. Louis.
> We have been denied a fair trial and hearing on appeal by racist and politically motivated courts, yes, including the United States Supreme Court. We have been denied pardon and reprieve by a politically opportunist Governor who, with callous indifference, disclaims the prerogative of his office. The merits of our case have been ignored by a moneygrubbing "free" press who would rather join the "conspiracy of silence" in order to sell advertising than to expose the corruption and the flagrant abuse of the judicial process that has condemned 15 innocent men and women to serve long jail terms because we fought for the poor and against the exploitation of man by man. When they have reached this judgment, the tortuous process of democracy will have affirmed once again the inescapable conclusion, that human rights are more precious than property rights, and that there is no place in our society for a judge, governor, or a newspaper who do not know it.[10]

At this point, it is important to consider Curtis' personal background. It was no accident that he was involved in the Jefferson Bank confrontation. Open resistance to racism had permeated Curtis' life. As a preschool child, he was with his mother when she refused to leave a railroad station's segregated dining room in Kansas City. A few years later, he was involved in desegregating public swimming pools in St. Louis. He possibly acquired some of his profound desire to contribute to the social betterment of man from having attended a Quaker prep school. By the time he received his B.A. degree at Illinois College, his social welfare thoughts included well-defined goals. While earning his law degree at Washington University, he was the very active president of the campus chapter of the NAACP, and he was arrested in 1959 for demonstrating. While he was fulfilling his military obligation, the Department of Defense found it necessary to come to his aid after civilian authorities arrested him for demonstrating in the proximity of Fort Hood, Texas.[11]

Because of the role Curtis played in the Jefferson Bank affair, the Bar Committee of the Twenty-second Judicial Circuit attempted to have him disbarred. It submitted a motion to the Missouri Supreme Court requesting that Curtis be disbarred because he had been found guilty of a crime involving moral turpitude and had thus violated legal canons of ethics.[12]

The Mound City Bar Association, composed mostly of black lawyers, immediately came to Curtis' aid and petitioned the Missouri Supreme Court to stop proceedings that would remove his name from the roll of practicing attorneys. It would be difficult to ascertain whether Mound City Bar members are among those who believe that black men should not be drafted into the United States Army unless black people serve on draft boards. But the Mound City Bar did inform the Missouri Supreme Court that black lawyers had been systematically excluded from becoming members of the Bar Committee of the Twenty-second Judicial Circuit which filed the motion to disbar a black lawyer, Robert B. Curtis. According to the Mound City Bar Association, the St. Louis Court of Appeals should not classify Curtis' conviction of contempt of court as a conviction of moral turpitude, but as a quasi-criminal action.[13]

Mound City Bar members argued that equating Curtis' conviction with conviction of a crime involving moral turpitude was in effect denying him due process of law because this procedure permitted summary disbarment without trial. They were additionally disturbed that their research failed to show any other case in Missouri where summary disbarment was sought where the defendant had not been entitled to a jury trial.[14]

The action of the Bar Association of Metropolitan St. Louis added to the resentment and smoldering anger in the black community. Disbarment came to have a special meaning to black people, whose new state of awareness had already increased their suspicion of the judicial system when they learned that the first lawyer threatened with disbarment without receiving an opportunity to have a jury trial was black. Mound City Bar members also used for argument the fact that the Bar Committee failed to inform Curtis of his specific activities that led it to request his disbarment.[15] According to Curtis: "I was not aware previously to my reading of it in the daily paper, that I was being investigated by any bar group. They made their announcement of their recommendation to the State Supreme Court without ever sending me a copy of their charges up to Tuesday."[16]

The *Argus* published a letter from the Greater St. Louis Community Council rallying to Curtis' defense. It accused the Bar Association of violating Missouri Supreme Court Rule #503 by releasing information to the press pertaining to Curtis' disbarment proceedings before he had been notified that proceedings had been instituted against him. The Community Council also charged the Association with violating Supreme Court Rule #4:20 in using newspapers to propagate information that could prejudice the anticipated litigation. It additionally said that: ". . . this Council is alarmed to the point of outrage that a body whose function it is to control the conduct of others, would itself be guilty of misconduct under laws and rules prescribed for pursuing its delegated duties."[17]

Although the Bar Association of Metropolitan St. Louis was concerned with the rule of law, it showed no similar sentiment in this case in that the defendants were not convicted for violating statute law, but for violating Judge Scott's law.[18] Nor was the Association concerned that: ". . . usually in a criminal trial, the defendant must be proved guilty beyond a reasonable doubt. If that standard had been applied in this case, the case would have been thrown out of court. And this is true even if one considers only the evidence offered by the prosecution."[19]

The Bar Association was cognizant that Judge Scott himself, and not a jury, found all nine of the original defendants guilty and that the St. Louis Court of Appeals ruled that there was insufficient evidence to convict four of the nine. This was true: ". . . even though less proof than beyond a reasonable doubt was required. In other words, given additional room for error, Judge Scott was still wrong in four cases out of nine."[20]

In addition, the Bar Association was aware that the single intent of requiring bail bond is to ensure that a defendant will appear to answer legal process. Since seven of the original nine defendants surrendered on their own accord, it is open to question whether or not it was necessary to set bond at $10,000, a figure required in St. Louis in less than 5 percent of heinous and gross felonies. The fantastically high bail put to question whether it was designed to impose undue and unnecessary financial burdens on the defendants since, more often than not, it will cost at least $1,000 to obtain such a bond in St. Louis. Action taken by Judge Scott becomes more questionable after considering that Washington University law students researched all reported contempt cases in this country and could not find one that remotely sanctioned the kind of sentences imposed by Judge Scott. It has been said that: ". . . Judge Scott can be shown to have acted arbitrarily and vindictively in a case in which he himself made debatable finding that the defendants were guilty of violating a law he himself made, and for which he himself imposed sentences that were without precedent in the United States legal history."[21]

When less than 5 percent of those charged with serious crimes are required to post $10,000 bail in St. Louis, it becomes difficult to believe that Judge Scott did not act arbitrarily and vindictively. If those white St. Louisans who have open minds were to examine this aspect of the Jefferson Bank confrontation, they no doubt would find it difficult to say that those black people in St. Louis who equated Judge Scott's brand of required obedience with white supremacy were in error.[22]

Evidently, there was an attempt to make it appear that the sentences handed down by Judge Scott had been approved by higher courts reviewing the case. But most black St. Louisans had acquired such a distrust of the judicial system that, even if the implication had been true, it is doubtful that approval by higher courts would have caused sizable numbers of black St. Louisans to place total faith in the courts. Furthermore, such an implication was misleading. It is highly doubtful that higher courts would have voiced their approval. Missouri laws do not empower higher courts to reduce sentences received for criminal contempt. A higher court can only determine whether a sentence is so flagrant that it denies the constitutional protection against cruel and unusual punishment.[23]

The belief that Judge Scott acted arbitrarily and vindictively caused many living in black neighborhoods to voice their outrage openly. Many white St. Louisans, along with members of the Bar Association of Metropolitan St. Louis, were aware of this fact. The *Post* informed its readers on April 26, 1967, that the situation was grave enough to cause concern. It also revealed that conservative black leaders were worried, a sort of follow-up to the *Argus'* March 17 warning that a time bomb was ticking in the community. The *Argus* was aware that not only were most black St. Louisans angry, but also that a few who were not known outside of the ghetto were totally alienated and unforgiving. Not only the general white public, but at least part, if not all, of official St. Louis expected the city to experience a major civil disturbance. This could be seen a few months later when, in September, Police Commissioner E. L. Dowd informed an audience that only about one-half of one percent of black St. Louisans were potential rioters, and that the police knew who they were and had files on them.[24] Regardless of whether it was true that the St. Louis Police Department could identify potential rioters (including those blacks not known outside of the ghetto), there did exist the belief that a riot was possible. But this did not move the St. Louis Bar Association to seek restoration of faith in the judicial system in black neighborhoods. Instead, it denounced ACTION.[25]

The denunciation of ACTION when it was demonstrating to support jailed CORE leaders only added another element to the underlying grievances in the black community. All of these factors make the warnings by the *Argus* and *Post* most relevant.

> . . . [A riot does] not typically erupt without preexisting causes, as a result of a single "triggering" or precipitating incident. Instead, it develops out of an increasingly disturbed social atmosphere, in which typically a series of tension-heightening incidents over a period of weeks or months became linked in the minds of

many in the Negro community with a shared network of underlying grievances.

There was, typically, a complex relationship between the series of incidents and the underlying grievances. . . .[26]

Amidst this tension "bad nigger" Percy Green saw to it that there were nightly demonstrations in front of Judge Scott's home: ". . . [It is] precisely because Judge Scott's decision was without principle—was, in fact, a rule of man and not of law—that the demonstrations are taking place.[27] Green's followers became increasingly angry during the more than a month of demonstrations. Finally, on Easter Sunday morning, they resorted to hanging Judge Scott in effigy from trees near his home. After this action the Bar Association of Metropolitan St. Louis publicly supported Judge Scott. John R. Barsanti, Jr., its president, issued a statement in its behalf condemning personal harassment of Scott. The Bar Association considered ACTION's techniques as dangerous dissent directed at personality in lieu of principle. Green, who had been disturbed in 1963 when the Bar Association was conspicuously silent over Judge Scott's severity with the defendants, responded to Barsanti in 1967 with "to hell with the Bar Association."[28]

Green was aware that justice has an impersonal quality, a quality which no man, however good, can attain. He realized discrepancies between this impersonal justice and Judge Scott's, which was not consistent with human dignity. It was not surprising that Green told the black community that the enemy was a white man and not abstract judicial principles.[29]

With Green's assistance, black St. Louis was soon to learn that among the conspiratorial racist forces intimidating and subordinating black people was an athletic club (Missouri Athletic Club—MAC), which even excluded the elites' "responsible Negroes" and maintained a lily white membership because, according to Percy Green: ". . . apparently whitey fears that some of the Negroes he has labeled as 'responsible' Negroes might overhear some of their white top secret planning and bring this information back to his so-called 'irresponsible' Negro brothers."[30]

To support this allegation, Green referred to what he believed to be the "conspiracy" to disbar Robert Curtis. According to him, MAC was composed of "heads of big business and top law officials who meet to conspire against Negro leaders and whites who openly support the Negro cause." Green revealed that John Barsanti, most of the members of the Bar Association of Metropolitan St. Louis, Wayne Millsap, and Judge Scott were MAC members. The ACTION chairman charged that after his organization hung Judge Scott in effigy on Easter Sunday, there was a special MAC meeting attended by sixteen members. According to Green, these members decided to research the possibility of getting an injunction against ACTION and to punish Robert Curtis ("teach a nigger a lesson") for remarks carried by television stations and published in newspapers criticizing Judge Scott and the judicial system. It was decided that Curtis must be disbarred because, according to Green's charges:

> . . . if att'y Curtis, being a Negro lawyer and allowed to denounce or bring embarrassment to the courts, what would prevent the other Negro professionals from getting out of hand? It was voiced that "we must make an example of Curtis to the Negro community, we will not tolerate disrespect for law and order, just for Negroes." Some club members compared atty. Curtis to Adam Clayton Powell. Another member remarked that if Negroes are unhappy with conditions here, why don't they go back to Africa.[31]

A white MAC member who held an unpublicized ACTION membership informed Green that MAC held a second special meeting immediately after constitutional lawyer Jules Gerard issued statements supporting Jefferson Bank demonstrators. At this meeting, it was decided that it was imperative to teach Gerard a lesson because he had soundly discredited Judge Scott's ability: ". . . because Gerard decided to openly support the bank demonstrators he must be willing to pay the price. . . . He is unfit to teach at Washington University's School of Law . . . thus plans were made to force the professor to resign."[32]

Most of those who supported Jefferson Bank's position perceived Judge Scott's actions as maintaining law and order; and by 1967, when his actions had the potential to lead to a "long, hot summer," they possibly had forgotten (or never realized) that only two of the original nine defendants had physically violated the injunction. The other seven defendants were influential in directing CORE; and the white community, aside from the establishment, possibly did not realize that instead of protecting bank property, the primary motive of Judge Scott's action was to jail leaders of the movement designed to improve black peoples' economic status. Therefore, the legal society's denunciation of ACTION was unfortunate. As Jules Gerard said:

> It was particularly distressing that a learned legal society should choose to hold up the virtually unreviewable exercise of a judge's discretionary contempt power as an example of "the rule of law." It is not too farfetched to say that the history of American law could be written in terms of the restrictions placed upon the power of judges to punish actions which occur outside the court-room as contempt. One could begin with James Madison's unsuccessful attempt to impeach Missouri's first federal judge for abuses of the contempt power, continue through the restrictions placed upon "labor injunctions" in the early years of this century; and conclude with recent cases from the United States Supreme Court severely limiting the sentences judges may impose without jury trials. Had these latter cases been controlling, by the way, they would have made the sentences imposed here unconstitutional.[33]

Although the Bar Association found it desirable to denounce ACTION, it was silent when both dailies criticized another circuit judge. Is being picketed at one's home more detrimental than being raked over the coals by powerful and influential newspapers? It also issued no public statement when there was agitation to impeach United States Supreme Court justices. Instead of attacking ACTION and further inflaming black people, it possibly should have attempted to find a way for the judicial process to function impartially as black people push to improve their economic and social positions. Again, in Gerard's words:

> What is needed is action by men of good will. This case raises directly the question of the proper role of the legal system in promoting the legitimate social aspirations of the Negroes, as distinguished from protecting their constitutional rights. Rather than inflame the situation by inappropriate statements, all of the bar associations of St. Louis should jointly offer their good offices to conciliate the dispute so that both sides may retire with dignity and honor.
>
> The Bar did not recognize that by picketing the judge and not the courts, the picketers distinguished between the man and the law. This we should welcome.[34]

Such efforts as Gerard suggests possibly could have, to a limited extent, helped in the restoration of black people's faith in the courts and possibly could have contributed to future peace and tranquility in the city. On the other hand, if the system continued to function as it did in the Jefferson Bank case, and if black people had become more convinced that this was the type of justice they could expect in St. Louis, it was highly possible that the city would have undergone almost unimaginable experiences.[35]

The fact that a few black people in St. Louis were alienated and unforgiving could have proved to have been very important. The Bar Association of Metropolitan St. Louis might have forgotten (or never knew) that slightly less than fifteen years earlier a handful of revolutionary-minded Moslems, unknown outside of their homes, had joined together to mobilize the Algerian population against the French Administration. According to E. Drexel Godfrey, Jr., the wave of terror on the part of Ben Bella and his associates did not cease when the French decided to suppress the revolt. The French learned that something had started that could not be easily nor rapidly rubbed out. As the French became more repressive, the Ben Bellas became more determined and skilled in guerrilla tactics.[36]

When one goes beyond the charge that black people in St. Louis did not receive impartial justice, the parallels become more similar. French exclusiveness in building Algeria meant that only cooperative Algerians were admitted to positions of influence. This system of exclusiveness is very similar to procedures followed by white people in American cities. Whether by design or accident, the St. Louis elite employed exclusiveness, as the North Central part of the city became in effect St. Louis' appendage. Charles Silberman suggests that in the United States this paternalistic attitude toward black people makes it imperative that the power structure select and place in positions of leadership those blacks who find it expedient to support and identify with the establishment.[37]

It has already been documented that ever since 1937, black St. Louisans have complained that their leaders usually proved more receptive to the immediate benefits of being associated with the establishment than to push for demands of the black masses. They remained leaders because the power structure protected them against rival interests within the black community. However, just as the French erred in Algeria, so did the power structure in St.

Louis during the Jefferson Bank confrontation. Both found themselves supporting discredited leaders. In St. Louis, establishment gestures of goodwill became fictions which were no longer accepted by the young Turks after the negotiations with Jefferson Bank opened their eyes. Since there is no way to seal off the black masses (not even with military power) from those who have lost faith in the courts, the Bar Association of Metropolitan St. Louis possibly should have attempted restoration of faith in the courts in lieu of attacking ACTION!

This point becomes very relevant when it is realized that in 1967 there were some unforgiving black people who were not known to the general white public and to most black people who supplied the power structure with news from the ghetto. Unforgiving militants and many others who openly advocated black power were not a homogeneous force and did not wholeheartedly accept identical ideologies and tactics. Many did not advocate that black power be violent, but: ". . . those who use violence . . . generally don't belong to any organization. They're just reacting spontaneously to a situation."[38]

In 1967, there appeared to be a steady influx into this camp of those who were not persuaded by the arguments offered by the traditional leaders, but who were influenced more by the fact that they and their families had experienced widespread economic suffering. Most of them did not align themselves with any organization because they feared that the power structure had paid spies in every black community organization. It appears that they went out of their way to avoid any contact with those they considered traditional leaders. It was no secret in the black community that many of the old-line leaders were disturbed because they felt there was an element in the community with which they could not communicate. More important, they could not readily identify them, thus destroying the utility and value of those leaders to the establishment. In early 1968, St. Louis' new Black Muslim Minister, Minister Joe X, admitted that he was experiencing difficulty preventing some of his young militants from deserting local Temple of Islam No. 28 to join the black power movement.[39]

The tension that developed after the Bar Association of Metropolitan St. Louis attempted to have Curtis disbarred in 1967 did not help improve relations between the races. On the other hand, the *Post* was hopeful that the Missouri Supreme Court's refusal to disbar Curtis would help to unify its black and white citizens:

> In tossing out disbarment proceedings against Robert B. Curtis . . . the Missouri Supreme Court has left new proceedings against him at least remotely possible. But the Judicial Circuit Bar Committee can no longer contend, the court indicates, that Mr. Curtis's contempt conviction constituted "moral turpitude" such as to require almost automatic disbarment. Instead, the committee would have to grant Mr. Curtis a hearing, which it has not done, and find and prove some further grounds for disciplinary action.
>
> This would seem neither worth the effort nor entirely wise. . . . After the Supreme Court's decision, any further efforts toward punishment could seem vindictive. Four years have passed since the Jefferson Bank demonstrations. It is time to wipe the slate clean, and to preserve community unity in behalf of civil rights and civil progress.[40]

The Jefferson Bank confrontation technically ended when Robert Curtis was not disbarred. However, in the next chapter the contention is made that the Jefferson Bank affair influenced practical politics by adversely affecting the strongest white politician in St. Louis.

NOTES

[1] Letter from Taylor Jones while in jail, as published by the *Argus*, March 31, 1967.

[2] *Ibid.*

[3] *Ibid.*

[4] *The Negro Family: The Case for National Action* (Washington: United States Department of Labor, Office of Policy Planning and Research, March, 1965), pp. 9, 16.

[5] Letter from William L. Clay, 26th Ward committeeman at the time the letter was written in city jail, April 27, 1967.

[6] *Ibid.*

[7] *Ibid.*

[8] Letter from Robert B. Curtis, chairman, St. Louis CORE, 1963, as published by the *Argus*, March 17, 1967.

[9] Christopher Jencks, "Limits of the New Left," *The New Republic*, CLVII (October 21, 1967), p. 20.

[10] Letter from Curtis, *op. cit.*

[11] Richard Jacobs, *Post*, September 1, 1963, p. 5A.

[12] *Post*, May 7, 1967, p. 1A.

[13] *Post*, May 19, 1967, p. 6A.

14 *Ibid.*

15 *Post*, May 19, 1967, p. 6A.

16 *Argus*, May 12, 1967, pp. 1A, 4A.

17 *Ibid.*

18 Jules B. Gerard, Letter to the Editor, *Post*, April 26, 1967, p. 26.

19 *Ibid.*

20 *Ibid.*

21 *Ibid.*

22 Jules B. Gerard, "Jefferson Bank Dispute Rocks St. Louis," *Focus/Midwest*, V (1967), p. 14.

23 *Ibid.*

24 *Post*, September 25, 1967, p. 3C.

25 *Post*, April 20, 1967, p. 3A.

26 National Advisory Commission on Civil Disorders, *Report of the National Advisory Commission on Civil Disorders*, A response to Executive Order 11365, issued by President Lyndon B. Johnson on July 29, 1967 (Washington: U.S. Government Printing Office, 1968), p. 111.

27 Gerard's Letter, *op. cit.* (n. 18).

28 *Post*, April 20, 1967, p. 3A.

29 Interview with Percy Green, chairman of ACTION, January 12, 1968.

30 *Argus*, May 26, 1967, pp. 1A, 4A.

31 *Ibid.*

32 *Ibid.*

33 Gerard, "Jefferson Bank Dispute Rocks St. Louis," *op. cit.* (n. 22), p. 13.

34 *Ibid.*, pp. 13–15.

35 *Ibid.*

36 E. Drexel Godfrey, Jr., *The Government of France* (New York: Thomas Y. Crowell, 1964), pp. 145–46.

37 Charles E. Silberman, *Crisis in Black and White* (New York: Vintage Books, 1964), p. 196.

38 *Post*, March 23, 1968, p. 3A.

39 Robert Collins, *Post*, March 26, 1968.

40 *Post* (editorial), November 15, 1967, p. 2D.

CHAPTER 11

The White Boss

After 1939, several Chicago political wards became thickly inhabited with black people whom the city's political machine desired to control. In reality, the machine leaders probably did not view this situation with the idea of utilizing a rational long-range plan which would help them control and sway votes in the black wards. Political racism only requires that black voters be controlled to the extent that they will support either black or white politicians, even though they fall short and become deficient in providing mutual government policy benefits and other advantages and services for black people to the same degree as for whites.

Theoretically, domination and subordination could have been effected in Chicago if the political machine had selected and supported one black man as political leader in each ward. This would have been easy since white people have a wealth of experience in selecting black leaders who will submit to their control. Technically, under this system of subordination each black leader would have been autonomous in his ward, but, in reality, would have been obligated to the machine's central committee, which had picked him. This is a type of subordination whereby black people were permitted "to produce a number of feudal barons in the kingdom of the Democratic Boss."[1] In terms of influencing and deciding how black people should vote, the machine had an option. It could have selected one black man in Chicago and charged him with the responsibility of organizing and keeping control of all black wards (for it). This is a subordinating process of subinfeudation, in which one black politician stands between the white boss and the black wards.[2]

Whether Chicago's white politicians proceeded with a rational plan of subordination, such as the one just outlined, or whether

164

a series of specifics and limited issues and decisions were determinant, is not as relevant as the fact that one black man, William L. Dawson, emerged dominant. In all probability, Dawson acquired much of his political power because the machine chose to side with him since he consistently withstood challengers and came out of political battles victoriously, displaying superior political astuteness. It was possible for Dawson to serve as the intermediary in subordinating black people precisely because there was a strong city machine which had control of enough patronage to support subinfeudation. Yet if the machine had been weak, with no central control over patronage, it is doubtful if it could have produced a single dominant black political leader.[3]

In contrast to Chicago, St. Louis was politically divided and held together by coalitions, regardless of which political party was dominant. On one side were generally found the dominant business interests and most of the middle class. In opposition were labor groups that had vested local interests, the lesser downtown interests, neighborhood business representation, or what has been called "stop sign-spot zoning groups." Black politicians belonged to both coalitions. The system of elected county offices helped maintain this power division. This division made it very difficult for any one white politician to gain control of enough patronage to dominate the city's political scene and install the subordinating process of subinfeudation—unless he were very astute, lucky, and held office for a very long time. Therefore, no white politician was able to bring a "Dawson" into being in St. Louis. Nevertheless, one black politician, Jordan Chambers, became somewhat more politically influential than any other black St. Louis politician. But because of the presence of elective county offices he could not completely dominate all other black politicians. Consequently, the black political structure in St. Louis was akin to that of the "feudal barons in the kingdom of the Democratic Bosses." Thus, primarily because of the lack of centralized political power, St. Louis' black people began to acquire a small measure of political power under circumstances somewhat different from those of their black brothers in Chicago. However, the differences were only of degree because in both cities blacks were subordinated.

Notwithstanding this acquisition of a small measure of political power by black St. Louisans, the very nature of the county office system made possible the rise of the entrenched older white politician who greatly subordinated the black community prior to and during the Jefferson Bank confrontation. This development also disadvantaged many young white politicians who might have possessed talent and ideas. According to a *Post* editorial: "One of the reasons the Democratic party apparatus in the city is so lacking in ideas and so relatively inhospitable to young talent is the power of the entrenched old-timers holding down public and party posts to freeze out opposition at primary time. Through judicious use of the patronage available in their public offices and shrewd use of their power as committeemen, they embrace one another and fight off outsiders."⁴

The freeze-out made it possible for a man to remain committeeman indefinitely, providing the opportunity for a politically astute committeeman to utilize patronage judiciously to enhance his political power beyond the boundaries of his ward. Thus, St. Louis did have a white politician who, in time, came to exercise a large measure of control over politics in black wards specifically, and in the city generally. He, John J. Dwyer, was a protégé of the old school of politics, in which people did things because they were indebted to someone. Dwyer's career began to ascend because of his association with St. Louis' then mayor, Bernard F. Dickman. In 1938, Mayor Dickman supported Dwyer's candidacy for Circuit Clerk in an effort to oust the incumbent, H. Sam Priest, who years later became President of St. Louis' Board of Police Commissioners. Although Dwyer lost what proved to be a lively campaign, Mayor Dickman was grateful that Dwyer was loyal enough to him to challenge Priest, and soon found an opportunity to reward Dwyer. That same year Henry C. Henne, City Treasurer, died, and Dickman appointed Dwyer as City Treasurer. A friendly test case was brought to determine if the mayor could fill the position of City Treasurer by appointment. Conveniently, the Missouri Supreme Court did not hand down its decision that the mayor could not fill the noncity position by appointment until after Dwyer had been elected to it later that year. In 1939, the state legislative body changed the statute so that the office could be filled by mayoral appointment.⁵

By the time the young Turks of the black community aggressively began to seek political power in the 1960's, Dwyer had become St. Louis' most powerful political figure, primarily because he was able to control and manipulate black voters to his advantage. Had he not been able to subordinate a large segment of the black electorate, it would have been virtually impossible for him to have been so politically powerful. His power was based on the fact that he was committeeman for the black Fourth Ward. This was most important because in 1943 he had become chairman of St. Louis' City Democratic Central Committee, and only a ward committeeman can serve in this capacity. Dwyer's political power was enhanced because in addition to the patronage available to a committeeman, he had at least sixty-five jobs under his control as City Treasurer. Once Dwyer became chairman of the Democratic Central Committee, his combined positions made it possible for him to control and influence hundreds of city, state, and federal jobs.[6]

Technically, the chairman of the Democratic Central Committee of St. Louis has limited power and simply presides over meetings of twenty-eight independent ward committeemen. In reality, the position provides ample opportunities for the chairman to enhance his political power as Dwyer did. According to the *Post:*

> The last chairman, the late John J. Dwyer, possessed two effective power bases independently of the chairmanship, and hence had muscle of his own. He controlled a large bloc of votes in his tightly-organized Fourth ward, one of the eight largest delivery wards in the city, and he also controlled both a bloc of patronage jobs and certain opportunities for fund raising among bankers by virtue of his public office as City Treasurer. Combining those with the chairmanship gave him access to state patronage; and until he picked the wrong horse in the Hearnes-Bush primary two years ago, he evidently had a real say in certain state matters. His support of former Mayor Tucker, who did not attempt to run the party, diminished his influence in the city still more.[7]

In addition to the black young Turks, there appeared in St. Louis a young white man who helped in the Jefferson Bank confrontation to the extent that Dwyer's political problems were enhanced. Eugene J. Tournour, CORE's Midwest Field Secretary, began to assume a measure of leadership in the Jefferson Bank confrontation. The twenty-six-year-old Tournour, whose wife was one of the nineteen demonstrators sent to jail by Judge Scott, was a St. Louisan and a graduate of Washington University of St. Louis.[8] Tournour helped reinforce the belief held by many black people in St. Louis that they could not expect to obtain quality education, better housing, and improved employment opportunities by relying on the existing political system and on older black political leaders. According to Tournour:

> For years . . . efforts to bring about fundamental changes in education, housing and employment policies were channeled through the existing political organizations. These met with no success.
>
> As a result, Negroes have become disenchanted with their older political leaders and with the solutions they propose.
>
> What must be realized is that the Negro rights movement is now solidly established and the challenge it poses to the old ways of thinking will not go away.
>
> What a majority of Americans may not realize . . . is that Negroes are no longer satisfied with the old processes of negotiations and discussion, and have resorted to a new spirit of militancy.
>
> I think political, business and religious leaders in the United States are coming to realize that we have a form of apartheid here, and that we are not so far removed from the South African situation as one might think.[9]

After the original nineteen Jefferson Bank demonstrators were sentenced on October 24 and 25 of 1963, Tournour urged several hundred people, who on October 27 were attending a rally at which funds were raised to pay legal fees for the jailed demonstrators, to participate in a new move against the bank. This newly proposed strategy revealed that they were going to attack the local Democratic boss, John J. Dwyer, with a "spirit of militancy." It included plans to demonstrate at Dwyer's City Treasurer's office, among other places, in order to urge that public funds be removed from Jefferson Bank.[10]

On October 28, Tournour led demonstrators to City Hall to confer with Dwyer. Dwyer admitted that the city had on deposit at Jefferson Bank at least $1,000,000 for general bills and a second account for payrolls that involved approximately $2,500,000 every two weeks. But he said that he believed nothing would be accomplished by removing the funds from the bank and flatly rejected the request of the demonstrators. Dwyer additionally informed the demonstrators that the Board of Fund Commissioners—composed of Dwyer, Mayor Raymond Tucker, and City Comptroller John Poelker—would have to make the final decision and that the Board has no plans to hold a conference on the matter.[11]

Thirty CORE members then picketed Dwyer's Plaza Square apartment, which was located well outside of the black ward that he had been elected to represent. On November 4, 119 demonstrators went to City Hall and Mayor Tucker rejected their request to remove funds from Jefferson Bank. But Comptroller Poelker informed the demonstrators that he believed the Board of Fund Commissioners would consider the request at its December meeting.[12]

Mayor Tucker's refusal to give immediate attention to CORE's request did not help ease tensions. On November 6, 1963, Percy Green, then a very active CORE member, was one of twenty-five people who participated in a demonstration outside Dwyer's office to show that they were aroused. After Dwyer's office closed November 6, all demonstrators except Green left. He continued to protest after closing hours. Green's strategy was to dramatize to the public that there had been a breakdown of relations between Dwyer and many in the black community, by conducting a silent hunger strike and reading. The police requested that he leave, but he refused and remained silent. Without verbally breaking his quietude, he acquiesced to their attempts to initiate communication by writing on a piece of paper that he would willingly leave when public money had been removed from Jefferson Bank. The police would not permit him to remain in the building and placed him on a stretcher as he clutched a copy of Lomax's *The Negro Revolt*.[13]

The demonstrations at City Hall were denounced by a white politician who said that he supported black people's struggle for equal economic opportunities. Donald Gunn, St. Louis' president of the Board of Aldermen, made a statement on a KMOX-TV program which revealed what black people call a "paternalistic" attitude. According to Gunn: "hardly anyone in St. Louis has done more for the Negroes in the city than Mr. Dwyer. . . . I am saddened that these demonstrations should take place in front of his office."[14]

The Board of Fund Commissioners at its December meeting re-approved Jefferson Bank as a depository with the actual distribution of funds left to Dwyer's discretion. This decision proved how politically powerless black St. Louisans were and provided CORE with undeniable proof that Dwyer, as well as Tucker and Poelker, were on the side of the bank and institutional racism. By 5 p.m. the very same day the decision was reached, CORE demonstrated at Dwyer's office.[15] The fact that in the minds of many CORE members Dwyer, as City Treasurer, blatantly ignored a request made by an organization in behalf of the black community indicated that he possessed willful disregard for black peoples' desires or that his lackey informants had misread the black community's mood, or both.

Thus, Dwyer's relationship with the Jefferson Bank set the stage for the harbingers of change to threaten the hold on the political and economic power which allowed him to subordinate black voters effectively. The protest threat was made with help from CORE's Midwest Field Secretary, Eugene Tournour, a white man. We will therefore examine why, today, some race-conscious blacks are not so very proud that it was not a black man who had initiated protest activity against Dwyer. This examination takes us back to the turn-of-the-century controversy between Booker T. Washington and W. E. B. DuBois.

In January of 1904, Washington was able to invite fifty black leaders to meet at Carnegie Hall in New York City primarily because their traveling expenses were to be paid by white philanthropist Andrew Carnegie. Upon Washington's request, DuBois helped arrange the meeting. Once it got under way, some in attendance voiced opposition to Washington and his policies,[16] policies that Stokely Carmichael and Charles Hamilton believed were inimical to black people making political and economic progress in this country because they helped cause black people to practice the "politics of deference" (a phrase which Carmichael and Hamilton attribute to Paul L. Puryear, a black political science professor).

An entire philosophy of race relations developed around Booker T. Washington's leadership in the late nineteenth century. This philosophy encouraged black people to concentrate their time and energy on developing their educational and economic potential. It de-emphasized political activity: Washington was not noted for advocating that blacks run for public office. The good white folks would take care of the political business and as black people proved themselves "worthy," they would slowly be "accepted" by their white neighbors. Always embedded in Washington's philosophy was the notion that black people had to prove themselves to white people. . . .

A most ironic aspect of Booker T. Washington's career is the context in which that career started. Tuskegee Institute itself was established precisely because, in 1880, the black people of Macon County possessed political power. . . . Blacks then constituted the great majority of the county population. A former Confederate Colonel, W. F. Foster, was running for the Alabama legislature on the Democratic ticket. Obviously needing black votes, he went to the local black leader, a Republican named Lewis Adams, and made a deal: if Adams would persuade the blacks to vote for him, he would—once elected—push for a state appropriation to establish a school for black people in the county. Adams delivered: Foster was elected and a sum of $2,000 per year was appropriated to pay teachers' salaries for a school. Adams wrote to Hampton Institute in Virginia for a person to come and set up the school. The head of Hampton recommended one of his best teachers, Booker T. Washington.[17]

Black people today can learn a lesson when analyzing how Washington, the master political strategist, replied to and counteracted the criticism of himself and his policies that was voiced at the Carnegie Hall meeting. He proposed that a Committee of Twelve be established for the "Advancement and Interest" of black people, and his proposal was accepted. Since DuBois was among his critics, he astutely made sure that DuBois would be one of the three to appoint the Committee. This was a meaningless gesture because the third person was Hugh Brown, a man who had an affinity for Washington. Later, when it came time for DuBois to go to New York to help decide on appointments, he arrived there and learned that Washington and Brown had already been meeting for at least twenty-four hours. As a result, the candidates recommended by DuBois were rejected by a two-to-one vote, and their candidates were selected by the vote of two to one. Later, DuBois became ill at the time the Committee of Twelve was to have met, and he wrote Washington requesting a postponement. DuBois' request was ignored; and the meeting was held with Washington being made chairman, whereupon he delegated the work to be done by the full committee to a subcommittee to be named by himself. After having been taught a lesson in parliamentary maneuverings, DuBois resigned with the realization that black men who opposed the "politics of deference" were not welcome.[18]

DuBois did not give up. In June of 1905, he sent letters to several black leaders requesting that they come together to organize for more determined and aggressive action in behalf of black people. In response to his letter, twenty-nine black leaders from fourteen states met July 11–13, 1905, on the Canadian side of Niagara Falls. According to the earlier plan, the conference was to have been held near Buffalo, New York, but DuBois' request for hotel accommodations was denied. (Did this transpire because DuBois and the others had not been endorsed by the national elite?) Because the meeting was held near the Falls, it has been labeled the "Niagara Movement."[19]

In 1910, a conference was held in New York City with whites in attendance. At this meeting, the NAACP was organized. (Also in that year the National Urban League was founded to assist rural blacks in adjusting to city life.) White Boston attorney, Moorfield Storey, was named president of the NAACP, with DuBois as director of publicity and research. In November of 1910, the first issue of Crisis, the official journal of the NAACP, appeared under DuBois' editorship. He resigned his position at Atlanta University and continued with the NAACP until 1933.[20] DuBois had accepted the invitation to teach sociology at Atlanta University after having held a position at the University of Pennsylvania that was never higher than that of an assistant instructor, in spite of his Ph.D. from Harvard. He was never given a teaching assignment, even in the face of his previous teaching experience at Wilberforce University in Ohio. In fact, he was at no time introduced to other members of the faculty. His work at the University of Pennsylvania was confined to research.[21]

The original Niagara Movement ceased to exist with the founding of the NAACP. But its spirit continued to live, at first, through the all-black National Equal Rights League established by William Monroe Trotter. Trotter's central theme did not gain widespread acceptance among many blacks until the late 1960's. While DuBois preferred an all-black organization, he helped organize the NAACP because a lack of financing made it impossible for him to found the type of viable organization of his choice. He was not alone.

The original NAACP included in its leadership most of the blacks involved in the Niagara Movement. However, Trotter, a man who refused to compromise on any issue and who was most instrumental in helping DuBois found the Niagara Movement, refused to attend the conference that led to the NAACP's coming into existence because he did not trust white people. His distrust of whites was not based upon any separatist political ideology. He was an open and avowed integrationist who demanded total integration of black people into all aspects of American society. His doubts and lack of confidence of and in whites had their origins in his belief that if white liberals were to become part of an organization dedicated to "complete integration" of black people into American society, they would "water down" demands for total integration.[22]

As the 1960's wore on, Trotter's attitude toward whites was adopted increasingly by many emerging black political and protest leaders. Many of them came to realize that it was necessary for every black man to develop a sagacious distrust of whites in general and of all white institutions. They also began to realize that it was necessary in daily dealings with whites who belonged to organizations dedicated to improving the lives of black people to demand that they prove themselves on each issue. Black people should never automatically assume that just because some whites had worked with black people for black people on a previous issue that they will automatically work with blacks for the benefit of blacks on the next issue. When and if the efforts are not mutually beneficial, self-interest could cause white people who had previously been helpful, to trade black interest in behalf of dimly cognizant indirect (or direct) benefits available because of institutional racism. Where most protest leaders and followers in St. Louis during the 1960's maintained their suspicions of whites in the spirit of Trotter, they did not rediscover his ideas pertaining to organizations and exclusion of whites until the late 1960's. Thus, today some St. Louis blacks are not so proud that it was a white man, and not a black man, who took the leadership role in initiating action against Dwyer pertaining to the deposit of city funds.

A comparison between part of Carmichael's and Hamilton's views pertaining to coalition politics, and Dwyer's denial of a request from an organization that represented black people, reveals an inherent weakness in the coalition between Dwyer and the black politicians who religiously supported him. Carmicheal and Hamilton believe that white politicians who become a part of a black-white coalition serve only at the leadership level and that their main objective is not to strive to improve materially the lives of the black masses.[23] They also believe that rights demanded by black people always remain negotiable and expendable to the white coalition leader in case they conflict with white interests.[24] It would have been a waste of time and energy to have attempted to convince Bill Clay and many others in the black community that coalition leader John Dwyer did not place the interest of the white Jefferson Bank above that of black people.[25] Dwyer's county office had given the black young Turks an additional issue to use against him politically when he was forced to choose between a demand from CORE and the interest of the bank and institutional subordination.

With Dwyer as the leader of the black-white coalition, whites received a disproportionate share of the advantages which present themselves when a political party or a coalition controls city government. White domination of the coalition ensured that black people would not receive benefits on an equitable basis. Dwyer's control over the coalition allowed him to exercise a measure of control over city government—including helping in the shaping and implementation of policies as they affected black St. Louisans. And since he also influenced appointments to many city (and some state and national) jobs, this form of political racism helped provide the energy to sustain other forms of racism.

The Jefferson Bank affair convinced many black St. Louisans that "King Dwyer's" priority was the protection of his own vested interests and those of the elite. And since he was unresponsive to the needs of black people, some young "barons" who officially had never been a part of his "kingdom" began aggressively to challenge him. Dwyer indicated concern and recognition of them as a threat to his "kingdom" when he attempted unsuccessfully to intimidate them with the age-old racist trick which, in effect, threatens blacks with what they could lose by asserting themselves. Dwyer publicly warned: "the split in Negro leadership over tactics involved in picketing the Jefferson Bank and Trust Company could result in lessening the effectiveness of the Negro voting population."[26]

However, aside from the fact that Dwyer could lose some of

his power and influence, he possibly revealed his greatest fears to the *Post*. Adolph J. Rahm, a *Post* staff writer, said that Dwyer was concerned as to whether the schism was severe enough to endanger the Democratic party's chances to maintain control of the city of St. Louis and the state of Missouri[27] (political racism).

Dwyer was supporting Governor John M. Dalton's choice, Lieutenant Governor Hilary Bush, for the Democratic nomination as governor. He was concerned because young Turk leader Bill Clay had become anti-Dalton. His uneasiness was enhanced because no one at that time truly knew whether or not Clay would emerge as the dominant black political figure in St. Louis. Dwyer believed that all black St. Louis political leaders were fighting to gain the influence once possessed by Jordan Chambers, who had died in August of 1962.[28]

There was a scramble for power to be sure, but the young Turks wanted more than the type of power held by Chambers. It was generally believed by those less well-established blacks who were political watchers that the young Turks sought the type of power which could be exercised in behalf of black people collectively. They had no use for that type of power which could only be used to help entrench the establishment they were fighting.

The Collector of Revenue (county office), Louis G. Berra, Democratic committeeman from the almost totally white Twenty-fourth Ward, realized what potential the cleavage held for white Democrats, but he showed no respect for the young Turks or the old-guard blacks who were seeking political power. He, too, attempted to frighten and browbeat them: "There isn't a Jordan Chambers among them. If they don't get together, they may lose much of what they have gained."[29]

Dwyer and Berra apparently believed that the demise of Chambers was partially responsible for the black political rift and loss of white influence in black wards. But there is some evidence that suggests had Jordan Chambers been living in 1964, he too would have been challenged by the young Turks. In 1960, before the young Turks became a cohesive force, Raymond Howard challenged Chambers for his Nineteenth Ward committee post and received almost 800 of the slightly more than 4,000 votes cast.[30] If Ernest Kirschten's description of Chambers is accurate, there is little doubt that the young Turks would have challenged Chambers in 1964. According to Kirschten:

> . . . Chambers is an organization man, or again to quote Mr. Priest, a structural leader. . . .
> Naturally enough, this businessman-politician sipping mineral water in his night club, held forth on the need for "sound" men and the danger of "leftists." He deflated the Wallace boom and he is no enthusiast for such things as fair-employment-practice laws. He is no trouble-maker. He is a little old-fashioned, but he is not the type that accepts appointments to Liberia or cares too much about being a trustee of a state college for Negroes.[31]

There is little doubt that the new consciousness of the young Turks would have allowed a black man who was "no enthusiast for such things as fair-employment-practice laws," and who was "no trouble-maker" for white people, to prevent them from attacking a white politician who helped to subordinate black people.

NOTES

[1] James Q. Wilson, *Negro Politics: The Search for Leadership* (Glencoe, Ill.: The Free Press, 1960), pp. 79–80.

[2] *Ibid.*

[3] *Ibid.*

[4] *Post* (editorial), October 1, 1964, p. 2D.

[5] *Post*, May 8, 1966, p. 3A.

[6] *Post*, May 4, 1966, p. 1A.

[7] *Post* (editorial), May 17, 1966, p. 2B.

[8] *Post*, November 6, 1963, p. 23A.

[9] *Ibid.*

[10] *Post*, October 28, 1963, p. 1A.

[11] *Post*, October 29, 1963, p. 3A.

[12] *Post*, November 4, 1963, pp. 1A, 6A.

[13] *Post*, November 7, 1963, p. 3A.

[14] *Ibid.*

[15] *Globe*, December 31, 1963, p. 1A.

[16] Bradford Chambers, ed., *Chronicles of Black Protest* (New York: Mentor Books, 1968), p. 159.

[17] Stokely Carmichael and Charles V. Hamilton, *Black Power: The Politics of Liberation* (New York: Random House, 1967), pp. 124–25.

[18] Chambers, *op. cit.*, pp. 159–61.

[19] *Ibid.*

[20] *Ibid.*

[21] *Ibid.*, pp. 154–55.

[22] *Ibid.*, p. 161.

[23] Carmichael and Hamilton, *op. cit.*, p. 59.

[24] *Ibid.*, pp. 62–63.

[25] Adolph J. Rahm, *Post*, November 17, 1963, p. 3A.

[26] *Ibid.*

[27] *Ibid.*

[28] *Ibid.*

[29] *Ibid.*

[30] Abstract of Votes Cast at the August 2, 1960, Primary Election Compiled and Certified by the Board of Election Commissioners for the City of St. Louis.

[31] Ernest Kirschten, *Catfish and Crystal* (Garden City, N.Y.: Doubleday, 1960), pp. 450–51.

CHAPTER 12

Attempt to Oust
a White Boss

Despite the fact that there was a Republican party (at least on paper) in St. Louis, the young Turks of the black community could hope to topple John Dwyer only if they fought and whipped him within the Democratic party. They were unable to play the party-switching game used so well in an earlier period by Jordan Chambers. When Chambers first became active in politics, he was a Republican and was among those who helped black St. Louisans switch political parties because he and others believed that black St. Louisans would obtain more patronage and make more political progress in a different party.

In the 1960's, the Republicans did not welcome blacks despite the fact that the Republicans had not come close to winning a city election in St. Louis since 1951. Black people began to defect from Republican ranks in 1949, and by 1964 when the young Turks were seeking political recognition, city Republican strength was declining fastest in that section of the city which was growing fastest—the black section. The lily-white image acquired in 1964 when many Missouri Republicans became associated with the Barry Goldwater campaign hurt the party in black St. Louis wards. However, there were other conditions predating Goldwater that also helped prevent young Turks from even remotely considering becoming Republicans.[1] Not only black people, but some white people were saying in 1964 that:

> Republican attitudes are still another problem. For instance, doctrinaire opposition to public housing that shelters so many Negro families; demands for elimination of political offices where Ne-

groes are employed; calls for increasing the strength of the police
canine corps, which is used largely against Negroes. It may be
asking too much to expect the leopard to change his spots, but
the public interest would benefit by an intelligent and continuing
attempt to revive a Republican organization in the city generally
and in the Negro wards in particular. . . .[2]

Missouri Republicans so disregarded black people that they held
their 1964 State Convention in St. Louis on June 13 and refused
to elect a black Republican even as an alternate delegate-at-large
to attend their National Convention. Furthermore, no black St. Louis
politician could entertain the idea of joining a state political party
that was preoccupied with utilizing campaign strategy, in behalf
of Barry Goldwater, which alienated black Missouri voters. Also,
black politicians were aware that Missouri Republicans who controlled the party in 1964 did not care if black people failed to
support Republicans because:

> . . . "for every Negro vote we lose in Missouri we will gain
> 10 from white Democrats who are opposed to the new civil rights
> law and disgusted with the unruly demonstrations by civil rights
> radicals," a top Missouri Goldwater supporter told the *Post-
> Dispatch.*
>
> After all, we haven't been getting many Negro votes in recent
> elections—not more than about 15 percent. So what do we really
> have to lose?[3]

Although Clay and his young Turks were dissatisfied because
they believed that white Democrats like Dwyer were using black
voters to perpetuate themselves in office, the Republicans were possibly guilty of hoping to use black people and their allies in a different manner so that they could control Missouri politically. Some
Republicans apparently decided to try and divide black and white
Missourians by dangerously exploiting racial tensions for political
ends. Those Missouri Republicans who were opposed to disruptive
tactics apparently hoped purposefully to evoke racial demonstrations
in order to gain a backlash support for Goldwater. They promised
efforts to:

> have Senator Goldwater bring his presidential campaign into
> Missouri.

His Missouri supporters said that they would expect members
of the Congress of Racial Equality (CORE) or other civil rights
groups to picket any Goldwater campaign appearances in the
state, particularly in St. Louis or Kansas City.

Many leaders frankly hope such anti-Goldwater demonstrations
occur, contending such events would only make more votes for
the GOP presidential candidate.[4]

The all-white Missouri Republican delegation went to San Fran-
cisco, and its actions there further demonstrated to black St.
Louisans that they were not wanted in the Republican party. The
Missouri delegation voted twenty-three to one in opposition to the
Republicans adopting a stronger civil rights plank and opposed a
proposed amendment specifically denouncing the right-wing John
Birch Society and the Ku Klux Klan. United States Representative
(St. Louis County District) Thomas B. Curtis of the Missouri delegation served as Assistant Parliamentarian of the convention and
actively opposed the stronger civil rights amendment by speaking
against it.[5]

In regard to the state of the Republican party in 1964 the *Post*
observed that Missouri was:

. . . already too much of a one-party state for its political good
health. But the situation is not likely to be improved by a Republican party which alienates itself from the main body of voters
and becomes the tool of the radical right.

If there is any moderate leadership in the Republican party
of Missouri it has gone underground. Not only is the state sending
a Goldwater delegation to the national convention, but it is doing
so with very little dissent from supposed leaders of the party.

Ethan A. H. Shepley, candidate for Governor, campaigns as
a moderate, but he has not lifted a voice against the domination
of his party by Goldwater radicalism. Jean Paul Bradshaw, candidate for Senator, also has elected the role of neutral in a crucial
struggle over the future of his party. Congressman Thomas B.
Curtis, who depends on independent and Democratic votes for
the seniority which is supposed to give him a position of leadership, is carefully not exercising leadership. Neither is Supervisor
Lawrence A. Roos, an allegedly modern Republican who once
crusaded for Eisenhower. . . .[6]

Aside from the fact that there was no balanced two-party system
in Missouri, young Turk Hugh White believed that another factor

helped prevent black St. Louisans from being a more effective political force. While serving as a member of the Missouri House of Representatives, White proclaimed that much of the effectiveness of St. Louis' black voting power had been nullified either because of reluctance or lack of capacity on the part of old-line black political leaders to work collectively when candidates for city, state, and national offices were being selected.[7] However, there is ground for belief that some of the old-line black politicians White criticized came together to back a black candidate, Curtis Crawford, for the citywide office of Circuit Attorney in 1964 in order to help "Boss Jack Dwyer."

> Quick endorsement of the Crawford candidacy was given by pro-Dwyer Negro political leaders. Some of these are under heavy attack from insurgent Democrats in their wards who are fed up with white bossism in the Negro area of the city. It is said that the pro-Dwyer faction intends to use the Crawford candidacy as a sort of decoy political maneuver which can be singled out and credited to Jack Dwyer, the white boss of the all-Negro 4th ward, who is struggling desperately to retain the committeeship there against Arthur J. Kennedy, a tough NAACP labor spokesman.
>
> Old Guard Negro leaders under the urging of a group of self-seeking job holders and paid spokesmen are pulling every trick out of the political bag to make Boss Jack Dwyer look good. For his strong support of the Jefferson Bank during the CORE job fight, Dwyer suffered a tremendous loss of prestige. . . .
>
> At one time, until he fell into the clutches of the Dwyer forces, Atty. Crawford was regarded as a strong contender for the 19th ward committee slot now held by the demure, quiet-spoken Judge J. H. Harvey, a strong Dwyer man. What happened to cause Atty. Crawford to back out of the race for committeeman has a lot of tongues wagging. Some say a judgeship was dangled in front of the ambitious young man for making the sacrificial race for white political bosses fighting for their political lives in the Negro community.[8]

"Insurgent Democrats" were well aware that pro-Dwyer blacks would pull "every trick out of the political bag" to help white boss Dwyer retain his committee post and thwart efforts in behalf of young Turk associate, Arthur Kennedy, to become the first black man to represent the black Fourth Ward as committeeman.

The 1964 race also provided restless moments for some in the white community. A considerable number of white Democratic political leaders in South St. Louis wards were uneasy and disturbed because they believed that if a black man were to win the Democratic nomination for Circuit Attorney, his presence on the ticket would cause the party to lose some votes in the November general election.[9]

Some people in the black community were confident that many of those whites who opposed black citywide candidates would resort to various subtle devices to eliminate them. There is evidence that sly devices had been utilized in the past. When in 1962 Fred Weathers, black Eighteenth Ward committeeman, ran for the city-wide office of Clerk of the Court of Criminal Correction, many people in the black community believed that some white ward organizations endorsed him at the last minute, and then most of them went fishing or on vacations on election day. Some black people believed that those white ward workers who did work for Weathers' election, worked in their own way, marking his race on the sample ballots in addition to circulating pictures to prove that he was black.[10]

Because of the opposition to Crawford expressed by some Southside white politicians, along with the belief that the circulation of a photo helped to defeat Weathers, those black politicians who advocated that Crawford's candidacy was not a sincere effort to elect a black man, but an effort to help Dwyer, found reason to increase their suspicions in April of 1964.

> Last week-end the St. Louis Globe Democrat featured Assistant Circuit Attorney Curtis Crawford on the front page. What is behind this splash of publicity? You can be sure it was not really intended to advance the candidacy of Atty. Crawford for the post of Circuit Attorney. The Globe political writer tried to spell out the effects of the Wallace vote in Wisconsin and the P. A. referendum in Kansas City on the Crawford candidacy.
> Most political observers in the central city feel that the St. Louis situation will not be affected in any material way by what has happened up in Wisconsin or over in neighboring Kansas City. And, if Atty. Crawford ever had any chance to succeed in his bid for Circuit Attorney, the feature story, complete with picture, in the Globe washed it up clean.[11]

Whether or not Crawford's candidacy was an endeavor to help Dwyer did not prevent some white politicians from striving to prevent him from winning the nomination. The *Globe* reported that white politicians who were attempting to block Crawford's nomination encountered a minor difficulty. Possibly because the secret leaked out, they found it necessary to cancel a scheduled meeting designed to cause white ward committeemen to agree to support one of the three white candidates because they believed Crawford would win if the white vote were split among three white candidates. Those who called the meeting attempted to spare Dwyer and two other white committeemen representing black wards embarrassment by not inviting them. Also the four black committeemen who had already endorsed Crawford were not invited to attend the meeting. Dwyer denied this explanation in the *Globe* and said, "I don't have any candidate for Circuit Attorney. I have not endorsed anybody for Circuit Attorney."[12] His denial put some of his black supporters on the spot:

> Dwyer's statement brought a flurry of counter statements from his Negro supporters who would be ridiculously embarrassed if Dwyer came out for a white candidate. They have made a tremendous effort to sell the idea to the Negro community that Dwyer was a "key bridge" between the Negro and the white community. But with Dwyer's reluctance to support a Negro city wide, the bridge seems to be collapsing.[13]

If Dwyer was part of the conspiracy with the white committeemen, or even if he was not a part of it and was not going to seek their active support for Crawford, there was little hope that Crawford could win. On the other hand, another happening affected Crawford's candidacy adversely. No one can predict with certainty what unforeseen incidents will occur and influence an election. But if the subtle device of circulation of a black man's picture in the white wards diminishes his chances to win white votes, then those white politicians who opposed Crawford could possibly have saved some of the energies they expended to block him.

If white people were going to vote against Crawford because he was black, and if they did not already know he was a black man, the *Globe* gave them a second opportunity through its front page April 29, 1964, article (including photo) to learn this fact.

The article informed readers that Crawford was a candidate for
the Democratic nomination for Circuit Attorney in the August 4
primary election and that as Assistant Circuit Attorney, he had
appeared at Police Headquarters between 2:30 and 3:30 a.m. on
a Sunday morning to dismiss a concealed weapons charge against
an eighteen-year-old woman delegate who was attending an
NAACP convention in St. Louis. The *Post* carried the same story
on page eighteen of its April 29, 1964, edition.

If there were not enough tension as a result of the efforts to
unseat Dwyer and of the Circuit Attorney's race, on April 28,
another element was added which possibly could have incited
violence. Three hours before the April 28 deadline for filing as
a candidate for Circuit Attorney, Wayne C. Millsap, Jefferson
Bank's lawyer, whose name had become synonymous with white
racism in the black community, decided to seek the office. Later
he withdrew. Many in St. Louis felt relieved after his withdrawal.

> Wayne L. Millsap's withdrawal as a candidate for the Republi-
> can nomination for Circuit Attorney coincides with what we be-
> lieve to be the public interest in the kind of candidate this office
> should seek. Mr. Millsap's private professional role last fall, when
> in effect he became Jefferson Bank's hired prosecutor in the CORE
> contempt case, constitutes an embarrassing and potentially divisive
> background for a candidate seeking to function as chief public
> prosecutor.
>
> As the Republican nominee Mr. Millsap could no more avoid
> opposition from the Negro community based on the Jefferson
> Bank situation than he could avoid support from racists in the
> white community. Such a contest could develop along ugly racial
> lines whether Mr. Millsap wished that result or not. Under the
> circumstances, it seems to us, his decision to withdraw is all for
> the best.
>
> The Circuit Attorney's post is the most important and sensitive
> of any of the city-wide offices for which St. Louisans will nomi-
> nate candidates in August. The occupant must be zealous in the
> protection of the rights of the accused as he is in the prosecution
> of the accused. And he cannot be, or even give the appearance
> of being symbolic of either the frustrations or ambitions of any
> segment of the population.[14]

The race then proceeded to a point where all white Democrats
except one finally withdrew, and the *Argus* writer, Buddy Lone-

some, conceded that Crawford's chances had dimmed somewhat.[15] He was correct. The white candidate, James S. Cocoran, lost only the nine wards centered on the black community as he defeated Crawford for the Democratic nomination for Circuit Attorney.[16]

Not only were Crawford's candidacy and the opposition of the black young Turks causing Dwyer personal political problems, but another political problem arose when a white man, John J. O'Toole, challenged Dwyer for his post as City Treasurer. Near the end of the campaign, O'Toole, speaking at a gathering of the Young Democrats of Metropolitan St. Louis, made statements that could have hurt Dwyer in his committee race if they had been made earlier in the campaign and had had an opportunity to circulate on the black grapevine. He charged Dwyer with helping to create a Mason-Dixon line in St. Louis. According to O'Toole, Dwyer would pledge to be a friend of black people when north of Delmar and when in white wards south of Delmar, he pointed out the virtues of white candidates.[17]

O'Toole's charges would have been welcomed by the young Turks earlier in the campaign, especially since they were made by a white man. Nevertheless, when the campaign began, the young Turks believed they had a black candidate who could unseat Dwyer as committeeman. He was not a member of CORE, but he had a long history of race involvement. Sheet metal shop operator Arthur Kennedy was persuaded to enter politics as an active candidate for the first time in his life. He, like the young Turks, believed that politics and black advancement could not be separated. Previously, this young Turk associate had been fighting to get trade unions in St. Louis to open apprenticeship training programs to black people. In addition, he was well known because he had led the fight for black students to enroll at the previously all-white Rankin Trade School. There were several reasons why Kennedy decided to oppose Dwyer, but he was particularly dissatisfied because Dwyer no longer lived in the ward which he supposedly represented. Kennedy was quoted as saying "that all elected officials should be responsible to the voters, and that the day of rule by political bosses is gone forever. We of the Fourth ward have been victims of this bossism, having received absentee representation by the committeeman who is never available and who does not even live in the ward."[18]

The knowledge that CORE and the young Turks were going to support Kennedy actively against Dwyer in a year when black people all over the United States were complaining about white people representing them caused some concern among pro-Dwyer black politicians. Some were concerned because they had previously worked to elect Dwyer, and in return he performed some small favors for them.

Old time Negro politicians who have sat beside the table of white committeemen and office-holders to catch the crumbs that fell, now find themselves faced with the possibility of being rejected by the Negro voters. In each of the predominant Negro population wards opposition has developed against those who advocated a "go slow" policy of integration. Many of the conservative Negro leaders . . . who at one time were looked upon as real leaders are now looked down on as puppets and parrots for Dwyer and Mayor Tucker. It is not by coincidence that . . . they always endorse the same candidates which Jack Dwyer does. It is by design of the white power structure that the established Negro politicians always support the candidates that have the backing of strong financial interests. . . .

In their zeal to retain Jack Dwyer in control of the all Negro ward . . . they are trying to sell the voters on the idea that we need Uncle Jack. What they are saying in effect is that a Negro is not qualified to represent Negro people. What they should be saying is that when the day comes that a Negro can be elected from a ward predominantly white then and only then should we let whites represent us. We need Dwyer about as much as we need . . . them. The policies and programs that they advocate are ones of appeasement of the white power structure. The policy of appeasement means that the interest of the Negro community is being side tracked and disregarded.

The actions of . . . pro-Dwyer Negroes in pushing a Dwyer over a well qualified Negro candidate like Arthur Kennedy shows racial irresponsibility on their part and puts their selfish interests above the interest of the total community.[19]

The fact that by early May of 1964 the black young Turks had been able to organize a measure of opposition to Dwyer and his black supporters indicated they believed the interest of the black community was being sidetracked and disregarded. Being able to organize also implied that they were not going to be merciful or amiable in their efforts to oust Dwyer and jostle old-line black politicians.

Despite the crescendo of opposition, pro-Dwyer black supporters remained loyal to him and campaigned in his behalf. On June 10, 1964, a page-two *Defender* article appeared along with a photo in which John Green, a black man, was standing beside Dwyer. The caption under the photo read: "The closeness of John Green and Jack Dwyer is shown as they stand side by side in this long hot summer political fight." The article said that John Green was the former Seventeenth District State Representative who was "spearheading the bi-partisan leadership for the re-election of Jack Dwyer. . . ." It then cited what could be called "personal materialistic reasons" why Dwyer should be reelected. According to John Green, the Fourth Ward was extremely fortunate to have Dwyer as its leader because he was the chairman of the Democratic Central Committee and therefore the party's chief patronage distributor (made possible because of political racism). The article continued and pointed out that John Green's opinions were shared by other leading politicians and then listed six black politicians and the offices held by them and four other people. Research has failed to turn up any evidence that the six politicians denied Green's statements or that any of them ever demanded a retraction.

On June 24, a related page-two *Defender* story informed readers that Dwyer had been chairman of the Democratic City Central Committee for twenty-two years and could only continue to serve in the top city political post if he were reelected as committeeman. And since the article was apparently written to help reelect Dwyer, it omitted the fact that black people in the ward were complaining because of a lack of actual representation of their views and because of bossism. But it did inform readers that black man Kennedy could not do as much for black people as white man Dwyer. It additionally informed its readers that black people were better represented by a paternalistic white boss and that if blacks were to defeat the white boss and elect a black man (who was interested in the collective black community), black people would lose because Dwyer's defeat "almost surely" would elevate certain other antiblack committeemen.

> St. Louis is the only major city in the country where the post is held by a leader who represents a predominantly Negro ward.

If we allow Mr. Dwyer to be defeated, this key position will not go to the man who defeats him. Instead, his successor as chairman of the Committee will almost surely be a committeeman from the far South St. Louis section. We already know that the aldermen from these wards have seldom supported any of the civil rights bills passed by the Board of Aldermen.[20]

The first sentence of the above quote could be considered most humiliating to those black people who have pride in their race. If that were not enough, the article continued and championed Dwyer purely because of materialistic reasons, disregarding any other qualities that black people might demand in a candidate. According to the article, Dwyer was responsible for many black people in several St. Louis black wards receiving city, state, and federal appointments. If the list of more than thirty positions that he supposedly helped black people obtain was factual, some of those who supposedly requested and received his help would be embarrassed today because of the new black awareness, pride in being black, and because of the emergence of younger blacks who condemn those black people they believe are indebted to the power structure.

Additional tricks employed to sell Dwyer to black people included a large photo in the June 24, 1964, *Defender.* It depicted Dwyer consulting with the then United States Senator, Hubert Humphrey from Minnesota, giving support for passage of civil rights legislation. Employing some basic propaganda techniques, transfer and glittering generality, it also conveyed the impression that Dwyer was so influential politically that, after just one hurried trip to Washington, he helped influence senators from other states to vote for civil rights legislation. The caption under the picture read:

JACK DWYER, Chairman of the Democratic Committee, of St. Louis and Committeeman of the 4th Ward, is seen shaking hands with Senator Hubert Humphrey (Dem.), Minnesota, the civil rights bill floor leader, after Dwyer had made a hurried visit to the Capitol's law making body for the purpose of aiding Missouri Senators Symington and Long to secure affirmative votes for the bill from other members of the Senate. The bill passed by a 73-27 vote.[21]

On July 31, 1964 the *Argus* carried Buddy Lonesone's reasons why black people in the Fourth Ward should vote for a white man who did not live in their ward over a black man who had gained a reputation fighting to help young black men obtain training and better jobs to provide for themselves and their families. According to Lonesome,

> . . . in the 4th Ward, heavily populated by Negroes, I find myself in the unique position of supporting the incumbent committeeman, Jack Dwyer, who happens to be white, against Arthur Kennedy. The fact remains that Jack Dwyer in addition to being the 4th Ward Committeeman, is also chairman, of the Democratic City Central Committee. This position carries with it a great deal of prestige and influence. As a consequence the 4th Ward has a heavy share of FAT jobs, being held by Negroes. Jack Dwyer, a shrewd politician has not only been the Democratic boss of the 4th Ward, but he has also dispensed patronage liberally among his Negro constituents. Compare this with the "nice guy" appeal of Kennedy . . . and you can see how it stacks up. Jack Dwyer has, with his position and influence hugely benefitted the Negro. Kennedy, if elected, would be a committeeman, but with nothing like the status of a Jack Dwyer. Therefore, in order to continue to obtain our Fair Share of municipal jobs, Jack Dwyer must be retained.[22]

If Dwyer were responsible for the patronage dispensed "liberally among his Negro constituents," it is easy to explain why some blacks assiduously supported him in 1964. They failed to understand or accept the new black political mentality which demanded that black people themselves possess the political power held and exercised by a paternalistic subordinating white man in a black ward. Or, if they understood the new black political mentality, they believed that the young Turks would fail in their efforts to topple the existing subordinating system and that they expected to benefit from supporting the oppressive political arrangement.[23]

Although the *Defender* carried articles giving reasons why Dwyer should be reelected, one of its writers, Jimmy Miller, did not get on the Dwyer band wagon. He criticized attempts to sell Dwyer to black people because of materialism: "Pro-Dwyer Negro politicians are crowing so loudly about what the Great White Father has done for us folks and how badly his kind of leadership is needed in the Negro community; several . . . have again come right out in the open with tearful pleas for the reelection of Jack

Dwyer as committeeman in the all-Negro 4th ward. Four years ago they did the same thing."[24]

Despite the "tearful pleas," Kennedy received doorbell-ringing support from those CORE members who continued to seek to redress their grievances within the existing political system.[25] The assistance he received from them made it possible for him to detect what he considered possible irregularities and, in early June, he requested that the Board of Election Commissioners provide deputies to monitor Fourth Ward polling places. This was essential for his candidacy since CORE canvassers could not locate many of those who were registered to vote in the ward. It was believed that, in past elections, some white people who had formerly lived in the ward returned to it on election day and voted for Dwyer.[26]

If Kennedy's suspicions that the election might be stolen from him were not enough to worry him, at this time he also became a very troubled father. The night preceding primary election day, his twenty-one-year-old son was accosted by a man who accused him of removing campaign signs from his automobile. Young Kennedy denied the allegation, but was pistol-whipped apparently because his father was challenging Dwyer. According to the *Post:* "Arthur J. Kennedy Jr., 4283 W. Easton Avenue, son of the principal opponent of City Treasurer John J. Dwyer for election today as Democratic committeeman of the Fourth ward, suffered a fractured jaw last night in a fight resulting from the bitter political race."[27]

Kennedy's first attempt to become elected to public office was undoubtedly disappointing to him. His son suffered a fractured jaw, and he lost the election. However, the young Turks did make themselves felt in the Fourth Ward. In the 1960 primary, Dwyer's black opponent did not carry a single precinct and only received 1,111 of the 5,124 votes cast.[28] But in 1964, Kennedy carried eight of the twenty-four precincts and received 2,012 of the 5,251 ballots cast.[29]

Strong and effective resistance to defeat black attempts to dislodge white incumbents is not unique to St. Louis. John Hadley Strange painted a very powerless picture of blacks in Philadelphia.

> But the City Democratic Organization is not content with keeping a close check on reapportionment. Moves to replace white

ward leaders with Negroes, on those rare occasions when they occur, are met with strong resistance. Patronage is withdrawn, rules are ignored, and the white political machine retains control. For example, in January 1965 the City Committee successfully defeated a plan to elect a Negro, Edgar Campbell, to the vacant ward leadership in the Fifty-second Ward, a ward that was approximately 65 percent Negro. Campbell was the expected (and some claim legal) successsor since he was then serving as chairman of the ward committee. But through the open use of its patronage and other threats, the City Committee had Campbell defeated 50–9 even though 41 out of the 71 committeemen eligible to vote for ward leader were Negroes. Herbert Fineman, whose brother Irving Fineman had been ward leader, was elected. Later Campbell lost his job as assistant to City Council Democratic Majority Leader, George X. Schwartz. Fred Handy, a Negro committeeman from the Fifty-second ward and one of Campbell's supporters, was also fired from his state job as the only Negro inspector in the Bureau of Weights and Measures. Herbert Fineman is reported to have said, "Ace (Handy) spearheaded that Edgar Campbell drive. Why did Ace do it? I don't understand him."[30]

The fact that forty-one of seventy-one committeemen who were eligible to vote in Philadelphia were black and Edgar Campbell received only nine votes to become the Fifty-second Ward leader indicates that black people need not necessarily expect black politicians to support a black man against the wishes of patronage dispensing whites. The Dwyer-Kennedy contest in St. Louis buttressed James Q. Wilson's conjecture that black people do not vote for other black people merely because of race.[31] We do not advocate that black politicians automatically support other black politicians, or that black people should vote for a man just because he is black. It would not help black people effect policies determined and designed by black people to help the total black community if black politicians automatically supported, or if black people automatically voted for, money-grubbing black men who would only echo what whites believe is good for black people.

We do condemn black politicians' failure to support a black politician because of the open use of patronage. We also condemn failure to support a black candidate whose record indicates that he had attempted and was willing to work in behalf of the black community. When such a black candidate opposes a white incumbent who, for years, subordinated black people, it becomes reprehensible to fail to support the black candidate just because the white incumbent had helped make it possible for a few black people to enhance their material status.

NOTES

[1] *Post* (editorial), April 10, 1965, p. 4A.
[2] *Ibid.*
[3] Herbert A. Trask, *Post*, July 19, 1964, pp. 1C, 8C.
[4] *Ibid.*
[5] *Post*, July 15, 1964, p. 5C.
[6] *Post* (editorial), June 25, 1964, p. 2B.
[7] *Defender*, March 24, 1964, p. 1.
[8] *Defender*, April 14, 1964, p. 3.
[9] *Post*, March 15, 1964, p. 4A.
[10] *St. Louis Crusader*, August 15, 1962, p. 4.
[11] *Defender*, April 14, 1964, p. 3.
[12] Ray J. Noonan, *Globe*, April 16, 1964, p. 3A.
[13] *Defender*, April 24, 1964, p. 3.
[14] *Post* (editorial), June 3, 1964, p. 2E.
[15] Buddy Lonesome, *Argus*, June 19, 1964, p. 7B.
[16] *Post*, August 5, 1964, p. 2D.
[17] *Globe*, July 29, 1964, p. 9A.
[18] *Post*, January 22, 1964, p. 4B.
[19] *Defender*, May 5, 1964, p. 4.
[20] *Defender*, June 24, 1964, p. 2.
[21] *Defender*, June 24, 1964, p. 7.
[22] Buddy Lonesome, *Argus*, July 31, 1964, p. 7B.
[23] See Stokely Carmichael and Charles V. Hamilton, *Black Power: The Politics of Liberation* (New York: Vintage Books, 1967), p. 179.
[24] Jimmy Miller, *Defender*, April 7, 1964, p. 4.
[25] *Argus*, August 31, 1964, p. 1A.
[26] *Post*, June 12, 1964, p. 13A.
[27] *Post*, August 4, 1964, p. 3A.
[28] Abstract of Votes Cast at the August 2, 1960, Primary Election Compiled and Certified by the Board of Election Commissioners for the City of St. Louis.
[29] Abstract of Votes Cast at the August 4, 1964, Primary Election Compiled and Certified by the Board of Election Commissioners for the City of St. Louis.
[30] John Hadley Strange, "The Negro and Philadelphia Politics," in Edward C. Banfield, ed., *Urban Government: A Reader in Administration and Politics* (New York: The Free Press, 1969), pp. 409–10.
[31] James Q. Wilson, *Negro Politics: The Search for Leadership* (New York: The Free Press, 1960), p. 38.

CHAPTER 13

Black People's Black Man

It has been shown that William L. Clay, Percy Green, and the young Turks and their allies were very persistent in their efforts to oppose institutional racism actively in St. Louis. Nevertheless, their creative protest politics were not sufficient to bridge the gulf between the racist "is" and the idealistic "ought." This gulf existed, in part, because much of the strategy of creative protest politics in St. Louis (and elsewhere) was based upon a flood of literature and propaganda which rehashed old formulas (traditional answers and clichés): "if all men were behaving like Christians," "if we would just realize that this or that minority would not be so obnoxious if given half a chance."[1] This school of thought was greatly influenced by Gunnar Myrdal's highly questionable assumption that the low "status accorded the Negro in America represents nothing more than and nothing less than a century-long lag of public morals."[2]

Attacking institutional racist subordination as if it only represents a "lag of public morals" does very little to uproot and eradicate institutional racism. It is highly doubtful that any line of reasoning concerned with morality greatly influences many organized or unorganized racists. If many of those who promote and propagate race hatred were greatly influenced by this line of reasoning the numerous organizations operating on the morality-lag idea and which attempt (in their various ways) to effect positive black-white relations would encounter great difficulty surviving. In fact, there would be little need for them. (In addition to fifteen labor unions and ten other groups—including the Americans for Democratic Action, Jewish War Veterans, and the American Civil

Liberties Union—six civil rights groups and seventeen church groups intensively lobbied for the Civil Rights Act of 1964.[3])

In other words, the very number of these organizations indicates the failure of their humanitarian appeals, and their fight against the practices counter to their abstract ideal is often met by ceremonials "designed to create enthusiasm, to increase faith and quiet doubt. It can have nothing to do with the actual practical analysis of facts." Furthermore, the ceremony or the literature surrounding such institutions need not be "consistent, logical, or rational because of the inherent nature of the psychological forces which bind men together in groups."

Yet, the budgets of these organizations reach million dollar figures; they all use similar techniques: propaganda and educational indoctrination; exhortation, stimulation of contacts, workcamps, community self-surveys, workshops, personal therapy; some of them even use threats of the application of anti-racial discrimination laws. Just like Myrdal, all these devices seem to operate on the basic premise that the survival of our democracy automatically necessitates the experimentation of such efforts to handle the problem.[4]

In spite of the fact that the budgets of some of these organizations reach million-dollar figures, they accomplish little in meliorating the relations between blacks and whites. Their failure, in part, can be ascribed to an explicit indisposition to regard black-white relations as an aspect of human power relations.[5]

Almost without exception, each human being desires to have his own way, to think and act as he likes. But because individuals live in a society each and every person cannot have his own way. Each person's freedom to act independently and arbitrarily ends when his actions interfere or infringe upon another human being. The pattern of individual assertiveness which conflicts with other human beings begins from the very first day of birth. The child has sway over his parents by crying, smiling, or kicking, and the parents maintain ascendency by feeding, frowning, scolding, or otherwise punishing the child.[6] As the child develops in the face of conflicting impulses and demands, he learns that each living soul secures advantages or suffers because of how he plays society's game of manipulative human relationships. This is a painful developmental process because of the strong urge to become independent.

Many predicaments are linked to the process of development. When a child ventures into life he faces gratifying possibilities but he also faces conflicting impulses and demands. Some of these are thrust upon him. Some of them arise as an outcome of his own striving toward maturity.

In his relations with his parents, it is comforting for a child to be dependent, but he also has a powerful urge to become independent. As a dutiful child he would like to obey his parents but he also has an impulse to assert himself, even to the point of being rebellious. He feels affection for his parents, but they also arouse his anger. Moreover, under the best circumstances he is likely to make demands which they either cannot or will not fulfill. And he has desires which his parents, representing the larger society in which he lives, forbid.

As a member of a peer group it is necessary for a child to conform to the ways of his fellows, yet it is also essential for him to preserve his individuality.

. . . Humanity is not an individual possession, but rather something held in common with others. A child finds himself through his relationships with his fellows, but he loses himself and his dignity as a human being if, in the name of social adjustment, he simply becomes a conformer, an "organization man."[7]

As individuals progress from childhood through adolescence to adulthood most not only are concerned with development of social skills to the extent that as adults they will possess dignity as human beings, but many desire to perfect their skills to the extent that they will be able to influence and impress others, even if faintly. This desire is somewhat more than the average person thinks it is. Influencing or impressing other people with technical competence, a beautiful voice, social prestige, or even sympathy is exercising power.[8]

If black politicians who desire to represent black people effectively harbor ideological wishes and goals that hopefully would benefit black people collectively, they will not see them fulfilled, primarily because of institutional racism, unless they acquire and effectively utilize power. The same holds true for any group or groups that desire positive benefits for black people. Through the effective use of power black politicians and groups can cause the elite to acquiesce or yield to many demands. Acquiescence may be voluntary or involuntary, conscious or unconscious. But most

important, it will occur for ends determined not by the establishment, but by black politicians or groups holding power. The person
or group which holds power uses it for purposes determined by
him (or it) in an outright, unrestrained, peremptory manner bound
by no law or principle except positive result. There is no such
thing as equality of parties in a power relationship; one side will
dominate and subordinate the other. Those who will accept this
hypothesis will better understand why the "lag of public morals"
surmise has not done very much in effecting better black-white
(also brown-white) relations.[9]

Analysis of America's ethnic power relationships reveals that
Jews are not subordinated to the same extent as black people, despite
widespread antisemitism in most parts of America. Real and
imagined power, for the most part, accounts for this. Many Jews
play important roles in the civil life of this country primarily because of the influence of some of their cultural patterns, and especially because of their real and reputed abilities to be successful
competitors in economic life (power). Thus, effective use of power
helps spare them much of the abasement and degradation experienced by black people. Despite this possession of power many Jews
face some restrictions in social life, where it is somewhat more
difficult to utilize power to effect change. In this sphere neither
vigorous and/or zealous appeals utilizing the highly questionable
assumption of a "century-long lag of public morals" nor reference
to constitutional or democratic ideology will help very much.[10]

This problem of social discrimination can be vividly shown by
examining the power exercised by the estimated 80,000 Jews who
lived in the Greater Miami Area around 1958 and the phenomenon
of the "5 o'clock shadow."[11]

> Minority groups and transplanted Northerners have an effect on
> Dade County politics. For one thing, they tend to keep the county
> isolated from the rest of the state. The badly apportioned state
> legislature, which is run by a "Pork Chop Gang" of rural county
> "rednecks," has always regarded Dade as a foreign land. The
> presence there of so many Jews and Yankees who are strongly
> sympathetic to the Negro puts the rural legislator on guard against
> it. In North Florida, the ultra-right thinks Metro [Dade County:
> Miami and environs] is the the next thing to Communism. . . .

The Jewish minority is politically powerful. It finds an issue of interest to it in almost every election and its members vote together. There is little discrimination in business or politics against Jews. Being Jewish or Catholic does not affect a candidate's chances for county-wide office, but a gentile might have problems running for office in the City of Miami Beach. There is social discrimination. The Anti-Defamation League complains of "5 o'clock shadow," meaning that contacts between Jews and non-Jews stop at the end of the business day.[12]

Black people will encounter great difficulty exercising power as effectively as Jews until blacks generally, and black politicians specifically, come to realize that power struggles are all-reaching. In reality they are catholic—no exceptions—because even those people who have no taste for power struggles and no desire to acquire and exercise power are guilty of playing power politics. Their unwillingness to play the game, in fact, makes possible greater opportunities for those in pursuit of power to acquire it to promote their selfish interests. It is most important that those black people who are nonassertive be made to realize that being deferential is inimical to the interest of the black community. Power-hungry racists welcome the lack of yearning after power on the part of blacks since black-white (and brown-white) relations are but another aspect of the universal struggle for power, modified only by the different conditions under which this struggle takes place as influenced by the mentality of the elite in each geographical locality.[13]

Power struggles in American politics are not new. Many people are familiar with John C. Calhoun's theory of nullification and secession. However, Alan Grimes's analysis of Calhoun concludes that his long and varied experiences in state and national politics helped Calhoun make a realistic and systematic contribution to political theory also in 1850 and 1851. At this time Calhoun saw imperfections in the constitutional system and attributed the defects to manifold (diverse) political forces that operated behind the law and gave it its life.[14]

Much of Calhoun's concern emanated from his belief that a primary function of government was to protect all of society. To him the power exercised by the majority prevented government from performing its protective function for diverse economic and social minorities. This was possible despite the fact that there was a written constitution which provided for limited governmental powers and separated the powers of government into three branches. The former was in itself no protection against the majority since the majority actually determined what was in fact the constitution. The latter was an insufficient check upon the misemployment of governmental powers, for the branches were but separate active elements representing the interests of the same majority.[15]

Where some today could agree with Calhoun's ideas as they pertained to the written constitution and the check-and-balance system, because of the suffrage many of them would not agree that the diverse economic and social minorities were powerless. But Calhoun considered the suffrage, indispensable as it was, a penurious check upon the majority's government, since the total community of voters was not a homogeneous society composed of individuals possessing selfsame interests. Additionally, since the interests of men were not exactly the same, the suffrage promoted dissonance and served to keep the government responsible only to the numerical majority of voters and not to all voters. When there were conflicts over constitutional construction, the majority interest would prevail, for the point of attaining office was to utilize power.[16]

Calhoun believed that the powerless could only counteract the power of the numerical majority by acquiring power of their own. His scheme was to develop adequate negative power, called the "concurrent majority." The scheme called for the manifold interests adversely affected by the majority's governmental policies to come together and pit their collective power against the majority's power. Calhoun was convinced that in this way the numerical majority's government would be willing to make adjustments and compromises. This would admittedly be difficult to effect inasmuch as his type of coalition called for near-unanimous cooperation. Nevertheless, he was driven to this type of thinking at mid-nineteenth century because he believed that government was necessary for the existence of society since man's "sympathetic or social feelings" were remote and since his "individual and self-regarding inclinations" were dominant. Calhoun believed that "self-regarding inclinations" motivated men to action to such an extent that if these inclinations were stronger, society itself would not be possible. There could be no society without government because each individual would find "his own interest of more particular and immediate concern than the interests of his fellow man."[17]

From among the established and emerging black leaders, those who will earn the designation as effective leaders during the 1970's must base their strategies upon the hard-learned lesson that man's self-interest is stronger than his social feelings. Otherwise, as in the 1960's, black people will continue to be subordinated because of too great a reliance on some type of nonexistent public moral consensus. Once this attitude has been adopted, black people must organize along the lines suggested by Saul Alinsky.

Alinsky distinguishes between a "movement" and an "organization." In a movement, efforts are undertaken to cause people to come together and carry out a protest demonstration. But after the demonstration little may be accomplished because of a lack of an effective vehicle to carry forward. Vigorous organizations are brought into existence for the sole purpose of generating power; therefore they must be organized on a mass-power basis. They must be built upon foundations of amoral power—power devoid of emotion and moral "oughts."[18]

If people desire to put their ideas into practice and or effect change it is imperative that they organize. According to Alinsky:

> If you are moving to have power, to have the ability to act, you must of necessity organize. As I said before, that is the only reason for organization. When people agree on certain religious ideas, and they want to put those ideas into practice—what they would call "to propagate their faith"—they organize to have the power to act, and they call it a church. When people are agreed on certain political ideas, and they want to put those ideas into practice, they organize to have the power to put those ideas into practice, and they call that organization a political party. So when we're talking about organization, we're talking about power.
>
> When people are organized, they have the only way they can act, the only way they can express themselves as citizens, the only way they can cause a change. We are talking about the kind of mass operation that is here not only for today, but for all tomorrows as well. Organization has the power to compel the opposition to agree. You must have organization to be able to communicate to the Establishment. In the world as it is, you never communicate with the Establishment through their ears;

you only communicate with them through their rears. Therefore, you must have the instrumentality to carry out this type of communication.[19]

The establishment and maintenance of this type of an organization makes possible meaningful concessions and not only a slice of the decision-making pie, but the possibility of helping to decide how the pie is to be sliced. Black leaders who were once active demonstrators in the movement, and who desire to lead in the 1970's, must quickly come to recognize that a movement is not an organization primarily because active "movement" people are accustomed to, and anticipate regular drama, demonstrations, and a measure of excitation. Many of them will consider organizational work wearisome. Effective black leaders will organize with the type of people who comprehend and appreciate—or at least have the potential to catch the idea and estimate justly—the necessity for tedious, boring organizational work to be performed by organizational staffs and members. Once these types of people have been recruited, the organization will remain viable only if at all times the staff and members are aware as to purposes, objectives, and whys.[20] Thus, it becomes imperative for the leadership to use effectively its network of communication to help achieve organizational objectives. This includes selecting the right words to use in communicating since some words do not carry the same meaning to everyone.[21]

Of great importance, the leadership itself must come to the point where it can interpret and react to the world as it is because this is the world in which it will be working. Ideally, it will simultaneously maintain its perception of the world as it would like it to be. This concept of leadership must be accepted on an emotional as well as intellectual level because acceptance only relating to the intellect is generally circumscribed and distorted. Accepting the world as it is should not in any way adulterate or restrict efforts to mold it into the world as black leaders would like for it to be. If black organizations are going to effect change, their leaders must work with what they have and with the way things are. In other words, starting from where they are, not from where they would like to be, is the central issue.[22]

CORE "movement" activist, William L. Clay, was moved to the point of recognizing the world as it is when he realized that it was not very beneficial for black St. Louisans to base strategies upon the assumption that St. Louis' white power structure and the vast majority of the city's whites would "behave like Christians." He had learned from the school of ward-level politics that organized power, not morality, moved whites.

Clay began voicing sentiments that St. Louis black people should have a greater voice in determining their political destinies. Immediately some of his political confidants and his academic associates (black high school teachers and junior college professors), who came to know him only because of their involvement in the Jefferson Bank episode, and who were familiar with St. Louis' city government structurally, encouraged him to seek the post of Twenty-sixth Ward committeeman. They realized that actual political power in St. Louis was vested in the ward committeeman, and not in the ward alderman. It could only help black people to have a strong black committeeman as a member of the City Democratic Central Committee. The academics promised to help in every way. Clay knew that they would keep their word for they had worked extremely well with his then close associate, Marion Oldham. He was also aware that they, and the many high school and college students who followed them, had worked long hours in his behalf, with Marion Oldham and Nathaniel Rivers, helping to keep the organization that he was building together while he was in jail.

CORE and the young Turks had been partially successful in their efforts to obtain more and better employment opportunities for black people primarily because the "movement," which was composed of such dissimilar membership, was able to maintain a united front during the early days of the Jefferson Bank episode. It has been shown how the movement lost Percy Green and other active members in 1964. Clay's decision to seek the post of committeeman further disrupted the united front. Nevertheless, both Green's and Clay's decisions benefited the black community.

The decision to seek the committeemanship meant that Clay would have to challenge a black incumbent, Norman Seay. Clay and Seay had been political friends, but they had begun to draw apart politically early in 1963, prior to their going to jail together in August of 1963. There is evidence that in the spring of 1963 they disagreed over candidates seeking to become the president of the Board of Aldermen.[23]

The academic associates who were encouraging Clay to run for committeeman realized that, even with help from Marion Oldham, they could not so persuade him. At that time they did not know him very well. Nevertheless, they believed Clay was willing to run and only had to be shown that he had widespread support. However, on October 17, 1963, the *Post* revealed that Seay had charged Clay with using demonstrations for political reasons. The academic group was angered because it considered this an attempt to lessen the appeal and influence of a man whom they believed profoundly desired to help black people. They considered it a cheap trick despite their belief that politics, economics, and black advancement were inseparable. This charge also angered Clay. Seay also accused Clay of having been associated with white labor leader, John L. Lawler (pipefitter), who Seay believed was antiblack.[24] However, by February of 1966, that association with Lawler enhanced Clay's image as a person who helps black men obtain meaningful employment. Ten black men became part of an on-the-job training program as journeymen pipefitters, and Edward Steska, president and business agent of Pipefitters Local 562 said that Clay had been very helpful in getting the group of craftsmen together.[25]

Where Seay accused Clay of using black advancement for personal political reasons, research failed to turn up any evidence that Clay directed any such charges toward Seay when a form letter for Seay, printed on very good quality paper, was distributed throughout the Twenty-sixth Ward. The letter, dated March 15, 1964, was signed by Seay and implied that Seay was a civil rights leader. It carried a shaded light blue photo of John F. Kennedy and the Kennedy name appeared in the extreme upper-left corner. Immediately below Kennedy's photo was one of Martin L. King with name identification. Further below was a photo of Seay, which was slightly larger than the other two, and which bore Seay's last name. The caption read: "In the tradition of leaders of the people— On Tuesday, August 4th ReElect Norman R. Seay." If that portion of the letter did not convince readers that there was a relationship between Seay, civil rights, and politics, then possibly the body of the letter did.

> I have just got out of jail as a result of my fight to get JOBS for Negroes. Now, most banks have Negroes working in white collar positions.

Even though my car was stolen while I was in jail and the loss of salary since October, 1963, was great, the PROGRESS OF THE NEGRO IS FIRST.

Tuesday, March 17, our Ward Organization will have its regular meeting. WILL YOU PLEASE COME??? WILL YOU PLEASE HELP ME TO OPEN ALL DOORS TO NEGROES???

For continued success I NEED your ACTIVE SUPPORT and PRAYERS!!![23]

Not only did Seay attack Clay, but white boss John Dwyer also struck at Clay and the young Turks. He attacked them as if he believed politics could or should have been separated from black people's overall efforts to obtain more effective and additional political power, more and better housing, and improved economic opportunities.[27]

On the one hand, Seay and Dwyer accused Clay of being politically motivated and apparently not interested in black advancement per se. On the other hand, a black man, Howard Woods, who was described by *Post* writer Richard Jacobs on July 21, 1963, as being one of those who opposed Clay, realized that contrary to what Dwyer believed, Clay had involved himself in the struggle to improve materially the lives of impoverished black St. Louisans. Woods began his assessment of Clay by calling him a leader in his ward.

If ever a politician has been anointed with the mantle of martyrdom just prior to a critical election year it has been Bill Clay, the ubiquitous alderman and leader of the 26th Ward. Clay is moving into one of the real test periods of his political career and today he rides the crest of the "new mood" sweeping the community, both Negro and white. The key figure in the Jefferson Bank demonstrations, he has emerged from his week in a jail cell renewed and fresh for new gains. A young man, or as he would best like to be known, as a young Turk, Clay has worked hard building his political empire in the 26th Ward, from which his chief opponent says he would like to expand. Clay has consistently challenged what he terms "old guard" political leadership. At the same time, he has worked hand in hand with this same "old guard" on community and civic programs. "Clay has every attribute for political greatness," one of his associates said one day last week. "If he maintains his balance." . . .

Clay as leader in the 26th Ward and also as its alderman, holds a unique position. There have been reports that Seay has teamed with Anna White, the committeewoman in the ward. . . . Even with Mrs. White Seay does not present to the public the hardened type of exterior so necessary in a rough and tumble intra-party scrap. Clay, on the other hand, with a real engaging personality history shows that he knows his way around in the infighting. In all fairness to him, he (Clay) has been identified with civil rights movements for sometime and he is generally credited with doing his home work on issues. He knows how to ride a hot issue and he is attuned to what his 26th Ward constituency wants. He has been smart enough to avoid open confrontations with Negroes, hence attacks by white elements tend to drive some fence straddling Negroes into his camp.[28]

The acknowledged leader of the young Turks not only had to fight Seay, boss Dwyer, and other politicians to advance his followers' cause. He found himself being opposed by the morning daily, the *Globe*, in a manner which had antagonized black people in St. Louis as early as 1937 when they objected to white people selecting the black man to represent black people. Woods, a black newspaperman who was not known to be one of Clay's friends, publicly acknowledged that Clay was a black man who had been elected by black people to represent black people and was "attuned to what his 26th Ward constituency wants." Also, according to Woods, Clay showed the ability to work with all political elements when it came to community and civic projects. But the *Globe* called for Clay to be removed from office, evidently because he had attempted to help black people obtain meaningful employment.

Of the nine found guilty yesterday, none is more so, nor his actions more reprehensible, than Alderman William Clay.

This man, this public official, who has so contemptuously disregarded a court order in a city in which he is an elected leader, has forfeited any claim to public office.

Just as one race cannot be condemned for the excess of one man so the city's deliberative body, the Board of Aldermen, should not be judged nor forced to put up with this kind among its numbers.

We urge that body to consider what can be done to cast him from their midst.[29]

It may be possible to measure the extent of Clay's political ascendancy and how well he represented not only black people living in his ward, but all black people living in St. Louis, by examining how he helped effect a fair housing law. There is strong and clear evidence that St. Louis did not adopt a fair housing law purely because of a simple response to majority sentiments or morality. Many people believed that the Board of Aldermen quickly adopted a fair housing law while Clay was in jail for demonstrating at the bank, thus attempting to prevent him from receiving any credit for its passage.

> Seasoned political observers say the swift passage of the St. Louis Fair Housing Law was due in no small measure to certain anti-Clay white politicians who wanted the measure passed while Alderman Wm. L. Clay was in jail so that he could not claim credit for its passage. An analysis of the aldermanic vote lends a great deal of credence to this belief. The measure was supported by a few aldermen who have traditionally opposed civil rights legislation. One such Alderman is A. Barney Mueller, 21st ward, whose committeeman faces a tough fight for re-election from a Clay-sponsored candidate, Bennie Goins, one of the convicted CORE demonstrators.[30]

It was easy for Clay to enter the ward-leadership campaign with a high degree of confidence. In addition to his political followers and his academic associates, he was conscious of the fact that many people—like black steelworker James Gaskins, who encountered difficulties at his place of employment because of the amount of time he devoted to the "movement"—were willing to support him in any way, regardless of whether they lived in his ward.

But what Clay did not know at that time was that some of his academic friends, as early as October of 1963, were already discussing with black physician Dr. John Gladney the need for, and strategies that would send, a black man from St. Louis to Congress. He also never knew, until 1968, that as early as January of 1964 that group had limited the "possibles" to William L. Clay and Hugh White. In 1964 they believed that a black man from St. Louis could be elected to Congress by 1970. We are confident that Clay never knew that when, in 1964, he ran for committeeman,

that in the minds of some of these academic associates he was building the foundation for a shot at Congress. Therefore, their promise
to help in any way possible in 1964 had a deep ideological meaning
for them. In 1964 Clay did not know either of Dr. Gladney's interest
in politics. Clay knew of Dr. Gladney at that time primarily because
this physician was responsible for assembling a pool of black physicians to administer, free of charge, physical examinations for black
high school (Vashon) graduates who were required to take physicals
as part of the college application procedure.

It became important for Clay's future that most of his academic
associates did not live in the Twenty-sixth Ward. They were scat-
tered throughout the black part of the city, making it easier for
him to receive widespread organized support when, in 1968, he
ran and was elected to Congress. It is a tribute to this man that
he was able, in 1968, to trust and rely upon, the academic group
which became associated with him in 1963. During the ensuing
years (1963–68) personal friendships within the group did not remain as close as they were in 1963, but in 1968, the members worked
in their individual ways to help Clay. It is highly doubtful that
even collectively anything they did spelled the difference between
winning or losing in 1968. But some of them were most helpful,
because of their relationships with some of the old-line blacks who
held various degrees of political influence, in lessening the degree
of opposition from established blacks. It is also probably true that
these same academic associates influenced some established blacks
to raise money for Clay's 1968 campaign.

Clay's decision to seek the committee post in 1964 provided the
old-line black politicians with an opportunity to co-opt a young
Turk. According to the *Post*'s Richard Jacobs, Eighteenth Ward
committeeman and constable (county office) Frederick N.
Weathers was a leader of the pro-Dwyer black faction; and the
Weathers faction began to promote Seay.[31] By backing Seay, the
pro-Dwyer faction possibly helped Dwyer on two fronts. First,
it would seem logical that if Clay and Seay had remained political
friends, together they would have presented more difficulties for
Dwyer by not dissipating their energies in the fight for Twenty-
sixth Ward committeeman. Second, by backing Seay, the pro-
Dwyer faction could promote a black politician who, like Clay,
was associated with black economic advancement.

At this point the *Argus* carried an article by Buddy Lonesome urging voters to elect Seay as committeeman primarily because Clay was so effective an alderman that his ward and the city could ill afford to lose his services. According to Lonesome:

> . . . However, the 26th Ward voters might overlook the most compelling reason as to why Seay—and not Clay—should get the 26th Ward Democratic Committeeman seat. As Alderman, Bill Clay has been a terror, in the Board of Aldermen, and this reporter has often seen his older, more experienced colleagues quake, when Alderman Clay presses them on an issue. It is good to see a young Negro adult, pushing for the advantages in such a municipal body. Yet, if Bill Clay is elected as Committeeman— then he will have to resign his seat as Alderman. Thus, the 26th Ward, one of the city's most heavily populated would be without the services of a competent Negro Alderman. This the ward, nor the city can afford.[32]

Most black people in the Twenty-sixth Ward believed that Clay had worked for their advantage and that he had been a good alderman. Therefore, they honored his request for their support and on August 4, 1964, elected him as their committeeman.

An analysis of the election reveals that Clay apparently possessed some type of charisma that caused Twenty-sixth Ward voters to remain loyal to him. While his running mate for committeewoman beat the incumbent committeewoman by only sixty-seven votes,[33] Clay carried nineteen of the twenty-three precincts and tied Seay in one. Of the three precincts carried by Seay, one was won by one vote and a second by only thirteen votes. Out of 5,132 ballots cast, Seay received only 1,971.[34]

Comparison with Seay's victory in the 1960 primary further illustrates the magnitude of Clay's victory. In 1960 St. Louis' sheriff (county office), Martin L. Tozer, and Austin Wright, a black man, both opposed Seay for the committeemanship. Tozer received 1,297 votes and Wright 1,797. In receiving 2,331 votes Seay held clear majorities in seven precincts against his two opponents and was the plurality winner in nine. Against two men Seay only lost seven precincts in 1960, but in 1964 he lost nineteen.[35]

Clay was made committeeman, in part, because of his image of being a black people's black man. During the campaign many residents of the Twenty-sixth Ward, like Leo Conley and his wife Emma, parents of eight children, were quick to tell potential voters that all during his political career, Clay had always done everything within his power to help any black person in the ward regardless of the person's economic or social status. They also told prospective voters how Clay would visit and chat with anyone in the ward in his home even if the person did not live in an elegant dwelling.[36] No doubt this image helped some voters to cast their ballots for Clay. Too, many believed the assessment of the black newspaper man Howard Woods that Clay knew his way around in the tough political infighting. No doubt this knowledge also helped elect Clay.

Thus, Clay became a burdened man (in a positive sense), a man who would have little time or energy for his family or himself. Because of the black community's problems, the anguished cries of black people would from this election forward dictate much of his daily pattern. He was burdened because he had achieved what every modern-day, aggressive (on race) black man would like to achieve—he had reached the top of the mountain. His climb to the top was made possible because of how his black constituents perceived him. When a black man's actions cause black people to believe in him, that is a great achievement.

Clay's relationship with his followers was and still is not based upon a large stock of favors, patronage, or other such inducements (Dwyer controlled them). This is why he could be instrumental in the fight to help oust "Boss Dwyer," for he could survive under conditions which would destroy black politicians who are an intimate part of a political machine. The politician with the type of personal following which supported Clay, and the politician who is associated with a machine are natural enemies. The politician with a following[37] like Clay is a disruptive force from the standpoint of those who are interested in the welfare of the political organization. Because a Clay-type politician's political strength is not dependent upon tangibles—favors, patronage, and other inducements that Dwyers have to give—it is a force that a Dwyer or any "boss" cannot discipline in the normal way. Therefore, Clay could, and his followers expected him to, fight Dwyer in behalf of black interests.

It is most important to realize that Clay's followers, on the whole, have not supported him for material reasons. The late Congressman

Adam C. Powell (Harlem) had a personal following and created an organization outside of the established organization. Until he underestimated the seriousness of the challenge for his congressional seat in 1970, he was able to call upon as many as one thousand workers for his campaigns. Many were from his church, but— a fact of great significance—most of them were volunteers. He was able to do this, in part, because black people in Harlem perceived him and his projective personality as a vivid and colorful manifestation of black people's collective aspirations and expectations.[38]

In the minds of some black people, these intangible appeals of race were endowed with a sacrosanct quality which made both Powell, their leader, and the goals he sought for black people superior to other leaders and their goals. To have compromised either the position of the leader or the essence of black people's goals would have been giving way to morally inferior persons or demands; in short, it would have been to have corrupted them. To oppose Powell in an election was to take the side of evil, or to be an "Uncle Tom." Since his power had not been received from the political organization of the city, the organization was not immune from his attacks in behalf of black people.

Because Powell did not hold his followers and workers by material benefits, they rarely felt cheated by his obvious material success. His material success (which included patronizing expensive restaurants and nightclubs) did not cause them to feel cheated because through his behavior he was able to manifest their collective aspirations and expectations; his tours of expensive restaurants and nightclubs meant that he was doing what many of them would like to have done.

Thus, on the one hand, not being part of the regular city organization made it possible for Powell to make demands in behalf of black people. On the other hand, inside such an organization, the late Congressman William L. Dawson (Chicago) discovered that rhetorical or other intangible appeals were not only not useful to a machine politician, but indeed that they could cause embarrassment to him and the machine. They were not useful because although he could only enhance his power by being able to distribute the material incentives which the machine held—patronage and favors—he could maintain the right to distribution only if he remained in good standing with the organization. He could not remain in good standing with the organization if he were to embarrass, divide, or weaken it by raising race issues which could require it to act against its own best interest. Black interest was of no significance. Only utilization of black votes to maintain the organization was important to the machine.

All of that is rather ironic, for early in Dawson's career, he was a frequent user of intangible (race) appeals. He was a well-known street-corner speaker with the type of magnetic personality which helped him build a personal following outside the machine. But once he entered the machine, his career as a purveyor of race rhetoric came to an end. He also became subject to constraints from which Powell was more or less exempted. Because Powell embodied the racial goals and private aspirations of many black people in Harlem, he could enrich his own position without weakening his status. He possibly enhanced it by doing so. In contrast, Dawson led a group of men whose underlying motives, although possibly not their sole motives, caused them to be in politics because of tangible rewards. Dawson would therefore have weakened his position by the extent to which he appeared to gain at the expense of his followers. It was necessary to convince his supporters that they could gain materially in proportion to the material gains of Dawson. If Dawson had gained disproportionately to his followers, he would have brought into being resentment, jealousy, and antagonisms. Therefore, Dawson lived carefully, drove secondhand cars, avoided ostentation, spent money freely on others, and generally minimized the visible material rewards of his position.

Because Clay's organizational cement is similar to that used by Powell and is not based upon the type of materialism that held Dawson's followers together, it will not be too difficult for him to live up to expectations as a black people's black man. The courage and leadership that he displayed during and after the Jefferson Bank affair well established him as a fighter against racism. Once a man acquires a given civic reputation, after his initial success or initial involvement, the reputation becomes cumulative. People who have faith in him expect him to continue to play that particular role because he did so in the past. Learning that people have such expectations frequently induces men to do more or less what is expected of them. Living up to expectations ought not to be too difficult, however, for a man who spent 105 days in jail for fighting racism as he sought to help black people collectively.

NOTES

[1] Joseph S. Roucek, "Minority-Majority Relations in Their Power Aspects," *Phylon,* XVII (First Quarter, 1956), p. 24.

[2] *Ibid.*

[3] *Revolution in Civil Rights,* 4th ed. (Washington, D.C.: Congressional Quarterly Service, June, 1968), p. 54.

[4] Roucek, *op. cit.,* p. 25.

[5] *Ibid.*

[6] *Ibid.,* p. 26.

[7] Arthur T. Jersild, *Child Psychology* (Englewood Cliffs, N.J.: Prentice-Hall, 1960), pp. 14–15.

[8] *Ibid.,* pp. 8–9.

[9] *Ibid.*

[10] *Ibid.,* pp. 9–10.

[11] Edward C. Banfield, *Big City Politics* (New York: Random House, 1965), p. 96.

[12] *Ibid.,* pp. 103–05.

[13] For general ideas pertaining to power, see Roucek, *op. cit.* (n. 1), pp. 103–05.

[14] Alan P. Grimes, *American Political Thought* (New York: Holt, Rinehart and Winston, 1960), pp. 268–75.

[15] *Ibid.*

[16] *Ibid.*

[17] *Ibid.*

[18] Saul Alinsky, "Directing Urban Discontent," in Jim Chard and Jon York, eds., *Urban America: Crisis and Opportunity* (Belmont, California; Dickenson Publishing Company, 1969), p. 140.

[19] *Ibid.,* p. 142.

[20] For general ideas, see *ibid.*

[21] Felix A. Nigro, *Modern Public Administration* (New York: Harper & Row, 1970), p. 187.

[22] Alinsky, *op. cit.*

[23] *Globe,* August 6, 1964, p. 4A.

[24] *Post,* October 17, 1963, p. 8A.

[25] *Post,* February 24, 1966, p. 14A.

[26] Form letter from Norman R. Seay, 26th Ward Democratic committeeman, March 15, 1964.

[27] Adolph J. Rahm, *Post,* November 17, 1963, p. 3A.

[28] Howard B. Woods, *Argus,* November 8, 1963, p. 4A.

[29] *Globe* (editorial), October 25, 1963, p. 8A.

[30] Jim Miller, *Defender,* February 11, 1964, p. 4.

[31] Richard Jacobs, *Post,* August 2, 1964, p. 3A.

[32] Buddy Lonesome, *Argus,* July 31, 1964, p. 7B.

[33] *Globe,* August 6, 1964, p. 4A.

[34] Abstract of Votes Cast at the August 4, 1964, Primary Election. Compiled

and Certified by the Board of Election Commissioners for the City of St. Louis.

[35] Abstract of Votes Cast at the August 2, 1960, Primary Election, *op. cit.*

[36] Interview with Leo Conley, 26th Ward voter, January 14, 16, 1968.

[37] For a discussion of a politician with a personal following, see Edward C. Banfield and James Q. Wilson, *City Politics* (Cambridge, Mass.: Harvard University Press, 1963), pp. 129–31.

[38] The comparison between Powell and Dawson is based upon James Q. Wilson, "The Negro Politicians: An Interpretation," *Midwest Journal of Political Science,* IV (1960), pp. 346–69.

CHAPTER 14

Black-White and Black-Black Ward Fights

Jefferson Bank's obstinate stand and the elite's decision to punish and make examples of the demonstrators helped the young Turks in their efforts to build a black political base not controlled by Dwyer or other members of the white Democratic organization. In fact, the young Turks helped politically powerless black people in St. Louis become organized to the extent that white people would no longer decide which blacks would serve as committeemen and aldermen in some black wards. Not only were black St. Louisans organized to the extent that they decided which blacks would represent some wards, but they were also able to influence the selection of a governor in 1964 and a mayor in 1965. Thus, what John Hadley Strange said in 1966 pertaining to Philadelphia could not be said about St. Louis. According to Strange:

> . . . Negroes do not participate in politics through a Negro political machine in Philadelphia. There is no Negro political organization in Philadelphia. There is no Negro political organization in Philadelphia now, and there never has been one. One white-controlled Democratic and Republican organizations exist in Philadelphia today; only the Democratic one is important. Negro politicians, successful and aspiring alike, publicly acknowledge that the city organizations determine which Negroes are nominated and elected.
>
> Negroes do, on occasion, suggest Negroes for slating by the white democratic organization, but it is the City Committee and its Chairman, not the Negroes, who decide when a Negro can have a particular office. . . .[1]

In St. Louis' Twenty-first Ward, young Turk Benjamin Goins challenged Leo Morrell, incumbent white ward committeeman, in

1964. It was to be a political contest that would test the belief that the Jefferson Bank confrontation had helped cause black St. Louis to acquire a new consciousness. Goins was armed with a Jefferson Bank jail record, and the *Defender*'s black political writer Jim Miller informed black people that Morrell was a die-hard segregationist who would not perform political favors for his black constituents and whose civil rights record was second only to that of Senator Eastland of Mississippi.

> In the complicated, confused network that comprises the Negro political power structure the last of the really die-hard segregationists, Leo Morrell the Democratic committeeman from the 21st ward, has adopted the political philosophy that it does no good to render political favors for his Negro constituents because when the ward becomes predominantly Negro they will kick him out anyway. Well the ward has now become predominantly Negro, at least 80% of the 21st ward is now Negro and Democratic. And Mr. Morrell, whose record on civil rights is second only to Senator Eastland of Mississippi, finds that his influence in the powerful Jack Dwyer machine has greatly lessened in recent years. At one time he was one of the main stays in the Dwyer-Weathers machinery. But his inability to deliver for Dwyer's hand-picked candidates renders him useless in the overall picture.[2]

The Twenty-first Ward Democratic Improvement Association endorsed Goins because he was black and because its membership believed Morrell to be antiblack. Also, Clarence Holly, the Association's chairman, was aware that between 1962 and 1964 the Twenty-first Ward had become predominantly black in at least fourteen of the nineteen precincts. He was additionally aware that for-sale signs were numerous in the four or five precincts that were predominantly white. In addition to Goins being black and Morrell being depicted as being antiblack, Holly had additional reasons to desire that Morrell be defeated. He believed that Morrell had insulted the intelligence of black people, provided no material benefits, and ruled the ward as an absentee white lord. According to Holly, Morrell ". . . insulted the intelligence of the Negro people of this ward, by not even inviting them to a Dem. Meeting. He has given no political jobs and no other jobs to Negroes, and has long since moved from the ward, and therefore has no interest and contact with the people. He now lives in the 1st Ward."[3]

Black political writer Jim Miller was aware as to how a committeeman controls the alderman from his ward. He used this fact as an additional reason why Morrell, who did not live in the Twenty-first Ward, should be defeated. As long as a white man is elected to represent a black ward he will vote for and push those measures he believes are best for black people, and not for what black people themselves desire.

> The reason advanced for the decline of Leo Morrell in Democratic circles has been attributed to his unyielding belief that the Negro is inferior and must not be recognized as a full citizen of the city of St. Louis. His record on civil rights is blemished from start to finish. Mr. Morrell is the person responsible for Alderman Barney Mueller's adverse votes in the Board of Aldermen on Public Accommodations and Fair Employment Legislation. On many occasions Alderman Mueller under the instructions of Leo Morrell voted against the Public Accommodations Bill. And even when the bill finally passed by a wide majority, Alderman Mueller voted present but not voting for the bill. This action is unforgivable! Even Aldermen from deep south side wards voted in favor of the bill while Barney Mueller who represents a ward 80% Negro refused to support such worthwhile battles for passage of the Fair Employment Law. Mr. Mueller and his committeeman Leo Morrell led the opponents in an effort to defeat it. On at least seven occasions, Mr. Mueller voted against Fair Employment and Public Accommodations. Recently, he refused to place his name as a sponsor of the Fair Housing Bill which is now before the Board for passage.[4]

The young Turks had a fight on their hands primarily, they believed, because a black man had been persuaded to enter the race against Goins in order to divide the black vote and enable Morrell to be reelected.[5] On the other hand, *Argus* writer Buddy Lonesome said that Morrell would possibly win because the best black candidate would lose some votes to Goins.[6]

Like the young Turks, Clarence Holly was unhappy because more than one black man was in the race against Morrell. Holly accused the black candidate, Ivory Mitchell, who could possibly prevent Goins from becoming committeeman, of helping a segregationist.

> One of these Negro Candidates is IVORY MITCHELL, Pres. of the Midtown young Democrats. MITCHELL DOES NOT LIVE IN THE 21st WARD NOW, and NEVER LIVED IN THE 21st WARD. Everyone that knows anything about Ivory Mitchell, knows that he lives with his wife and 4 children at 4415a Elmbank, which is in the 20th ward. . . . His wife is employed on a political job in the Marriage License Bureau of the Record of Deed's Office. We are ashamed of IVORY MITCHELL, stooping to such vicious politics, as to secure a voting address in another Ward, to run for an office, just to split the Negro vote, and help MORRELL, A SEGREGA-TIONIST to win over THE Negro people that he simply ignores, MITCHELL SHOULD RESIGN as the Pres. of the Midtown Young Democrats.[7]

Jim Miller said that Morrell kept blacks locked out of the regular meetings of the ward's club. Despite this and other antiblack charges, Miller believed that Morrell would attempt to dupe black people into voting to reelect him by finding a black woman to run as his running mate for committeewoman, and then he would open a "Jim Crow" headquarters in the heavy black section of the ward.

> In the 21st ward it is reported that this longtime Democrat committeeman of that ward, Leo J. Morrell, is seeking re-election with a Negro woman . . . as his running mate. This is interesting; only a few months ago this same committeeman kept Negroes locked out of the regular meetings of the Ward's Club headed by Mr. Morrell. They plan to open a "Jim Crow" headquarters in the South end of the ward near Sarah and Ashland.[8]

Jim Miller, Clarence Holly, and the young Turks were not disappointed. Results of the Goins-Mitchell-Morrell race showed that it was largely decided along racial lines. They also indicated that if blacks living in other wards thought along the lines of their sisters and brothers in the Twenty-first Ward, then black people in St. Louis had in fact acquired a new consciousness.

Morrell received a clear majority in four of the nineteen precincts and was the plurality winner in one precinct. Those five precincts were located in the northeastern part of the ward, the area Clarence Holly said was filled with for-sale signs. From those five precincts, Morrell received 967 of his 1,664 votes. Goins received a clear majority in ten of the nineteen precincts and was the winning plurality candidate in four additional precincts. But he only received 136 of his 2,276 votes in those five "for sale signs" precincts. Mitchell failed to carry a single precinct, but his vote indicated that the election was decided along racial lines. Mitchell only received 55 of his 713 votes in the five predominantly white precincts. Many black voters must have believed, as Clarence Holly felt, that an attempt was being made to split the black vote in order to help Morrell. The alleged conspiracy failed by 612 votes.[9] Of great importance, black people of the Twenty-first Ward recognized and rewarded Benjamin Goins, a black man who went to jail in 1963 because he sought economic betterment for black people in St. Louis.

During the 1970's, those black people who attempt to play the game of electoral politics can profit by familiarizing themselves with the Goins-Mitchell-Morrell and Dwyer-Kennedy 1964 primary races. The latter race teaches black people that when a white candidate has material advantages (jobs, favors, etc.) to offer, it is extremely difficult to get black people to vote for a black candidate, even though he had been assertive on race issues, over a paternalistic white candidate. The former race teaches blacks that when a white candidate has been shown to be antiblack, black people are willing to vote for his black opponent if he has been assertive on race issues.

Therefore, throughout America's large cities during the 1970's, those blacks who desire to play winning electoral politics must devise strategies accordingly. They must utilize every form of communication necessary to convince black voters that job-and-favor dispensing white politicians only benefit a few material-worshiping black people, and in the process, subordinate the collective black community. This type of political educational process also helps to point out how such a white politician is antiblack. Thus, it would help a black candidate who is assertive on race and demonstrates interest in the collective black community. The political education for the black community must include information showing why the power vested in the particular office at stake should be held by a black politician who will use that office to help provide benefits for black people.

Where the Goins-Mitchell-Morrell and Dwyer-Kennedy election results indicated what could happen in black-white campaigns, blacks who are interested in the total black community need guidelines to help them determine campaign strategy when a supposedly conservative black politician is challenged at the polls by a black man who is assertive on race issues. On the surface, St. Louis appeared to have had such a black-black contest in 1964 when young Turk Hugh White opposed incumbent Eighteenth Ward committeeman Fred Weathers, who had been called the leader of the pro-Dwyer black faction.

However, those blacks who are willing to analyze election results so as to better formulate winning strategies must examine more than the results precinct by precinct. Basing strategies solely upon precinct results involves a great deal of work and would be better than basing them upon no analysis at all. Nevertheless, this will not be enough for blacks in the 1970's. Black people must do more in order to ensure victory. Analysis must include other factors and incidents that appeared or occurred during given campaigns. On the surface, one could analyze the 1964 Weathers-White results by precincts and conclude that just as Dwyer had utilized materialism to help defeat Kennedy, Weathers, being the alleged leader of the pro-Dwyer black forces, had used it to defeat White. Such a conclusion could be detrimental because it could cause some blacks who are organizing to acquire political power to become discouraged and lessen their efforts on the assumption that materialism is too great an element to overcome.

In the Weathers-White election, it is apparent that two factors, in addition to Weathers' allegedly being tied to Dwyer and White's aggressive record on race issues, were determinant in that primary election.

In 1960 young Turk Raymond Howard challenged the black establishment by opposing its acknowledged leader, Jordan Chambers. As a young Turk, Howard had been one of the original nineteen in the 1963 Jefferson Bank confrontation and was one of the four released by the St. Louis Court of Appeals because of insufficient evidence in January of 1964. After acquiring his Jefferson Bank jail reputation, Howard joined the black establishment in 1964 instead of opposing it as in 1960. He challenged young Turk Hugh White for his seat in the Missouri House of Representatives. Partly because of Howard, White lost not only his bid to unseat Weathers, but his house seat to Howard as well.[10]

Young Turk White carried only one of the twenty-two precincts against Weathers in the contest for committeeman.[11] On the surface, it would appear that a black man who had been assertive on race issues could not garner black ward-level political support against a less assertive incumbent black politician who allegedly was associated with a white paternalistic jobs-and-favors dispensing politician.

Such a conclusion would be too superficial. There is no question that materialism helped Weathers. But of great importance also was the fact that Weathers had built an organization upon the foundation of amoral power—power devoid of emotion and moral oughts. Weathers had a well-oiled political organization that was impressive enough to attract young Turk Raymond Howard to it. No doubt, having a Jefferson Bank demonstrator on his ticket helped Weathers beat White. Twelve of the Eighteenth Ward's precincts were in Hugh White's House district. Howard carried all of the twelve except one.[12] It would not be too farfetched to assume that, to a small degree, Howard helped Weathers in those eleven precincts.

One could conclude that Weathers' well-oiled organization and the addition of Howard spelled the difference in favor of Weathers in the committeeman contest. One could continue this line of reasoning and conclude that in the contest for White's seat in the Missouri House of Representatives, since both White and Howard had impressive records of being assertive on race issues and since both were young Turks, the voters chose the more popular of the two (and that this factor also helped Weathers). These assumptions may hold small measures of truth, but it may be that another factor greatly influenced the outcomes of both elections. This additional factor helps point out why black people must use more than election results as guides for formulating winning electoral strategies. They must also look for reasons as to why the results are what they are.

This additional factor was that in February of 1964, Hugh White was arrested and charged with writing a twenty-five-dollar check without sufficient funds. That in itself was detrimental to White's candidacy, but the fact that the check was used to pay for liquor, in all probability, added to his troubles. White attempted to explain the incident and replied that:

> . . . in the heat of a legislative session a person might reasonably allow a deposit to his home bank to be delayed, but it is difficult to understand how the holder would wait so long to say anything about it. . . . The whole thing was simply an oversight which could and probably has happened to many people. . . . This is an excellent example of the fact that a man who will stand up and fight for his people can't afford to make any mistake.[13]

White realized he had made a costly mistake, and although political writer Jim Miller did not specifically say so, he apparently believed that White would be discredited to the point that he would lose to Weathers: "Hugh White will have to learn the hard way that when you step on certain toes in this town no stones will be left unturned by those who seek to discredit him. Had he been going along with the program and policies of the old line conservative Negro set, the advocates of a go-slow approach, nothing would have happened in this case."[14]

White soon learned that it was no longer possible to conduct the campaign along the lines of an established young Turk opposing a conservative. Buddy Lonesome of the *Argus* reported that:

> . . . in the 18th ward, Democratic Committeeman Fred Weathers, a prominent civic leader, in addition to having attained a real political stature, is being opposed by Hugh White, a young man whose greatest publicity to date has been for his amazing penchant for writing rubber checks. . . .
>
> . . . This corner can hardly imagine the voter dropping Weathers, at the peak of the affable committeeman's powerful political career—for the likes of a Hugh White! Not hardly.[15]

Several things can be learned from White's two defeats. Blacks seeking political power during the 1970's cannot select a candidate solely because he has an impressive assertive record in behalf of black people and assume that he will automatically defeat a black politician who is less assertive. This is true, especially, if the less assertive black politician is associated with that city's subordinating jobs-and-favors dispensing political organization and has a well-oiled ward-level organization of his own. Strategies to defeat a nonassertive black politician must include the realization that materialism influences some votes. Therefore, the organized and entrenched black politician needs only to concentrate on those voters who are not seeking personal gain. In the Weathers-White contest, no doubt, White's being arrested and charged with writing a check without sufficient funds in his account (along with White's lack of a tight-knit organization) was all that the astute Weathers and his political organization needed to convince many Eighteenth Ward voters who were not self-seekers to vote to retain Weathers in office.

Those black people who are seeking in the 1970's to gain control of elective offices for the benefit of the collective black community must not lose sight of the fact that materialism influences some voters. Therefore, they must build an organization upon a foundation of amoral power which will be capable of conducting the type of political education that will help undermine self-interest (materialism) as a major determinant in outcomes of elections.

The Weathers-White and Howard-White elections should serve to remind blacks who support assertive race men—potential black people's black men—that old-line conservative blacks and their white allies will leave no stones unturned to try to discredit assertive race men. For this reason, organized blacks seeking political power for the collective black community must review the backgrounds of all potential candidates they are willing to support. And since any minor incident will be blown up and utilized, they will, out of necessity, select candidates who have been and then are, above reproach. This is not "democratic," for it means that black people will be forced to run candidates who are "better," not equal to, white handpicked black candidates and whites running for similar posts in white wards.

NOTES

[1] John Hadley Strange, "The Negro and Philadelphia Politics," in Edward C. Banfield, ed., *Urban Government: A Reader in Administration and Politics* (New York: The Free Press, 1969), p. 409.

[2] Jim Miller, *Defender*, January 14, 1964, p. 15.

[3] *Defender*, June 12, 1964, p. 14.

[4] Miller, *op. cit.*

[5] *Defender*, June 12, 1964, p. 14.

[6] Buddy Lonesome, *Argus*, July 31, 1964, p. 7B.

[7] *Defender*, June 12, 1964, p. 14.

[8] Jim Miller, *Defender*, February 18, 1964, p. 4.

[9] Abstract of Votes Cast at the August 4, 1964, Primary Election. Compiled and Certified by the Board of Election Commissioners for the City of St. Louis.

[10] *Post*, August 5, 1964, p. 2D.

[11] Abstract of Votes Cast at the August 4, 1964, Primary Election, *op. cit.*

[12] *Ibid.*

[13] *Defender*, March 3, 1964, p. 1.

[14] Jim Miller, *Defender*, March 3, 1964, p. 5.

[15] Lonesome, *op. cit.* (n. 6).

CHAPTER 15

Black Influence on the 1964 Missouri Gubernatorial Race and the 1965 St. Louis City Mayoralty Race

Aside from fighting to obtain political power in the various wards, the young Turks became involved in statewide politics and influenced the nomination of the Democratic candidate for governor of Missouri in 1964 (Democratic nomination was tantamount to election). The two candidates who were seeking the Democratic nomination for governor of Missouri Warren Hearnes and Hillary Bush, worked assiduously to influence black votes in St. Louis. The *Defender* reported that Hearnes was going to receive support from many of those black politicians who were known because they were assertive on race; it also reported that old-line conservative black politicians who were influenced by boss John J. Dwyer were supporting Bush.[1]

In the Jefferson Bank dispute, the young Turks believed that they were fighting the St. Louis establishment, and that the bank was an integral part of it. During the gubernatorial primary campaign in 1964, the *Post* made it easier for the young Turks to support Hearnes when it reported that Bush was being supported by the Missouri establishment, which was controlled by a bank.

> Bush has an advantage, too, in getting support from bankers, business and professional leaders, some of whom are friendly to or want favors from the Establishment which is backing the Lieu-

223

tenant Governor. The Establishment is a politically-influential group centered on the Central Missouri Trust Co. of Jefferson City, which has had a strong voice in the selection of Missouri governors for 20 years.[2]

On June 22, 1964, the *Post* said that Missouri governors were seldom brilliant, possibly because the Missouri establishment did not bestow its magic blessings on a candidate until its selection process had eliminated innovators or caused them to become fatigued and weary. Establishment candidates usually were past fifty-five and not particularly receptive to new ideas. Young Turk leader William Clay had denounced Governor John M. Dalton (Democratic incumbent, but not eligible for reelection) early in September of 1963. The Hearnes candidacy not only provided Clay with the opportunity to hurt a Dalton man, but gave him an opportunity to try to elect a man who was young enough to be receptive to new ideas that would be advantageous for black people in Missouri.

> Secretary of State Warren E. Hearnes, the non-Establishment candidate for Governor on the Democratic ticket, is striving to disrupt this pattern, and we think disrupting it is a good idea. Mr. Hearnes will be 41 next month. Had he been willing to wait for 10 or 15 years, getting himself re-elected to one minor job or another, growing gray in the state service and proving himself "sound" in the Establishment's eyes, he might well have looked forward to arriving at the Governorship someday in the same way his predecessors arrived at it. But he might be a different man in that case, and a less promising potential Governor.
>
> The very qualities that led Mr. Hearnes to reject his properly humble place on the official escalator, and to seek nomination on his own, recommend him for the post. His 10 years of experience as legislator and Majority floor leader, together with four years in the executive branch, have given him a thorough knowledge of all aspects of state government. His relative youth and his independence from the Establishment are extra assets. The Democrats would bring a fresh breeze into state politics by nominating him.[3]

Black people in St. Louis were restless and participated in disruptive protests between 1959 and 1964 because they were dissatisfied with their subordinated lot; the establishment had politically controlled Missouri immediately prior to and during the restless period.

However, despite the fact that Bush had been labeled an establishment man, the *Argus* apparently decided to support him. It said that "the team around Gov. Bush had been labeled 'an establishment' by his opponents. The assumption seems to be—that if honest men come together in the interest of a person, or a cause, and remain together for a period of time, then the net result of this collective thinking or activity is something less than honorable. Incredible as it seems, that is the line against Gov. Bush. . . ."[4]

The *Argus* informed its readers that Hearnes was receiving support from J. V. Conran of New Madrid, Missouri; and it believed that Conran was powerful as a "boot hill" leader and influential with the antiblack cotton planters. It also said that an Ozark group which opposed a public accommodations law for Missouri supported Hearnes. (The "boot hill" group, cotton planters, and Ozark group were all active in the same southern section of the state.) And it discredited reports that Hearnes had gathered legislative support for the proposed public accommodations bill, apparently because a state legislator (David Rolwing) who was from Hearnes's own Mississippi County Missouri District came to St. Louis and spoke on television against it. The *Argus* also said that Steamfitter Doc Lawler supported Hearnes and that Bush was surrounded by more respectable individuals.[5]

It apparently makes a difference who charges a candidate with being antiblack. Had Bill Clay or Benjamin Goins made the antiblack charge against Hearnes, Hearnes perhaps would not have done well in St. Louis' black wards. Also, it evidently makes a difference whether or not a candidate has been charged with having associates who are antiblack, or whether the candidate himself has been charged with being antiblack.

Thus, the young Turks, in their support of Hearnes, were able to make themselves felt in the 1964 gubernatorial race. Table 15.1 shows that in 1960 Governor Dalton carried Clay's Twenty-sixth Ward by 3,131 votes; but in 1964, Dalton's choice for Governor lost Clay's ward by forty-two votes—a net loss of 3,173 votes for the old guard in comparison with 1960 results. In 1960, Dalton carried Goins's Twenty-first Ward by 2,016 votes, but his candidate lost the ward by 805 votes in 1964—a net loss of 2,812 votes for the Dwyer forces. In 1960, Dalton carried Frederick N. Weathers' Eighteenth Ward by 4,237 votes; but in 1964, Bush only carried

TABLE 15.1

Comparison Between 1960 and 1964 Gubernatorial Races in Four St. Louis Wards

	1960		1964		Net
Ward	Dalton	Cox	Bush	Hearnes	Loss
26th	3,355	224	2,321	2,363	3,173
21st	2,139	132	1,908	2,713	2,812
18th	2,959	192	3,490	1,549	826
4th	4,368	131	3,902	1,224	1,559

SOURCES: Abstract of Votes Cast at the Primary Election August 2, 1960; Abstract of Votes Cast at the Primary Election August 4, 1964. Compiled and Certified by the Board of Election Commissioners for the City of St. Louis.

the ward by 2,678 votes—a net loss of 1,559 votes to the Dwyer forces. Put differently, the young Turks were mainly responsible for the Dwyer-Weathers-Bush camp receiving 8,369 fewer votes for their choice of governor in 1964 than in 1960 in the four wards. Thus, the young Turks proved that it is possible for assertive black politicians to organize and mobilize much of a big city's black electorate and simultaneously induce it to change its voting pattern in statewide politics.

The young Turks' belief that more civil rights legislation would be enacted under a younger governor, even if he were from Mississippi County, than under an old, establishment candidate, cannot be proven true or false. But there is evidence that the *Post* was not in error when on June 22, 1964, it strongly implied that Hearnes's relative youth would possibly cause him to be different from past Missouri governors who were seldom distinguised for progressive leadership or flexibility of thought. After the election, when the legislative body ended its sixth-month session in June of 1965, there *were* new civil rights measures on the books. And some of civil rights legislation had been pushed by the new rural governor with a southern type of background, Warren Hearnes. It could be said that Governor Hearnes was attempting to demonstrate progressive leadership. However, one should not overlook the fact that Hearnes, as an astute politician (especially if he held future political ambitions), sought to dispel doubts and suspicions harbored by black people pertaining to him. He himself commented pertaining to the legislative session: "I think it is interesting . . . that more civil rights legislation was approved in Missouri than ever before under leadership of a Governor from Mississippi County, just as most of the Federal Government's civil rights legislation was passed through the urging of a President from Texas."[6]

As governor, in addition to seeking passage of public accommodations and employment practice laws, Hearnes put a little life in the State Commission on Human Rights. When he became governor, the commission had had a $48,000 budget, one man, and a secretary for two years. Hearnes increased the budget to $164,812 for one year; and, because of his efforts, it received an additional $12,000 in emergency funds to be used in 1965 prior to the date the new budget went into effect.[7] No doubt some black St. Louisans did interpret Hearnes's actions pertaining to the State Commission on Human Rights in a positive light. Nevertheless, human rights commissions do very little to uproot and eradicate individual or institutional racism. By 1968, many black people in Missouri had become dissatisfied with Hearnes. Young Turk Robert B. Curtis filed for the Democratic nomination as Governor in an attempt to garner a protest vote against Hearnes.[8]

With the 1964 election experiences added to their arsenal, the young Turks set out to help elect their candidate as mayor of St. Louis in 1965. They were able to use statements in their cause made by a black politician who apparently was anti-young Turk, but possibly not pro-Tucker. Joseph W. B. Clark was Jack Dwyer's Fourth Ward alderman; and a few months before Mayor Raymond Tucker decided to seek an unprecedented fourth term, Clark made a public attack on Tucker, planting seeds of distrust and suspicion that the young Turks nurtured and helped grow into maturity by the time of the 1965 primary election.[9] According to Jimmy Miller of the *Defender:* "Clark's . . . classic attack on Mayor Tucker for his concealed attempt to close Homer G. Phillips Hospital has supplied Tucker's opposition with a major campaign issue in sepia wards that is going to cost him many votes. . . ."[10]

Clark made public what he said had been a suppressed management survey of St. Louis' public hospitals in which Homer G. Phillips had been praised and City Hospital (white) had received some unfavorable comments. Ever since Homer G. Phillips opened in 1937, it had served as the primary center for black St. Louisans to receive medical treatment; it also served as an institution which trained black physicians and nurses. Politically, it was located in Clark's and Dwyer's Fourth Ward. Clark made the report public because there were rumors of a plan to close Homer G. Phillips. It was possible for Clark and the black community to believe such rumors because the city's Director of Health and Hospitals had forced Homer G. Phillips to cease using a privately financed subsidy that was designed to attract interns. It was believed that such action resulted in handicapping the hospital's teaching program because from July 1, 1964, until Clark made his charges public in October, the hospital had only one intern. However, Mayor Tucker immediately proclaimed that there was no substance to the rumors that the hospital would close.[11]

What the black community did immediately after Mayor Tucker made his statement clearly points out that black people do not always believe white people when white people believe that black people should accept their statement, or statements, as a matter of truth or fact. The action on the part of the black community after Clark's revelation also showed clearly how information filters through the black grapevine regardless of what white people want black people to believe. Immediately after Clark made his remarks and Tucker proclaimed that they were unfounded, on October 12, 1964, more than 350 black people met at Antioch Baptist Church and organized a citizens' committee to work for the retention of Homer G. Phillips.[12]

The citizens' committee met with Tucker on November 18 and demanded his long-range assurance that Homer G. Phillips would continue to operate. Tucker replied that immediate steps would be taken to strengthen the hospital but that he could not assure them of long-range continued existence since his term of office ended in April of 1965. It is not known whether he was playing politics with that statement. But at the meeting he was presented with petitions bearing 40,000 signatures.[13] Young Turk associate Arthur Kennedy, as co-chairman of the committee, played a major role in obtaining the signatures, especially those from white South St. Louis.[14]

In January of 1965, the *Defender* informed its readers that the primary election could become a contest between Mayor Tucker and the black community. The first reason cited was the Homer Phillips issue and the economic loss for black people if it were closed; the second, that Tucker was believed to have been largely responsible for the Mill Creek Urban Renewal project, which to many meant "black removal." Tucker was also discredited because of a lack of black faces on his staff, and his Jefferson Bank stand.

> Just recently the entire Negro community was up in arms when Mayor Tucker and high officials in his administration attempted to close Homer G. Phillips. And had it not been for the efforts of an aroused Negro community, Mayor Tucker might have been successful in putting almost a thousand (1000) Negroes out of work. Even more important he would have closed the last effective training institution for Negro doctors in this country. Most certain the H. G. Phillips issue will loom to its true proportion in the coming election. In addition, many Negroes who were uprooted from their overcrowded homes in the Mill Creek area and herded into an already overcrowded West-end area still have bitter resentment against Mayor Tucker. Obviously many of them who had paid for their homes or were renting flats for $10.00 per month are now financially overburdened with $100.00 per month notes or $75.00 per month rental fees.
>
> Most of the young, militant civil rights leaders are opposing Mayor Tucker because of his refusal to enforce strong civil rights legislation. This young militant group . . . point to the fact that Tucker has refused to hire a Negro on his staff. . . . They also point out that he defended the Jefferson Bank in its discriminatory hiring policies. So as things seem to be shaping an accurate slogan for the coming Mayoral campaign might be "Mayor Tucker versus the Negro community."[15]

Many factors were determinant in the 1965 Democratic primary deciding who would become Mayor of St. Louis. In addition to the rumors pertaining to Homer G. Phillips and the Mill Creek "black removal" theory, there were suggestions that Mayor Tucker was aloof and separated from average citizens. It is not inconceivable that those black people who could be convinced that the incumbent mayor was indifferent to white people could come to believe that black people could expect less from such a mayor. Whether or not there was such a plan as the closing of Homer G. Phillips and whether or not the mayor was, in reality, indifferent is not as important as the actual fact that something of this sort was being publicized when the young Turks began to devote their energies to helping A. J. Cervantes to become mayor of St. Louis in 1965. They received some help in the form of reprints from South St. Louis. One of the reprints widely circulated read as follows:

> When Tucker was elected in 1953 he was elected by the downtown press, downtown business interests and the independents. With the help of the press and downtown, he did get much done in his first term.
>
> But since that time, Tucker has become aloof and has lost touch with the problems of the average taxpayer and the small businessman. . . .
>
> A man such as A. J. Cervantes, who realizes the importance of the small businessman to a city and who won't set himself apart from the average taxpayer, will certainly take steps to eliminate many of these problems and thus put our city back on the road to progress.[16]

The *South Side Journal*'s editorial vividly revealed the two major political coalitions in St. Louis. A few days later a *Globe* editorial acknowledged that the Jefferson Bank confrontation was politically significant in the black community, but the *Globe* clearly underestimated its significance. The editorial said that William Clay had been in "jail as a result of his activities in the wretched Jefferson Bank demonstration" (Clay was supporting Cervantes and the *Globe* apparently hoped that his support of Cervantes would help Tucker). Such a remark clearly revealed that the *Globe* did not realize the full impact of the bank demonstration in the black community, especially if it were attempting to influence black votes. Indeed, the statement indicated that the demonstration held one meaning for the *Globe* and something entirely different for black St. Louisans. Although the *Globe* condemned Clay, a few months earlier black people in the Twenty-sixth Ward had elected him as their committeeman. In citing Clay as one of the reasons why Tucker, and not Cervantes, should have been nominated in 1965, the *Globe* editorial possibly hurt Tucker in Clay's ward. Results of the Tucker-Cervantes contest show that black people in the Twenty-sixth Ward listened to Clay, and not to the *Globe,* giving Cervantes a larger majority than any other ward in the city.

> Al Cervantes served 14 years on the Board of Aldermen, from 1949 until 1963, the last four years as President of the board. What was his Aldermanic record?
>
> He voted 55 times to override the Mayor's veto of spot zoning bills. He backed rooming house operators seeking changes in the City Plan Commission declared harmful to neighborhoods. . . .
>
> A most frightening aspect of Mr. Cervantes' candidacy is the caliber of unsavory backers. Among such choice characters are John L. (Doc) Lawler, Second Ward Committeeman, boss of the Steamfitters' Union and Henchman of Larry Callanan, who served a prison term for labor racketeering. Another is ex-Alderman William L. Clay, Twenty-sixth ward Committeeman and rabblerouser, who went to jail as a result of his activities in the wretched Jefferson Bank demonstration.
>
> These are ward-heeling politicians who don't labor in the vineyards just for love of public weal. They will demand payment if Mr. Cervantes gets to City Hall. For years they and their ilk got only the gate from the Tucker administration. They crave political pie and think they can get a fat slice if Ray Tucker is turned out of office.[17]

The editorial attack on Clay, and the black Twenty-sixth Ward's response in the 1965 Tucker-Cervantes contest makes it easy to believe the talk in the black community that every time the *Globe* attacks Clay, black people more vigorously support him. On November 1, 1963, the *Argus* published Howard Woods's statement pertaining to Clay that "attacks by white elements tend to drive some fence straddling Negroes into his camp." Although Woods did not identify the white elements, one only needs to read a few of his articles to discern that Woods was too astute a newspaperman to criticize the *Globe* directly.

The *Post,* too, criticized Cervantes as being a "stop sign-spot zoning" candidate. It also included Lawler in its criticism, but evidently realized that the Jefferson Bank confrontation helped Clay acquire whatever type of charisma he possessed and did not include him in its reasons for not supporting Cervantes.

> The phalanx of Democratic ward bosses lined up against Mayor Tucker is a distressing reminder of what the March 9 city primary is all about.

Each of the committeemen supporting A. J. Cervantes aspires to be mayor within his own ward (and police chief too if that can be arranged). Each knows from experience over the last 12 years that Mayor Tucker insists on being mayor for all the wards. One such important field is zoning. Mr. Cervantes's record and his generally superficial approach to city government suggests he would be a willing cooperator in spot-zoning. As an alderman he voted for at least 48 spot-zoning bills that helped destroy property values in established neighborhoods by introducing incompatible uses. Mayor Tucker has consistently followed the advice of the City Plan Commission and vetoed spot-zonings, only to be overridden by the Board of Aldermen, controlled by Cervantes supporters.

The ward organizations also want unhindered control over traffic in their wards because, as with zoning changes, there are friendships, votes and perhaps money to be made that way. The monumental traffic jam at the South Broadway-Jefferson-Chippewa wedge each day is a testimonial to the power of the committeeman Louis Buckowitz (became Cervantes' Director of Parks) a Cervantes supporter, to frustrate the Tucker administration's efforts to move traffic, instead of accommodating a few merchants.

Some of Mr. Cervantes's supporters have interests of the wider nature. Committeeman Matt O'Neill of the twenty-second ward, an official of the Bricklayers' Union, wants the Building Code rigged to require the use of brick construction, necessary or not. Doc Lawler, committeeman in the Second Ward and boss of the Steamfitters, wants a mayor who will look at Building Code Amendments with the eyes of a steamfitter.

Mayor Tucker has a 12-year record of deciding zoning, traffic, building code or other disputes in the over-all public interest as recommended by the appropriate technical agency. Mr. Cervantes's approach has been more a matter of testing the prevailing winds.[18]

Despite the fact that both dailies and the *Argus* supported Tucker, Cervantes won the nomination. On March 10, 1965, immediately following the March 9 primary, *Post* staff writer E. H. Thornton analyzed the election results on the basis of complete unofficial returns. He concluded that Cervantes had carried eighteen of the twenty-eight wards and had defeated Tucker by 14,442 votes partly because of the type of ward support Cervantes received. According to Thornton: "Dwyer, whose Fourth Ward Democratic

Organization was one of the few regular ward organizations that indorsed Tucker, said that the Tucker organization thought it would carry the Fourth ward and some other wards in the Tucker camp 'by much larger margins.' He mentioned specifically the Eighteenth. . . .

Complete unofficial returns showed that Tucker carried the Fourth ward by only 214 votes, the Eighteenth by 342. . . ."[19]

In those two wards where some believed that Tucker would do well, official election results show that he actually lost a little ground in comparison with his 1961 vote. In 1961, Tucker carried Dwyer's Fourth Ward, where Homer G. Phillips is located, by 372 votes; but in 1965, he carried it by only 262 votes, or 110 fewer than in 1961. Tucker carried Weathers' Eighteenth Ward in 1961 by 548 votes and in 1965 by 447, or 101 fewer votes than in 1961.[20]

The *Globe* believed that in most black wards Tucker did not receive as many votes as he desired because "the smear sheets created unrest over the fate of Homer G. Phillips Hospital, and thus cut down the Mayor's vote in these areas, as did the baseless charge that he callously moved Negroes out of Mill Creek Valley."[21]

The *Defender* gave Clay, the young Turks, and others who were not a part of the Dwyer-Weathers coalition much credit for Cervantes' victory.

> In a magnificent display of raw political power, Bill Clay and the Democratic Committeeman of the 26th ward emerged from last Tuesday's primary election as the number one delivery politician in the city of St. Louis [overcoming] tremendous odds in an effort to unseat an entrenched political machine run by Tucker, Dwyer and Weathers. . . . But the margin of victory for Cervantes was delivered in mid-town Negro wards. More than a 9,000 vote majority for Cervantes came from the 10 predominantly Negro wards in mid-town. James Troupe of the 5th ward delivered a 1900 vote majority; Leroy Tyus delivered 1800 vote majority; Ben Goins delivered 1200 votes majority; Matt O'Neil delivered 1400 vote majority; and Bill Clay delivered 2600 vote majority.
>
> Committeeman William (Bill) Clay of the 26th who became the target of the Globe Democrat, Post-Dispatch and the Argus, proved his ability to deliver in a crucial election. His ward organization gave A. J. Cervantes the biggest majority of any ward

in the City of St. Louis. The 26th Ward posted a majority of more than 2600 votes in a smashing defeat of the Tucker forces led by the former committeeman Norman R. Seay. Mr. Seay who campaigned for Tucker was thoroughly humiliated by the sound defeat at the hands of Bill Clay.

The prowess of the organization built by Clay in the 26th ward brings back to memory the heydays of the late Jordan W. Chambers. Many veteran political observers believed that the young, energetic Bill Clay has reached the political stature once held by the late Jordan W. Chambers. Clay who was instrumental in the election of Governor Hearnes and A. J. Cervantes had been able to put together a political machine in the Negro community that has completely destroyed the stronghold once controlled by Jack Dwyer and Fred Weathers. Both Mr. Dwyer and Mr. Weathers who once headed strong delivery organizations were embarrassed by the returns of last week which showed them almost losing their wards to rump groups headed up by Arthur Kennedy and Hugh White.[22]

As indicated by the *Defender*, young Turks and some other black politicians who were not official members of the Dwyer-Weathers camp did play a key role, especially in two wards. In 1961, Mayor Tucker carried the Twenty-first Ward by 689 votes, but with Benjamin Goins as committeeman, he lost the ward by 948 votes in 1965, or a net loss of 1,637 in comparison with 1961 results. Clay made even a greater contribution to Tucker's defeat. In 1961, Tucker lost the Twenty-sixth Ward by 137 votes, but with anti-Tucker Clay serving as committeeman in 1965, Tucker lost the ward by 2,888 votes.[23]

Tucker was hurt in three additional black wards. In the 1961 primary election James Troupe (black) was defeated as a candidate for committeeman in a three-way race in the Fifth Ward. The white candidate won. However, in the 1965 primary election Troupe won on his second try. Research has failed to reveal any evidence that he considered himself an official member of the young Turk family. But he helped Cervantes in 1965 as much as most of the young Turks. Tucker carried the Fifth Ward in 1961 by 367 votes but lost it in 1965 with Troupe as committeeman by 2,030 votes. Tucker also lost the Twentieth Ward by 1,641 votes; and although a white man served as committeeman of the black Twenty-second Ward, Tucker lost it by 1,872 votes.[24]

The *Post* recognized that the black vote was determinant in the mayoral election along with that of independent or nonorganized voters.

> Mr. Cervantes won by carrying most of the South Side wards with a lead of 7600 votes, and the eight Negro wards by 8200 votes. . . .
>
> . . . Clearly the Negro vote, which Mr. Cervantes failed to carry when running for President of the Board of Aldermen two years ago, was crucial to him this year, and the most interesting question of the election is why it switched. Those wards whose leaders supported Mr. Tucker turned in only slight majorities for him, while the others registered heavy pluralities for his opponent.
>
> While the base of Mr. Cervantes's victory was his command of the most effective Democratic ward organizations, he could not have won with them alone. He succeeded in appealing to non-organization voters as well . . . largest primary vote in 20 years.[25]

Thus, because of the Homer G. Phillips issue; urban renewal; attacks upon Clay by the *Globe;* black ward leaders in the Fifth, Twentieth, Twenty-second (rump leaders) wards; and effective political organization on the part of the young Turks, black St. Louisans were able to help determine which man would be elected as mayor of St. Louis in 1965.

NOTES

[1] *Defender*, April 28, 1964, p. 3.
[2] Herbert A. Trask, *Post*, June 28, 1964, pp. 1A, 29A.
[3] *Post* (editorial), June 22, 1964, p. 36.
[4] *Argus* (editorial), June 19, 1964, p. 2B.
[5] *Ibid.*
[6] Ronald D. Willnow, *Post*, July 4, 1965, p. 6A.
[7] *Ibid.*
[8] *Post*, April 29, 1968, p. 3A.
[9] *Post*, October 11, 1964, p. 8A.
[10] Jimmy Miller, *Defender*, February 18, 1965, p. 4.
[11] *Ibid.*
[12] *Post*, October 13, 1964, p. 1A.
[13] *Post*, November 18, 1964, p. 21A.
[14] *Globe*, November 6, 1964, p. 5A.

[15] Jim Miller, *Defender*, January 6, 1965, p. 4.

[16] *South Side Journal* (editorial reprint), February 10, 1965.

[17] *Globe* (editorial), February 23, 1965, p. 26.

[18] *Post* (editorial), March 1, 1965, p. 26.

[19] H. Thornton, *Post*, March 10, 1965, p. 6A.

[20] The 1961 and 1965 election results cited are from the following sources: Abstract of Votes Cast at the Primary Election March 7, 1961; Abstract of Votes Cast at the Primary Election March 9, 1965. Compiled and Certified by the Board of Election Commissioners for the City of St. Louis.

[21] *Globe* (editorial), March 11, 1965, p. 8A.

[22] *Defender*, March 18, 1965, p. 2.

[23] Abstract of 1961 and 1965 Votes, *op. cit.* (n. 20).

[24] *Ibid.*

[25] *Post* (editorial), March 10, 1965, p. 2B.

CHAPTER 16

Black Political Paranoia

The young Turks' being able to organize black people to the extent that the black vote became an influential variable in the 1965 mayoralty race in St. Louis pointed out a significant political reality that blacks must not lose sight of during the 1970's: black political support to help a white man become mayor does not necessarily mean that blacks are helping to elect a mayor whose administration will give top priority to the pursuit of legitimate black demands. Nor does it automatically mean that the new city administration will be genuinely committed to making policy and substantive decisions affecting blacks *with* black people, rather than for black people. If the decision or new policy to be adopted will cause the mayor to realize financial rewards and simultaneously takes something away from the very black people who helped to put him in office, they, no doubt, helped the wrong man. Black people must realize that when they help elect a white man to public office, he is capable of taking not just "something" from them; but if it is to his advantage, he may take away from black people that which they desire and believe performs a useful and necessary service for much of the black community.

In fact, what happened shortly after Mayor Cervantes took office in 1965 indelibly impressed this political reality upon the minds of those blacks in St. Louis (Clay, Curtis, Goins, Green, M. Oldham, White, and others) who had learned how to use protest not as an end in itself, but as part of the effort to arouse black people and develop momentum and organization to push for political power. If and when black people decide to support a white candidate for a citywide (also state or national) office, awareness of this political fact should cause black people to distrust that candidate in the

same way the reformers' moral fervor led them to distrust the political spoilsman and the professional politician.

Black psychiatrists William H. Grier and Price M. Cobbs
acknowledge that ". . . for a black man survival in America depends in large measure on the development of a 'healthy' cultural
paranoia. He must maintain a high degree of suspicion toward the
motives of every white man and at the same time never allow this
suspicion to impair his grasp of reality. It is a demanding requirement and not everyone can manage it with grace. . . ."[1]

We recognize that for collective black communities to survive
and enhance themselves politically in American cities depends, in
large measure, on the development of a "healthy" black political
paranoia. Black communities generally and black politicians specifically must maintain a high degree of suspicion toward the motives and actions of every white politician—especially those who
have received political support from black voters. At the same time,
blacks should not allow this suspicion to impair their perspective
of the political community as it is. Development and maintenance
of a "healthy" black political paranoia is a demanding requirement,
but it must be accomplished if black people ever hope to achieve
equitable recognition in this country. If this is not accomplished,
no form of repression will stop those blacks who advocate various
forms of urban guerrilla tactics from dominating subordinated and
politically powerless black communities.

In 1965 black St. Louisans underwent an experience pointing
out the need for a black political paranoia, one which provided
them with a reason to question whether or not Mayor Cervantes
deserved the political support he received from black wards. Many
black St. Louisans used jitneys for transportation to work and elsewhere. The jitneys were owned and operated by the Consolidated
Service Car Company, in which Cervantes held at least 40 percent
interest. When a purchase agreement was announced which was
designed to eliminate the jitneys, many blacks were angered. The
purchase agreement meant that for $625,000 the Bi-State Transit
System was being assured that service car (jitney) competition
would be eliminated for the present and future. No real property
was involved.[2] According to black Alderman Joseph Clark:

> . . . in the first place . . . the city charter prohibits the sale
> or transfer of a franchise. Certificates of convenience and necessity

issued by the city's Board of Public Service for operation of service cars constitute a franchise to operate over fixed routes.

Bi-State reportedly proposes to seek assurances from the Board of Public Service that they will not authorize operation of service cars in the future because they will not be needed.

How could the public service board possibly state that there never would be any necessity for service car operation. In my opinion there is ample ground for a finding of convenience and necessity at the present time.

Many of the persons riding these service cars (most of the riders are Negroes) are poor people. . . . The proposed change to busses would mean an increase in fare for them from 20 to 30 cents a ride, an added expense that many of them cannot afford.[3]

Alderman Clark apparently underestimated the pervasiveness of institutional racism when whites have an opportunity for economic gain. Apparently, the fact that poor black people would find themselves paying thirty instead of twenty cents for a ride was not as significant as the estimate that the annual revenues for all service cars was approximately $700,000 and that Bi-State lost 3,465,000 passengers annually to the jitney service.

It also appeared the Bi-State at the time stood to lose additional revenues because of the service cars. In 1965 a confidential report stated that ". . . it is the present intentions of the management of the Consolidated Service Car to expand their operations to the West. . . . where more than 10,000 persons per day are using these Bi-State lines."[4] The report additionally predicted that black people living in the expansion neighborhoods would use the jitneys because of their frequency and low fares. This meant that Bi-State would lose additional money; and it was recommended that Bi-State purchase the operating rights of Consolidated to help save public transportation.

Acceptance of this recommendation meant that the new policy adopted by the Cervantes administration decreed that service cars would be banned from the streets of St. Louis (streets in black neighborhoods), thus taking away from poor black people a jitney service which provided frequent transportation at low fares. The Board of Public Service which approved of cancelling the jitney franchise consisted of a mayoral appointed president and six city

department heads who served in the Mayor's cabinet. According
to *Life's* Denny Walsh: ". . . Mayor Cervantes was asked if he
had discussed the board's decision with Sansone or any member
of the board before the board okayed the cancellation. His answer:
'I don't remember.' "[5]

The $625,000 purchase agreement for Consolidated Service Car
Company, which operated the jitneys, was signed by Anthony F.
Sansone, Consolidated's president. Sansone had also served as
Cervantes' manager in the 1965 campaign. Cervantes had owned
one-half interest in Consolidated in the name of Mrs. Victoria
Karches, his sister. But the mayor informed the *Post* on June 30,
1965, that he had sold his interest. Many black people and some
white Republicans began to question this because Consolidated's
1965 Corporation Registration Report filed with the Missouri Secretary of State, dated June 25, 1965, listed Mrs. Karches as Vice-President and as a director of Consolidated.

Almost five years later, Denny Walsh cited the service car sale
in his *Life* article of May 29, 1970, which alleged Cervantes had
personal ties to the underworld. Walsh explained the sale in the
following manner.

> Was Cervantes flouting Missouri's conflict of interest laws?
> The mayor says no. He has said publicly that he sold his 40%
> interest in Consolidated to his partner Sansone for $125,000 in
> a "straight cash" deal eight days after he took office in April
> 1965—before the trust was set up. But had he?
>
> An Internal Revenue Service investigation turned up a check
> from Sansone dated April 28 and canceled stock certificates and
> corporate minutes that showed Cervantes had sold his shares that
> day.
>
> Sansone's check, however, had been written on an account
> with insufficient funds. Cervantes held it until Dec. 24—more
> than a month after the sales agreement with Bi-State and more
> than eight months after he took office. On that Christmas Eve
> Sansone borrowed $125,000 from Lindell Trust. The loan was
> secured by a certificate of deposit for $125,000 purchased the
> same day by Cervantes with Sansone's original check.
>
> A federal investigator later described this as "a paper transac-
> tion, designed to substantiate the appearance of a money flow."
>
> The mayor will, of course, get his $125,000 as Sansone pays
> off his loan. The loan is being paid from the same checking ac-

count into which Bi-State makes its monthly payments for the purchase of Consolidated.

Cervantes' lawyer Jack Murphy later acknowledged to IRS that after the Bi-State sale agreement, he had reconstructed Consolidated's stock record book because Sansone told him the originals were lost.[6]

Because of the service car "deal," Cervantes received heavy criticism in black wards. Two black aldermen, Joseph Clark and Dewittee Lawson, were among the black politicians who put Cervantes under fire. They were not young Turks nor were they among those black politicians that research revealed worked to elect Cervantes. The action taken by Clark and Lawson could be interpreted as an attempt by black politicians associated with the Dwyer-Weathers coalition to embarrass a white leader of the young Turk stop sign-spot zoning coalition. A *Post* editorial suggested: "Most of the aldermanic opponents include Mayor Cervantes' political enemies who suspect he may still be a silent partner in Consolidated."[7]

This was possibly true, but the suspicion that Cervantes was still a silent partner in Consolidated evidently only partially explained the motives of Clark and Lawson since the economic-political battle that developed involved many in the black community and was one of the reasons that the Clay-Cervantes marriage headed for divorce court. Aldermen Clark and Lawson jointly introduced a resolution calling for an aldermanic inquiry into the proposal that Bi-State Transit System buy the operating rights of Consolidated Service Car Company.[8] They were concerned as to the welfare of the black drivers. The Consolidated Service Car Company was owner of all of the separate operating certificates for each of the at least eighty vehicles. Most of them were old airport-type, eight-passenger limousines, and a few six-passenger cars.

The cars were either owned by, or were being purchased from or through the Consolidated Service Car Company by, individual drivers and were operated independently, but with some supervision. The service car drivers who were buying their cars determined their own working hours and used other drivers so that some cars were on the streets from 5 a.m. until 1 a.m. weekdays and Saturdays. As a result, there were at least 120 service car drivers. Each driver hand-collected twenty cents from adults and fifteen cents from children as fares. From this, each car owner had to pay Consolidated a fee for the operating certificate, and for insurance and general administrative costs; and he had to pay other costs such as gasoline, oil, tires, repairs, and a helper driver in many cases. Whatever was left was his salary.[9]

In order to lessen the drivers' resistance to the purchase agreement—especially since the prospect of economic loss might influence their thinking—they were made a promise: employment with Bi-State. But Alderman Clark did not put much faith in the promise that all service car drivers would receive full-time permanent employment with Bi-State, and feared that the move might deny them an opportunity to care for their families.[10] Clark also believed that many service car drivers did not possess the type of training and experience that would enable them to find meaningful employment in the private sector. He voiced concern that they would become members of the army of unemployed and find it necessary to seek public assistance.[11]

In addition to receiving support from Clark and other black politicians, the drivers attempted to help themselves. On November 30, 1965, many of them were in the delegation of sixty that went to see Mayor Cervantes. They carried petitions containing 15,000 signatures requesting that the service cars not be denied the right to continue operating because they offered faster and cheaper transportation than Bi-State. The signatures had been obtained by the service car drivers themselves. On that same day, about twenty service car drivers picketed City Hall with their limousines as the Board of Public Service met and approved of the sale. Some of their signs read "Mayor Unfair to the Negro Group," "Mayor—We Helped Elect You, Now Help Us," and "We Need Insurance From the Cervantes Insurance Co."[12] The latter was displayed because ". . . the insurance on the service cars had been handled by Cervantes since the Consolidated company was organized in the early 1950's. . . ."[13]

ACTION's Percy Green dispatched a letter to the mayor threatening immediate direct action. CORE also came to the assistance of the drivers, and Norman Seay (1964 CORE Chairman) accompanied some of the drivers to talk with the mayor in an attempt to persuade him to intervene in behalf of the drivers.[14] A few seconds prior to that meeting there was an attempt to intimidate Seay.

According to the *Argus*: "While waiting to see the Mayor, Seay and the drivers saw Samuel Bernstein, newly appointed director of the St. Louis Human Development Corporation, hurry into Cervantes' office. When the Mayor appeared with Bernstein, Seay's boss at his side, he remarked: 'Hi, Norman. You must be on your lunch hour, because I know you work for HDC.' "[15]

Not only did Seay and CORE, Green and ACTION, and black politicians support the service car drivers, but the *Argus*, too, championed their cause. The *Argus'* "healthy" black paranoia caused it to harbor less than one hundred percent confidence concerning whether or not Bi-State would provide adequate service in black neighborhoods after the demise of the service cars. It believed, further, that elimination of service cars was an example of the poor being victimized by the more affluent. Specifically, the *Argus* said:

> Even if Bi-State's pledge to hire all of the ex-drivers who desire employment will come to fruition, the problem of public service and convenience will remain.
>
> While it is true that additional bus runs have been added to the Page, Wellston, Hodiamont, and Delmar-Forsyth lines, it will be the first of the year before any true evaluation of Bi-State adjustment to the service car areas can be made. Additional buses are always added to the lines during the Christmas season. The significant point is whether or not these extra services will be continued after the holiday season ends.
>
> The least affluent members of our community are, again, the victims of the more affluent. The increase in transaction costs to the area of the city served by the service cars will, undoubtedly, work a hardship on the residents.
>
> It now seems as if every recourse—save the boycott which has been proposed by the service car drivers—has been exhausted. Petitions, pickets, mass meetings, discussions, and investigations have brought the 124 drivers no relief. Bi-State will employ the ex-drivers; at least, they and their families will not suffer.
>
> And the citizens in the northwest area of the city—the ones most dependent on the service cars for cheap, efficient transportations? Well, after all, they are only voters![16]

Many of the citizens living in the northwest area were voters, but the election for a new mayor was more than three years away. Therefore, among other reasons, a CORE-sponsored boycott was initiated against Bi-State in behalf of the service car drivers. Cars participating in the boycott displayed American flags and signs saying "Freedom Rides." The Republican City Central Committee, pledged money to help CORE buy gasoline. It also decided to investigate the sale of Consolidated with emphasis on Cervantes' involvement.[17]

Freedom-car passengers were not charged a fee, but most made donations that in many cases exceeded the twenty-cents fee charged by service cars. Also, more people began to ride freedom cars and thus helped to strengthen the boycott. It soon became very effective. The city then retaliated and began to issue summons to drivers of freedom cars because they did not possess service car licenses and liability stickers.[18]

The fact that Samuel Bernstein of the St. Louis Human Development Corporation spoke to CORE chairman Norman Seay early in December when Seay escorted some drivers to see Cervantes caused some questions to be raised the last part of December. In the midst of the successful boycott Seay resigned as chairman of CORE and simply said that his role in the antipoverty program had forced him to curtail his activities.[19] Despite Seay's resignation, freedom rides continued into early 1966 with overwhelming black community support. At the same time, the forces that were determined to take the jitney service away from black people continued to try to break the boycott. And for reasons that are unclear to us, black taxi drivers working in the areas served by former service cars decided to seek an end to the freedom rides.

> A group of taxicab drivers presented to Mayor Alfonso J. Cervantes yesterday a petition protesting against the operation of Freedom Cars in the city where the cabs operate. The petition was signed by 450 drivers of five companies.
> The drivers said Freedom Cars were unfair competition and took as much as $3000 a day in income away from their companies. Some of the drivers said they were making $5 to $10 a day less since Freedom Cars started operating.[20]

It is possibly true that some of the drivers were earning less because of the freedom cars. But were there other pressures being exerted to cause the 450 taxicab drivers to submit their petition to Cervantes? There are grounds to believe that the petition was not just the result of spontaneity. Bi-State admitted that it was losing approximately $30,000 monthly because of the boycott. Also, there were behind-the-scenes maneuverings. After a midnight meeting held in the Sheraton Jefferson Hotel—which even most CORE members were unaware of until March 3, 1966—CORE agreed to end the boycott by midnight March 3.[21] According to the *Globe:*

> Under the agreement made during the meeting at the Sheraton Jefferson Hotel, Bi-State agreed to hire all former Consolidated drivers who have not been hired thus far.
>
> This applies to drivers under 65 who can pass a physical examination.
>
> Mr. Sansone agreed to assume the outstanding mortgages on former Consolidated service cars which have not been paid for.[22]

One of the reasons cited by CORE's new chairman, Bill Bailey, for ending the boycott implied that he believed the affair had become too political.[23] But that answer did not prevent Buddy Lonesome of the *Argus* and many black St. Louisans from becoming suspicious:

> The Freedom Car episode, which just closed here in St. Louis, has literally left this jaded old reporter, gasping for air. . . . Pure, FRESH, AIR—unsmelly, and not putrid with the odor of suspicion. . . . One day there was a bus boycott going on. This corner felt it was well-deserved concern at the plight of a group of Negro workers, forced from their jobs . . . and a large segment of the Community, forced to accept a one-third increase in fares. Yoicks . . . on waking up the very next morning, the bus boycott was over! No preamble, no waiting period . . . just OVER, no ifs and buts about it.
>
> Wonder how it happened? A talk with some of the CORE officials turns up a big, FAT NOTHING. . . .[24]

This "sale," which was politically damaging for Cervantes in black wards, was removed from the public arena when in December of 1966, the 1,392 charges against 100 freedom-car drivers were dismissed. However, the service car episode, no doubt, caused Cervantes to recognize that he was in political trouble in black wards. Young Turk leader William Clay, Cervantes' most prolific vote producer in 1965, soon proved that he would cease to be associated with a white political coalition leader if that white politician's actions were inimical to black people.[25]

Anthony Sansone, Mayor Cervantes' former Consolidated Service Car Company partner, was brought into the city from his country residence in Afton and with Cervantes' help was installed as committeeman in the nondelivery Twenty-fifth Ward over the objections of the pro-Tucker forces (white) who carried the ward in 1965. Cervantes then proceeded to back Sansone for the post of Democratic Central Committee Chairman of St. Louis when Dwyer died in May of 1966.[26] But Clay and other black committeemen refused to support Sansone. A *Post* editorial stated: "The Mayor evidently worked diligently for Anthony Sansone. But he was unable to attract a single vote from among the eight wards of the Negro community, and that was fatal to the Sansone candidacy. . . ."[27]

The *Argus* reported that Clay had become dissatisfied with Cervantes. It also said that the service car episode contributed to the black community's displeasure with Cervantes:

Mayor A. J. Cervantes failed to attend a meeting scheduled for the ending of 107 years of street-cars in the City when it was learned that all the elected officials from the ward would be absent. Word of the boycott had been circulated around city hall for the past week. It was reported that Committeeman William L. Clay, the biggest supporter that Cervantes had in the last primary election, had become displeased with Cervantes administration.

The fact that Committeeman Clay, Committeewoman Ida L. Harris and Alderman Nat. J. Rivers were not present at the ceremony . . . was evidence that Mayor Cervantes was not in good standing in the Negro community. . . . Veteran political observers conclude that Cervantes is in serious political trouble in the powerful midtown wards. Just one year ago, Bill Clay delivered the 26th Ward by a majority of more than 2900 votes for Cervantes over Tucker. . . . That majority represented the greatest amount of any ward in the City.

The rift that now apparently exists between Cervantes and the Negro community was openly expressed by many rank and file citizens who did attend the gatherings. Several persons interviewed by an ARGUS Staff reporter defined the primary contentions of disagreement with Mayor Cervantes as the (1) the bungling way in which he and his business partner, Anthony

Sansone, handled the sale of the Consolidated Service Company. . . ."[28]

The case of Mayor Cervantes of St. Louis shows that black voters must come to realize that when they help elect a white man to office that he is capable of adopting policies inimical to black people. Therefore, it may help if the elected white official is aware that black voters generally and black politicians specifically, have developed and are maintaining a "healthy" black political paranoia. Such knowledge should cause the white official to realize that despite having received black political support to obtain his office, he must prove (with actions) that he travels a positive road when it comes to legitimate black demands. Whenever, in any American city, an elected white official adopts policies or takes action inimical to the black community, what elected black officials do is of great importance. They should follow the example of Clay, Committeewoman Harris, and Alderman Rivers. They should not only disassociate themselves from him and refuse to support him, but should also work to defeat his choice or choices for other public offices.

NOTES

[1] William H. Grier and Price M. Cobbs, *Black Rage* (New York: Basic Books, 1968), p. 135.

[2] *Post*, November 9, 1965, p. 6A.

[3] *Post*, November 14, 1965, p. 3A.

[4] *A Confidential Report on the Consolidated Service Car Operations in St. Louis, Missouri*. Prepared by the W. C. Gilman & Company, Inc. (St. Louis, Missouri, October 28, 1965), pp. 1–2.

[5] Denny Walsh, "The Mayor, The Mob and The Lawyer: A Two-Faced Crime Fight in St. Louis," *Life*, May 29, 1970, p. 26.

[6] *Ibid.*, pp. 26–27.

[7] *Post* (editorial), November 15, 1965, p. 2B.

[8] *Post*, November 12, 1965, p. 6A.

[9] *Confidential Report, op. cit.* (n. 4), pp. 1–2.

[10] *Post*, November 12, 1965, p. 6A.

[11] *Post*, November 14, 1965, p. 3A.

[12] *Post*, November 30, 1965, pp. 1A, 8A.

[13] *Ibid.*

[14] *Argus*, December 3, 1965, p. 1A.

[15] *Ibid.*

[16] *Argus*, December 3, 1965, p. 2B.

[17] *Post*, December 8, 1965, p. 5A.

[18] *Post*, December 22, 1965, p. 7A.
[19] *Post*, December 12, 1965, p. 1C.
[20] *Post*, February 26, 1966, p. 3A.
[21] *Globe*, March 3, 1966, p. 1A.
[22] *Ibid.*
[23] *Ibid.*
[24] Buddy Lonesome, *Argus*, March 11, 1966, p. 3B.
[25] *Post*, December 12, 1966, p. 8A.
[26] *Post*, May 17, 1966, p. 2B.
[27] *Post* (editorial), May 19, 1966, p. 2B
[28] *Argus*, May 27, 1966, p. 1A.

CHAPTER 17

Black Urban Organizations

It is a well-known fact that nonblack and nonbrown major ethnic groups in America used the political potential of being herded together into natural neighborhoods to acquire advantages in securing jobs and numerous other benefits, especially including major inputs into the political decision-making process. On the other side of the coin, blacks were herded into natural neighborhood communities, but have been subjected to political and economic decisions made from without their communities. In fact, despite being crowded into natural neighborhoods that held raw political potential, blacks have remained power-poor. This is beginning to change at a slow, incremental pace. Nevertheless, those blacks who are interested in accelerating the pace must come to accept the fact that initiation of meaningful black participation in the political life of their cities comes at a time when political participation, in the traditional sense, without major system change, could result in very few gains and an increasing sense of frustration.[1]

In other words, there must be structural changes that will allow natural-neighborhood residents to have a greater voice in shaping the policies that directly affect them. But black political activists of the 1970's will find it rather difficult to effect the necessary structural changes since the current holders of power have demonstrated unwillingness to relinquish meaningful power to citizen groups.

Ways must be found to cause the ruling elites in American cities to acquiesce. If not, the call for black power, the cry that reflects the urgency to make the system more responsible to the needs of black natural neighborhoods, could end up as empty verbalism, and not as concrete reality.[2] It is our belief that effective use of the

black vote can help cause the elites to resign themselves to the
necessary structural changes.

Effective use of the black vote, among other things, includes
being aware of how important the black vote is in presidential
elections. Approximately 85 percent of the 1968 black presidential
vote went to the Democratic candidate, creating a situation in which
roughly one out of every five Democratic voters was black.[3] If,
during the 1970's, the black vote does not become splintered and
if blacks are not attached firmly to any particular political party,
black votes will be crucial in presidential elections.

Of great importance for the 92nd Congress was the fact that
black people comprised more than 30 percent of the population
in 59 of the 435 congressional districts. Ten of those districts had
a black population of over 50 percent and were represented by
nine black congressmen and one black congresswoman.[4]

Table 17.1 shows that for the 92nd Congress, twelve congressional
districts had from 38 to 49 percent black populations, but only
one of them was represented by a black man, George Collins (Chicago). Ronald Dellums (Oakland) was the only black congressman
elected from a district with less than a 30 percent black population.

Redistricting changed some of the population percentages, and
in January of 1973 when the 93rd Congress convened, there were
three additional blacks. Two of the newcomers are Yvonne Braith-
waite Burke (Los Angeles) and Barbara Jordan (Houston), former
President Pro Tempore of the Texas Senate. The third, Andrew
Young, Jr. (Atlanta), comes from a district that is only 38 percent
black.[5]

Black people will attempt to unseat some white congressmen
in districts that have between 38 to 49 percent black populations.
In those districts where blacks comprise 30 percent or more of
the population, it is also possible that black people may be able
to exert a great deal of influence and persuade particular white
congressmen to support certain measures that benefit black people.
However, to influence and persuade the white congressman and
make sure that he pursues some policies not determined by him
or other whites, black people must not organize around some "lag
of public morality" surmise.

Blacks must establish vigorous urban organizations to carry forward once blacks have made their demands known. The urban

TABLE 17.1
92nd Congress
Congressional Districts with 38 to 49 Percent
Black Populations

State	Dist.	Blk. % of Pop.	Principal City	Name of Rep.	No. of Terms in Office
California	31st	41.3	Los Angeles	Charles H. Wilson	5
Georgia	2nd	38.2	Albany	Dawson Mathis	1
	5th	39.2	Atlanta	S. Fletcher Thompson	3
Illinois	3rd	49.8	Chicago	Morgan F. Murphy	1
	6th	42.3	Chicago	George W. Collins	2
	7th	44.2	Chicago	Frank Annunzio	4
Mississippi	1st	46.2	Greenville	Thomas G. Abernathy	15
	3rd	43.1	Jackson-Vicksburg	Charles H. Griffin	3
	4th	41.0	Meridian	G. V. Montgomery	3
North Carolina	2nd	43.3	Rocky Mount	L. H. Fountain	10
Pennsylvania	1st	47.9	Philadelphia	William A. Barrett	13
South Carolina	6th	40.7	Florence	John L. McMillan	17

SOURCE: Joint Center For Political Studies, *The Black Electorate: A Statistical Summary*, A Research Bulletin Prepared by the Joint Center For Political Studies, I, No. 3 (Washington, D.C.: Joint Center For Political Studies, 1972), Table III.

organizations must not consist only of black elites, but they must have a mass power base built upon the foundations of amoral power—power devoid of emotion and moral oughts. The organizations must deal with the world as it is in each congressional district and work to make conditions as blacks would like for them to be—starting from where they are.

All black people associated with these urban organizations will owe it to black people collectively to help the black members of Congress come up with meaningful legislative proposals. Such help will be needed for it will not be easy to push legislation through Congress that only benefits blacks. In fact, collective black minds must come up with proposals that benefit blacks, poor whites, and middle-class whites since it is highly doubtful that any bill will get through Congress if the white middle class does not, in some way, feel that it, too, will benefit.

Table 17.2 shows that for the 92nd Congress, there were some congressional districts in which the black population was 30 percent or more and in which the white incumbent had served only one or two terms. Such a congressman will not have been in Congress long enough to acquire bits and pieces of power under the seniority system and possibly will not have become an imposing political power. Thus, such congressmen can effectively be challenged at election time by blacks.

TABLE 17.2
92nd Congress
Districts In Which the Black Population Was 30 Percent or More and the White Incumbent Had Only Served One or Two Terms

State	Dist.	Blk. % of Pop.	Name	No. Terms Served	Principal City
Alabama	5th	36.3	Walker Flowers	2	Bessemer
Georgia	2nd	38.2	Dawson Mathis	1	Albany
Illinois	3rd	49.8	Morgan F. Murphy	1	Chicago
South Carolina	1st	36.0	Mendel Davis	1	Charleston
	2nd	33.2	Floyd Spence	1	Columbia

SOURCE: Joint Center For Political Studies, *The Black Electorate: A Statistical Summary*, A Research Bulletin Prepared by the Joint Center for Political Studies, 1, No. 3 (Washington, D.C.: Joint Center For Political Studies, 1972), Table III.

As important as presidential and congressional politics are, it is improbable that black people will realize anticipated results unless they view city politics as the center of all black political activity. For it is highly unlikely that any political strategy will yield positive results for blacks if the potential black vote is splintered and/or apathetic, and cannot be mobilized. As we have suggested, one important way to avoid a fragmented, indifferent, and/or unconcerned potential black vote is through viable mass-based urban organizations. It seems logical that a more effective black power-seeking organization can be built, maintained, and sustained if its foundation is built upon precincts and wards in various cities, in lieu of organizing along state legislative, congressional district lines or state boundary lines during presidential elections.

Organizations that are viable enough to interest black people to support or not support particular candidates, bond issues, and the like are absolutely essential. Raw, potential black votes are not sufficient to help ensure that public policies adopted by elected officials and administered by bureaucracies will not be inimical to black interests. Black people must cast their ballots in increasing numbers if there is to be any hope of electoral politics helping to serve as one of the mechanisms that will contribute assistance as black America attempts to move from its state of powerlessness. Furthermore, with effective black precinct-ward organizations, there is a greater likelihood that blacks will participate in presidential and congressional elections.

It is essential to view city politics as the central nervous system of black political activity because there are 89 American cities that have total populations of 50,000 or more in which at least 20 percent or more of the total population and at least 16 percent of the total voting-age population are black. Collectively, these cities represent 33,192,868 total inhabitants, of which 31.6 percent or 10,487,432 are black. The total voting-age population in these 89 cities is 23,743,032, and 28.3 percent or 6,722,060 of the total voting-age population are black.[6]

If we include Atlanta's 496,976 inhabitants, Table 17.3 shows that there are 10 American cities of over (or near) 500,000 population in which black people comprise from 32 to 71 percent of the total population, and from 31.1 to 66 percent of the total voting-age population.

However, black people must do more than just make a statistical analysis of cities prior to devising electoral strategies. Electoral structure must be thoroughly understood. It will be easier to build vote-swaying organizations in some cities than in others because of local governmental structure. Therefore, all black electoral strategies must include consideration of structure, as well as other factors. Primarily because of the numerically smaller and somewhat more homogeneous populations in small wards or natural neighborhoods, and the abridged geographical area, it is easier to build the necessary

TABLE 17.3

Cities of Over (or Near) 500,000 Population: Black Percentages of Population and Voting-Age Population

City	Tot. Pop.	Tot. Blk. Pop.	Blk. % of Pop.	Tot. V.A.P.	Blk. V.A.P.	Blk. % of Tot. Pop.
Atlanta	496,973	255,051	51.3	354,642	167,796	47.3
Baltimore	905,759	420,210	46.4	625,011	272,973	43.7
Chicago	3,336,957	1,102,620	32.7	2,398,930	677,379	28.2
Cleveland	750,903	287,841	38.3	524,991	184,451	35.1
Detroit	1,511,482	660,428	43.7	1,072,953	423,032	39.4
Memphis	623,530	242,513	38.9	423,432	153,172	36.2
New Orleans	593,471	267,308	45.0	413,905	164,257	39.7
Philadelphia	1,948,609	653,791	33.6	1,405,828	437,345	31.1
St. Louis	622,236	254,191	40.9	444,486	159,406	35.9
Washington, D.C.	756,510	537,712	71.1	555,869	371,592	66.8

SOURCE: Joint Center For Political Studies, *The Black Electorate: A Statistical Summary*, A Research Bulletin Prepared by the Joint Center For Political Studies, I, No. 3 (Washington, D.C.: Joint Center For Political Studies, 1972), Table III.

effective organizations in cities where councilmen are elected from small wards.

Some cities elect part of their councilmen from wards and the others at-large. In combination ward/at-large cities it is possible to build the precinct-ward, black power-seeking organization by using the existing boundary lines from which the non-at-large councilmen are elected. However, black people must not lose sight of the fact that when it comes to representation on city councils in combination ward/at-large systems, blacks suffer from political racism equal to the percent of councilmen elected at-large. This is primarily true because with their vast resources, the white elite will have been largely responsible for electing the at-large councilmen.

Most of the cities in which blacks comprise 20 percent or more of the population make use of the at-large system to select city councilmen; that at-large system is apt to create problems for blacks who are interested in a precinct-ward type of organization. However, rather than be frightened by the prospect of a lack of small wards, pragmatic blacks in at-large cities have little choice except, with varying tactics, to work with the system as it is and simultaneously attempt to promote positive change. In at-large cities it is possible to build viable black urban organizations by using the existing precincts. As far as possible, those precincts that are contiguous and reflect black natural neighborhoods need to be grouped together. Thereby, wards will be created in which blacks can operate effectively.

In cities where small wards exist, black people are justified in considering utilization of any instrumentality necessary to resist any proposals to change to nonpartisan and/or at-large systems. It is absolutely necessary, moreover, that black people who live in at-large cities fight with a missionary zeal to change such electoral systems to small-ward arrangements. Hopefully, elites in at-large and/or nonpartisan cities will recognize that such a structural change in American cities has the potential not merely of transferring power to black natural neighborhoods, but also of staving off igniting the fuse that could lead to the destruction of society.

Black people in at-large cities must recognize, of course, that to effect the necessary structural changes will be extremely difficult. Many businessmen and upper-class civic leaders will realize that they invariably will have less influence under a small-ward, natural-neighborhood system than under an at-large or even a combination at-large-ward system. In fact, theoretically, businessmen and civic dignitaries become minority groups among other minority groups under small-ward systems. If an at-large system city were to adopt small wards, in reality, such a realization would no doubt cause the elites to utilize some of their resources to help expand their influence beyond the boundaries of the elite wards. Astute utilization of their resources would help the elites maintain their dominance.

The crux of the matter is that city government structurally based upon the natural neighborhood holds the potential of making subordinated racial groups a small part of the system. Councilmanic representation based upon the natural-neighborhood concept affords more decentralization and a greater dispersal of power than under other systems, and thus gives blacks more points of access or avenues to influence city governmental policies. Nevertheless, black people living in cities where small wards exist and in cities where

they may become operative in the future cannot jump to the conclusion that the natural-neighborhood arrangement automatically
causes blacks to receive councilmanic representation roughly in proportion to a city's black population.

Black people in Cleveland comprise 38.3 percent (see Table 17.4)
of the total population and hold 39.4 percent of the councilmanic

TABLE 17.4
Cities In Which Councilmen Are Elected By Wards
1970

City	Blk. V.A.P.	Blk. % of Tot. V.A.P.	No. in Council	No. Blk. Councmn. 1972	% of Tot. Councmn.	Blk. % of Tot. Pop.
Chicago	677,379	28.2	50	14	28.0	32.7
Baltimore	272,973	43.7	19	5	26.3	46.4
Cleveland	184,451	35.1	33	13	39.4	38.3
St. Louis	159,406	35.9	28*	10	35.7	40.9

SOURCE: Joint Center For Political Studies, *The Black Agenda: Proportional Repre-
sentation*, A Research Bulletin Prepared by the Joint Center for Political Studies, 1,
No. 4 (Washington, D.C.: Joint Center for Political Studies, 1972). Table V, The
Municipal Year Book, *Governmental Data For Cities Over 5,000 and Council-Manager
Places Under 5,000*, 1968, pp. 64–68.
* President of Board of Aldermen is elected at-large.

representation. St. Louis blacks comprise 40.9 percent of the whole
population and hold 35.7 percent of the aldermanic seats. Chicago
blacks comprise 32.7 percent of the city's entire population and
hold 28 percent of the councilmanic seats. A person interested in
promoting natural-neighborhood government could look at Cleveland, St. Louis, and Chicago and assume that black people in natural-neighborhood cities have representation that roughly reflects
black numerical strength. But before anyone accepts a conjecture
of that kind, another natural-neighborhood city should be examined. Although blacks comprise 46.4 percent of Baltimore's total
population, they claim only 26.3 percent of the councilmanic
representation.

Examination of Table 17.5 ward and at-large combination cities

TABLE 17.5
Black Councilmanic Representation In Combination Cities

City	Blk. V.A.P.	Blk. % of Tot. V.A.P.	No. in Council	At-Large	Ward	No. Blk. Councmn. 1972	Blk. % of Tot. Councmn.	Blk. % Tot. Pop.
Gary, Ind.	57,212	49.7	8	3	6	6	66.7	52.8
Memphis	67,264	36.2	13	6	7	3	23.1	38.9
New Orleans	164,257	39.7	7	2	7	0	0.0	45.0
Newark, N.J.	123,093	48.6	9	4	5	3	33.3	54.2
Philadelphia	437,345	31.1	17	7	10	4	23.5	33.6

SOURCE: Joint Center for Political Studies, *The Black Agenda: Proportional Representation*, A Research Bulletin Prepared by the Joint Center for Political Studies, I, No. 4 (Washington, D.C.: Joint Center for Political Studies, 1972), Table V, The Municipal Year Book, *Governmental Data for Cities Over 5,000 and Council-Manager Places Under 5,000*, 1968, pp. 64–68.

also indicates a mixed bag. In Gary, Indiana, blacks comprise only 52.8 percent of the entire population but command 66.7 percent of the councilmanic representation. In Newark, New Jersey, blacks comprise 54.2 percent of the whole population but only have title to 33.3 percent of the councilmanic representation. Philadelphia blacks comprise 33.6 percent of the population and hold only 23.5 percent of the councilmanic representation. Memphis blacks comprise 38.7 percent of the total population, but hold only 23.1 percent of the councilmanic seats. Political racism shows up strongly in New Orleans, where 45 percent of the entire population is black and there are no black councilmen.

With one exception, examination of the at-large cities cited in Table 17.6 is very discouraging to those who hope to see black representation in city legislative bodies roughly comparable to the black proportion of the entire population. In Wilmington, Delaware, blacks comprise 43.6 percent of the city's people population and command 41.7 percent of the councilmanic representation. But in Detroit, blacks, who comprise 43.7 percent of the city's population, only have 22.2 percent of the Common Council's representation. Prior to the 1974 reorganization, Atlanta's blacks were in the numerical majority with 51.3 percent of the inhabitants, but held only 26.3 percent councilmanic representation. The black population of Oakland, California, comprises 34.5 percent of the total, but only

TABLE 17.6

Black Councilmanic Representation In At-Large Cities

City	Blk. V.A.P.	Blk. % of Tot. V.A.P.	No. in Council	No. Blk. Councmn. 1972	Blk. % of Tot. Councmn.	Blk. % Tot. Pop.
Atlanta	167,796	47.3	19	5	26.3	51.3
Detroit	423,032	39.4	9	2	22.2	43.7
Oakland, Calif.	80,501	29.4	8	1	12.5	34.5
Richmond, Va.	69,068	38.0	9	1	11.1	42.0
Wilmington, Del.	20,994	36.7	12	5	47.1	43.6

SOURCE: Joint Center for Political Studies, *The Black Agenda: Proportional Representation*, A Research Bulletin Prepared by the Joint Center for Political Studies, I, No. 4 (Washington, D.C.: Joint Center for Political Studies, 1972), Table V, The Municipal Year Book, *Governmental Data for Cities Over 5,000 and Council-Manager Places Under 5,000*, 1968, pp. 64–68.

12.5 percent or one of eight councilmen is black. Richmond, Virginia, is 42 percent black, but only one of the nine city legislators is black—11.1 percent.

There are many reasons why the problem of achieving black representation on city councils in at-large cities is such a discouraging one for black partisans. Among these are the various and sundry styles of politics which appear to take place under the facade of nonpartisanship and which allow the elite to exercise great influence. The nonpartisan ballot itself contributes to the discouragement of blacks. This ballot emphasizes the individual candidate over coherent group effort—especially confusing when voters do not have the aid of familiar party labels. Because of these facts, the most likely strategy for blacks to employ in tackling this problem is to work to secure black advantages within a particular structural system as it is, while simultaneously trying to change the arrangement. There must be precinct/ward-like, black power-seeking organizations in nonpartisan cities so that blacks will be able to play collective and not individual politics. The black urban political organizations will be able to help identify and promote black candidates who identify with the collective black community.

There is another important factor that black urban organizations in nonpartisan cities must face—the long list of candidates on the ballot which tends to confuse both black and white voters. If a black-led organization that commands the respect of much of the black community directs attention to black candidates who identify with the collective black community, then black voters will not have to face the quandary created by the long list by voting for candidates who have a favorable position on the ballot or a familiar-sounding name, as has been done in many nonpartisan at-large elections.

Of course, the black power-seeking organizations in at-large nonpartisan cities will do very little to help black people gain councilmanic representation roughly in proportion to black numerical strength unless the organizations find ways of financing black candidates. No black person can afford to lose sight of the fact that in at-large elections candidates are more likely to be dependent on special interest groups that have large bank rolls, or upon wealthy private individuals. Groups and wealthy individuals that have helped finance successful candidates exercise more than just ordinary democratic influence in the council. It is unlikely that many, if any, white interest groups or wealthy white individuals will willingly help finance campaigns for black people's black men who are seeking some of the white power to use to benefit black people.

It is more likely that since the mass media influence many voters in at-large elections, the elite will use its influence and cause the media to support so-called black men who are nonassertive on race and who are willing to work for policies that whites think are best for blacks. This would not be too difficult a task for the elite to perform since the instruments of communication are disproportionately controlled by them and their supporters. If the elite were to decide to support a black man who has a reputation as being a black people's black man, black people in that community had better initiate the search for another strong, assertive black man.

Of course, in natural neighborhoods, black urban organizations can overcome elite control of communications and help assertive black candidates because of the narrowness of their formal and informal communication channels, the homogeneity of the population, and the minimizing of conflicting messages. Thus urban organizations are essential to help blacks overcome their powerlessness.

NOTES

[1] Harold M. Rose, *The Black Ghetto* (New York: McGraw-Hill, 1971), pp. 102–04.

[2] *Ibid.*

[3] Joint Center for Political Studies, *Black Presidential Power,* A Research Bulletin Prepared by the Joint Center for Political Studies, I, No. 2 (Washington, D.C.: Joint Center for Political Studies, 1972), p. 1.

[4] Joint Center for Political Studies, *The Black Electorate: A Statistical Summary,* A Research Bulletin Prepared by the Joint Center for Political Studies, I, No. 3 (Washington, D.C.: Joint Center for Political Studies, 1972), Table II. The ten blacks were Augustus F. Hawkins, Los Angeles; Ralph H. Metcalfe, Chicago; Parren J. Mitchell, Baltimore; John Conyers, Jr. and Charles C. Diggs, Highland Park and Detroit; William L. Clay, St. Louis; Shirley Chisholm and Charles Rangel, New York City; Louis Stokes, Cleveland; and Robert N. C. Nix, Philadelphia.

[5] *Denver Post,* November 8, 1972, p. 27; *Denver Post,* November 11, 1972, p. 13.

[6] *The Black Electorate: A Statistical Summary, op. cit.*

CHAPTER 18

Blacks and Public Goods–Services Distribution

Elite support of nonassertive blacks will not strengthen democracy in America. If there is ever to be more meaningful democracy in America, there must be devolution of as much authority as possible to natural-neighborhood communities. Of course, greater participation by natural-neighborhood inhabitants holds the potential, in most cases, of creating conflict at every turn with elites who have well-entrenched interests. But this price must be paid if America is ever to experience a perceptible democracy which does not carry one meaning for blacks and another for whites.[1]

Greater natural-neighborhood inhabitant participation must not only include direct representation on the city councils, but also on the boards of education, police commissions, and other significant policy bodies and at all levels of the public service in far more than token numbers.[2] The preponderance of white people, both liberal and conservative, have come to the conclusion that it is now time for considerable administrative decentralization in America's big cities. They are also in agreement that there is a direct relationship between good administration and its responsiveness to credible client aspirations and desires.[3]

We also call for administration decentralization, as benefiting black people living in big city natural-neighborhoods; and we agree that a decisive test of good administration is responsiveness to credible client aspirations and desires. It is highly likely that city administrations will be more responsive if there is a greater dispersal of power by giving blacks more points of access or avenues to exert influence.

As soon as white bureaucracies know that they are accountable to boards or commissions that have effective black representation, they will gear many of their activities toward responding to the needs and desires of natural neighborhoods.[4] As black faces begin to appear throughout the bureaucracies in more than token numbers, there should also be a greater trend toward responding to legitimate natural-neighborhood needs. However, it would not be very wise for black people to assume that as increasing numbers of black faces appear among a city's bureaucracy, that the strategy of natural-neighborhood government will automatically cause city government to move in the direction desired by black people. Blacks must take notice of eminent black psychologist Kenneth C. Clark's warning: "It [community control] may be used and exploited by those who are concerned with personal profit and power."[5] In other words, some new black city bureaucrats may not necessarily be concerned with the collective black community.

The strategy of natural-neighborhood government is based upon despair and a loss of hope. Many blacks have come to support various forms of natural-neighborhood government because of the realization of the broken promises of the elite. It is a historical fact that whites, not blacks, resisted integration. In fact, those few white liberals who say that they genuinely desire full integration have not been able to deliver it. Since they are a very definite numerical minority, it is highly improbable that they will be able to deliver integration in the foreseeable future.[6]

Since most whites resist integration, it seems logical that natural-neighborhood government will evolve. However, despite most white attitudes pertaining to integration, it will be extremely difficult to effect natural-neighborhood government.[7] Natural-neighborhood government should not accelerate black movement into white neighborhoods. Therefore, it is rather ironic that black people will find it necessary to fight for natural-neighborhood arrangements since it is fairly safe to say that most whites have no profound desire to see blacks move into white neighborhoods.

Based upon survey data from 15 major American cities, it has been determined that 19 percent of the white population surveyed would "mind a lot," and 25 percent would "mind a little," if a black family with about the same income and education moved next door.[8] If 44 percent of whites say that they do not want blacks to live in their neighborhoods, the real percentage is possibly much higher. According to Alan A. Altshuler: ". . . comparing survey with referendum results on open housing one is led to the conclusion that whites talk a more integrationist line than they vote. The reason is quite likely that their fears are easily stirred during referendum campaigns, on the other hand, it may simply be that whites are more prone generally to resist integration in practice than when answering pollsters."[9]

It is understandable that some whites resist integration in practice and talk pro-integration with pollsters. No loyal American white likes to be called un-American; yet resisting black efforts to obtain decent housing is racist, and racism is antidemocratic and thus theoretically un-American. However, racism so permeates this society that, in reality, it is as American as cherry pie (in Rap Brown's words).

By taking advantage of the fact that many whites have no desire to accept large numbers of blacks into white neighborhoods, blacks can gain some support for natural-neighborhood government. It is highly unlikely that there will be widespread natural-neighborhood government until and unless the white middle class accepts the idea. Some middle-class whites possibly will accept natural-neighborhood arrangements if they are convinced that that will help keep blacks out of their neighborhoods. Of course, no black person pushing for natural-neighborhood government should put such a middle-class white on the spot by trading off fewer blacks in a white neighborhood in order to gain some white support. In fact, whites will probably not admit to such an un-American argument as a reason for supporting natural-neighborhood government. No matter—the only important factor is to gain enough support so that black people can acquire a high measure of control over their lives. Strange people sleep in political beds, and natural-neighborhood government is a political bed.

Despite the call for natural-neighborhood government being based upon a strategy of despair, whites themselves may "mess up the game." Black people must be perpetually watchful or the establishment and its supporters will use a semblance of natural-neighborhood government to deceive them. If this is allowed to happen, blacks, more often than not, will be driven to employ strategies based upon complete and utter hopelessness. If strategies of that kind are put into action, blacks and whites both may lose: whites more, for blacks have far less to lose. Constant watching is absolutely necessary because the hoodwinking can come about quickly.

If the thinking of some whites is not altered, natural-neighborhood government would, in reality, be something very short of what is necessary. Many of those whites who are willing to advocate decentralization generally have in mind the delegation of authority within bureaucracies to field officers. This is the hoodwink. Field-office bureaucrats will be instructed to seek "good community relations"—a facade. More probable than not, any field-office bureaucrat who, perchance, rocks the boat by responding to legitimate needs of the black community when the central agency has no such inclination, would be slapped down at will by his superiors at central headquarters.[10] He would be slapped down because one of the important reasons central headquarters decided upon decentralization was recognition that it was experiencing difficulty decreeing and directing its uniform rules and procedures throughout the entire city. This difficulty would be encountered primarily because of the diverse nature and character of many neighborhoods.[11]

Schoolboy fiction teaches that democracy promotes unity, not conformity and/or uniformity. However, top bureaucrats realize that the elite allows them to function only as long as the lid is kept on tight. With this in mind, the elite's bureaucratic supporters may seize upon decentralization as a matter of administrative necessity or efficiency rather than as a genuine response to legitimate natural-neighborhood needs. A side effect is that the move away from centralized decision making may improve employees' morale and possibly cause them to show a measure of initiative and creativity.[12]

Decentralization is not a 1970 elite invention. It is a practice long followed by many large corporations which discovered that decentralization was sometimes more effective and profitable than absolute control at the center. Administrative decentralization of city government, however, must not be mistaken for natural-neighborhood participation. On the other hand, true decentralization could facilitate citizen participation by locating the decision-making agencies closer to the people. But even this would not necessarily guarantee natural-neighborhood residents an opportunity to participate if the particular governmental agency lacked sufficient decision-making authority. Indeed, administrative decentralization could aggravate frustration in natural neighborhoods by employing decentralized agencies which have insufficient authority so as to deflect neighborhood desires from the real seat of decision making. In other words, the real decision making remains at central headquarters with authorities who are high enough to be almost impervious to all but massive pressure, bordering on violence, from poor, uninfluential citizens.[13]

When there is no real reallocation of decision-making power, administrative decentralization does not add very much, if anything, to guarantees that municipal governmental agencies will respond to the legitimate needs and desires of poor and/or subordinated citizens. Even if there were genuine reallocation of power and authority, a determined headquarters could still be a hindrance to meaningful natural-neighborhood government. Headquarters personnel has a psychological influence over whatever field people do. Bureaucrats, in general, are products of traditional merit or civil service systems. Therefore, most field officers will be found looking upward, to an administrative superior, and not into the community they are supposedly assigned to serve.[14]

The vast majority of field officers will be aware that whether or not they are judged to be competent has much to do with whether they will receive future promotions. They are also aware that the competence of an employee is determined by his superiors in the hierarchy, and not by the people he is supposed to serve. His superior has possibly won a promotion or two, moving from one level of competence to a higher level of competence, thus qualifying for still another promotion. However, for each individual the final promotion may be from a level of competence to a level of incompetence (Peter Principle).[15] And if the field officer's superior has reached his level of incompetence, he will probably rate his subordinates in terms of institutional values. Competence then is described as the behavior which supports the rules, rituals, and forms of the status quo. This is possibly one of the main reasons that, particularly among minor officials with no discretionary powers, one sees an obsessive concern with getting forms filled out correctly, whether the forms serve any useful purpose or not. No deviation, however slight, from the customary routine will be permitted.[16]

Laurence J. Peter refers to such an employee as a "professional automaton" because the employee considers means to be more important than ends. The paper work is more important than the purpose for which it was originally designed. Such a bureaucrat no longer sees himself as existing to serve the public: he sees the public as the raw material that serves to maintain him, the forms, the rituals, and the hierarchy.[17]

Many people do not accept the Peter Principle and its concomitants. And it is possible that every employee does not rise to his level of incompetence. However, black people can ill afford totally to disregard the ideas of Laurence J. Peter. For if his principle only applies to most employees, it, in part, explains why mere administrative decentralization holds the potential to serve black people ill. Since many city bureaucrats are products of traditional merit or civil service systems, internal consistency is valued more highly than efficient service (Peter's Inversion). Such employees invert the means-end relationship (Peter's Inverts). Therefore most hierarchies are nowadays so overloaded with rules and traditions, and so bound by public laws, that even top-level employees do not lead. They simply learn how to follow precedents, religiously obey regulations, and move at the head of the crowd.[18]

Are the Peter Principles valid? John M. Pfiffner and Robert Prestus have acquired strong academic reputations in public administration and political science, and in a slightly different way they have said much of what has been said by Peter:

> Bureaucratic inflexibility is aggravated by the legal framework in which public officials work. Their conduct is bound up with the "rule of law," a principle brought to America from England. . . .
> . . . The administrator will be dependent upon his legal and financial aides, who can furnish a path through the maze of legal minutiae confronting him. . . . Strict conformity to established procedures and legal regulations necessarily reduces dispatch and economy.
> Administrators are conditioned also by cultural values and the dominant opinions of their colleagues. Generally they develop a value system which satisfactorily identifies their role with that of the organization, and in turn, the role of the latter with the values of society.[19]

We feel that it is safe to say that when it comes to most city governmental agencies and their relationships with natural-neighborhood residents and problems, there is little, if any, comprehensive scrutiny and evaluation of various alternatives. Since bureaucratic inflexibility is aggravated by the legal framework, most decision makers focus only on those policies that differ incrementally from existing policies. This course of action (or inaction) only makes possible consideration of a small number of policy alternatives and permits manifold ends-means and means-ends accommodations that help make the immediate problem more manageable. Add this to the fact that the greatest number of bureaucrats are influenced by the administrative culture, and it is not difficult to understand why city bureaucrats generally never reach one decision or produce an unswerving solution. Their never-ending serial analyses, evaluations, and attacks on the contemporary problem are remedial and geared more to the alleviation of current social imperfections that cause the powerless to disturb the elite's tranquility, than to the furtherance of positive future social goals for natural neighborhoods.[20]

There must be meaningful devolution of authority so that the pro-inertia and anti-innovation forces prevalent in city bureaucracies will not be able to continue mainly to seek marginal change in public policies and actions that are viewed negatively by most natural-neighborhood residents. To oppose devolution of power is to support drifting—traditional bureaucratic action (or inaction) without positive direction—when it comes to blacks, browns, and power-poor whites.[21]

For these reasons, under mere administrative decentralization, headquarters will continue to have uniform policies that the local officials will not be allowed to disregard—this, despite the fact that the present centralized system has proved itself incapable of responding effectively to the diverse needs of subordinated blacks, browns, and poor whites. Since blacks, browns, and poor whites find city government remote and unresponsive to their needs, the need for natural-neighborhood government takes on new urgency.[22] If this urgency is not met there is a great likelihood of increased alienation and feelings of isolation that could cause very serious disillusionment with big city government and its services. The remedy is a genuine redistribution of power through the natural-neighborhood mechanism.[23]

Responsible administration transpires only if all groups to be served by an agency have an opportunity to make their views known. This has been attempted (sincere, sham, or otherwise) to some extent since the mid-1960's with the technique of creating advisory committees on which the different interest groups are represented. Technically, the advisory committees can make known to the bureaucrats points of view of which they otherwise might not be aware. In a strict functional sense, advisory committees hold the potential to prevent agencies from making mistakes by sounding the alarm when agencies' expert staffs propose policies that overlook practical difficulties that might arise in putting them into effect. However, the more powerful groups represented on advisory boards and committees may dominate the deliberations and possibly provide the bureaucracy with a distorted view of interest and opinion, providing a focus through which strong and strategically-located interests may exert a disproportionate amount of influence.[24]

Part of the fear of and opposition to natural-neighborhood government may be traced to the belief among many in the white community that blacks, especially low-income blacks, are not capable of creating and implementing positive public policies for their communities. This fundamentally paternalistic impression, with all of its implied stereotyping and subtleties, overlooks the fact that when and if blacks were to make public-policy errors, the mistakes could hardly be more serious than the ones made by bureaucrats and elected public officials who are white. Also, there would be the possibility that during the initial stages of meaningful natural-neighborhood government, black errors would not be as long-standing in the minds of blacks as white errors.[25]

The paternalism, implied stereotyping, and generally racist subtleties of whites were probably reinforced after the community action projects of the antipoverty programs revealed that, early in the game, many blacks were unfamiliar with power and status and lacked some specific organizational skills. Those paternalistic whites who would oppose natural-neighborhood government are, no doubt, also aware of apathy, disunity and fighting over crumbs, and cynicism associated with extended repression and subordination; and they easily conclude that these elements are associated with blacks and antipoverty programs. Those whites also possibly can see how such factors weaken blacks' capacity to compete and make the natural neighborhood vulnerable to those who would exploit it for their own ends.[26]

However, any white person who uses the examination of black involvement with the antipoverty program during its early stages to oppose natural-neighborhood government, should update his thinking. It is undeniable that during the direct-action period of the early 1960's and even later, many blacks were not familiar with power and status and lacked some organizational skills. This should have been expected from a people long subordinated. However, updating should effect the realization that out of the direct-action movement, antipoverty program, community control, and welfare rights movements, an indigenous black leadership cadre began to emerge.[27] This homegrown leadership cadre is capable of bringing into being and implementing positive public policies for black natural neighborhoods.

Black tacticians must not overlook the fact that some of the opposition to natural-neighborhood government is based crudely on unadulterated self-interest. Many bureaucrats fear for their jobs and promotions while various contractors worry about their profits.[28] These fears have possibly increased with the realization that black arrival in the various cities possibly did not initiate white flight to suburbia, but helped serve to accelerate it. But many of the city-deserting whites did not relinquish their natural-neighborhood properties nor did others give up their bureaucratic jobs: policemen, teachers, sanitation men, welfare workers, and the like.[29]

As whites continue to hold jobs in central cities in which they refuse to live, black people are becoming increasingly familiar with how whites maintain their jobs through pseudo-professionalization. Plumbers have become "sanitary engineers," and in places like New York City, formal educational requirements have been established where there were none a dozen or so years ago. Title changes and added educational requirements are not as harmless as they seem. Why? When it comes to firemen, maintenance men, mechanics' helpers, and the like, neither the official descriptions of the tasks to be performed nor the jobs themselves have changed. Is this an effort to make it more difficult for others to gain new entry? Not only is this type of thing happening all over, but pseudo-professionalism is receiving enthusiastic cooperation from unions and management.[30] Therefore, many blacks have come to realize that numerous jobs in education, law enforcement, fire fighting, sanitation, and social-welfare fields can be performed by natural-neighborhood residents who are incapable of meeting the arbitrarily stringent requirements of merit systems. This is why there is growing pressure to change the recruiting and hiring procedures. This pressure is likely to continue to grow, especially for nonprofessionals in education, health fields, and so on. On the other hand, many lower-middle-class whites who hold natural-neighborhood-based jobs as policemen, sanitation workers, firemen, and even teachers, possibly feel threatened.[31]

On this account, and contrary to the earlier expectations of most reformers, it is now clear that neither the democratic ideology of equality of opportunity nor good government notions concerning public-regarding motivations are automatically served by civil service and/or merit. In fact, they help secure bureaucratic autonomy and shield patterns of institutional racism.[32]

Not only are the pseudo-requirements a sham, but those employees who possess formal education do not necessarily have all the skills to perform sufficiently in their jobs. Even work experience for such employees is inadequate. Modern technological advances and constantly changing situations that did not exist a few years ago make in-service training and updating of skills necessary. Natural-neighborhood residents can benefit and learn to perform sufficiently in their jobs with in-service training and updating as well as whites. Updating will become increasingly important as skills and knowledge in many areas become obsolete.[33]

Advocates of natural-neighborhood government believe written examinations which typically require rote memorization and formal academic requirements that rise and rise (creating shortages of personnel) are not based on evidence that they are valid predictors of job performance. They also believe oral examinations help exclude already underrepresented blacks from the bureaucracy.[34]

There are several ways to overcome black bureaucratic underrepresentation. Some of them hold the potential to reduce white fears pertaining to loss of employment. True natural-neighborhood government would include earlier retirement plans on full pension for older white workers in natural neighborhoods. Thus, blacks could be hired without those whites being left helpless and insecure. Another way to attack the problem would be the expansion of the work force with new jobs going in a prime manner to blacks.[35]

It is true that these two proposals would call for increases in already strained city budgets and would be difficult to effect due to the fact that state funds would possibly be necessary. These proposals could also mean removing, in part or fully, the tax-exempt status of some institutions, organizations, and their properties. Or, part of the necessary capital may be raised by taxing every vehicle that enters the city. There are many possibilities. However, all would require concerted political activity on the part of black urban, political power-seeking organizations and those whites who, for varied reasons, support the idea of natural-neighborhood government. However, black and white neighborhood government advocates both must find ways to raise the level of political understanding and awareness of many whites.[36]

Another way to help increase black representation in the city bureaucracy is to encourage civil servants who work in natural neighborhoods to live within them. There are some cities that make it mandatory for city employees to live within the city limits, and many more cities had such a requirement when unemployment rates were high. Moreover, it is a near-universal American requirement that elected officials live in the district they represent. There is no constitutional reason why United States congressmen must live in the districts which they represent. However, custom and practice decree that congressmen at least maintain an address in their districts. If they should be required to live in districts they represent, no less should be required of bureaucrats.[37]

Also, it seems logical that those white bureaucrats who would choose to live in a natural neighborhood would be or become sensitized public servants. Although some civil servants may move into natural neighborhoods just to maintain their jobs and fail to increase their susceptibility to legitimate neighborhood demands by overcoming the administrative culture, if they are hostile to black interests, getting rid of them would be healthy for the entire city. Nevertheless, it is probably true that most whites would refuse to live in natural black neighborhoods. Thus, in the normal course of events, most of those recruited to fill vacancies in these neighborhoods will be black.[38]

Michael Lipsky refers to many city employees as "Street-level Bureaucrats" since they "represent" city government to the people through their face-to-face encounters with citizens. Lipsky, too, suggests that some Street-level Bureaucrats not only protect bureaucratic functions but experience inherent difficulties in serving black, brown, and other stigmatized clienteles. Certain of their behavior patterns are said to make them incapable of responding to pressure from natural-neighborhood residents. If Lipsky is correct, then the employee who fails to increase his susceptibility to neighborhood needs may be incapable of responding. In such a case, his removal would not only be healthy for the whole city, but would be a necessity.[39]

Another factor that will help effect a smoother transition to natural-neighborhood government is the high turnover rates in so-called ghettos. Turnover can be used to help phase-in natural-neighborhood government.[40]

Opposition to natural-neighborhood government remains strong and effective because civil service unions are not politically neutral. To some degree they have replaced old-style political machines. Their members are on the city payroll and dues-lugs are assessed to support the organization. They lobby vigorously on policies of interest to them and if they fail to win support for a given policy, they generally demand referenda and mount passion at campaigns for general voter support. If the turnout is not too heavy, they will be particualarly effective as a result of hustling votes from their friends and relatives. Thus, in effect, civil service unions attempt to help their friends and seek to punish those who have defied them.[41] One of the most significant urban political developments throughout the last decade or so has been the rapidly increasing power and militancy of municipal employee unions. They have become new centers of power and influence in cities and influence terms and conditions of employment, as well as major policy decisions. One reason employee unions have become powerful is their proven ability to disrupt vital municipal services.[42] They possibly pick up some additional public support for their activities from members of other social or secondary groups to which some public employee union members belong.[43]

Ethnic diversity in big cities creates a situation whereby various religious and fraternal groups compete for the loyalties of municipal employees. There are diverse societies and associations for Catholics, Italians, Puerto Ricans, Germans, and Poles. And of great importance, recently different groups for blacks have come into being. Within some civil service unions one can detect patterns of ethnic politics analogous to politics played citywide as the diverse ethnic groups seek to control employee unions. However, evidence indicates that in recent years differences among white ethnic groups have submerged, and dissension between blacks and whites has increased. Therefore, blacks and whites both feel the necessity to utilize fraternal groups to protect and promote what they consider their vested interests.[44]

Increasing unionization of public employees has enhanced white city bureaucrats generally. But unionization has affected blacks somewhat differently. Most black people are aware that historically public servant-unionization relations partly helped cause blacks to be excluded from the more desirable-paying public jobs and to be largely relegated to lower-paying positions because restricted procedures were supported by the trade union movement.[45]

Historically, when from their nineteenth-century inception craft unions excluded blacks, the die was cast to exclude blacks from skilled public service employment. The irony was that black slaves and freed bondsmen at one time dominated the skilled-craft force in the South. However, the exclusionary policies of the consolidated craft unions drove most blacks out of the trades by the beginning of the twentieth century.

Most members of crafts employed by cities held membership in private industry unions. Therefore, the exclusion of blacks from unions meant that in city departments throughout every part of the country skilled work was done by white men. Consequently, blacks became effectively blackballed from a considerable proportion of municipal jobs solely because their color prevented them from qualifying for membership in craft unions that were influential enough to have their municipal members' salaries set by the prevailing rate in private work.[46]

The increasing strength and militancy of city employee unions are two of the reasons that most cities are facing fiscal crisis. However, many people believe that because poor blacks came to cities in increasing numbers, they are mostly responsible for the financial predicament of cities. If this is true, why did it take two decades to discern? Black people began to flock to urban areas during World War II, and the precipitous rise in municipal costs began during the 1960's. In fact, apart from public welfare—which is not the major factor in the increase, accounting for only part of it—the bulk of the increases in expenditures did not go to black people. The greatest share of increased expenditures was harvested primarily by the organized producer groups that depend on the public services for their livelihoods—city workers, building contractors, and health field people who provide reimbursable services.[47]

In the era of bosses and machines, political uses of municipal services were common occurrences. Maintenance of allegiance of diverse groups was accomplished by quietly distributing public goods in an informal, personal favor style. Today, other than Chicago's Mayor Richard Daley, effective bosses are gone; and public service bureaucrats distribute public service goods in a somewhat more formalized manner as the struggle between various groups has become more public. Style alteration has not changed the functions of public goods distributions, however. Schools, sanitation departments, and the like are not politically neutral because such agencies bear a whole variety of benefits. Indeed, it is through the dispensation and redistribution of those benefits that city political leaders attempt to maintain and build allegiance. As a result, jobs, contracts, and actual services performed by city housekeeping agencies are as political today as yesterday.[48]

If there is a momentous derangement in the administration and financing of city services, the implicit cause is likely to be a serious disturbance in political relations. This transpired during the 1930's when grave economic dislocations energized classes that previously made very few demands of government. In a like manner, momentous derangements may occur when groups enhance themselves economically, become more politicized, and press city administrations with new demands. In addition, large-scale migrations hold the potential to modify the balance, especially between races or classes.[49]

As the new groups augment their influence, power, and political sophistication, there usually ensues a period of uncertainty when established political relationships between political leaders and older groups become shaky. If during this period of uncertainty political leaders began to feel insecure, political alignments may shift.[50]

Black migration to cities has had a greater impact on other urban problems than upon budgets related to service needs. The influx of blacks that helped cause many middle-class whites to leave for suburbia made it necessary for city political leaders to form new alliances with the new constituents. However, for a long time white political leaders resisted forming new relations with blacks and withheld the services, symbols, and benefits that possibly might have gained some black allegiance just as the loyalty of other groups had previously been won. White political leaders remained firmly attached to the remnants of the traditional inhabitants of the cities and further placed themselves in positions where they could make no concessions to black groups. In the meantime, race and class polarities worsened as white ethnics who lived near black natural neighborhoods feared blacks would move into their communities and attend their schools.[51]

The change in style of distributing public goods and services caused the little concessions later made to blacks to become insidious matters. Since public favors could no longer be dispensed covertly, white political leaders could not conceal, say, public housing and the like for blacks from white groups. Therefore, as blacks became a greater percentage of the American urban population during the 1940's and 1950's, they received very little of the municipal pie. There was one exception. In Chicago, where a facsimile of machine politics remains, blacks received a little piece of the pie in the form of increased AFDC rolls and some political jobs. But in most cities service bureaucrats resisted blacks. In fact, some major southern cities found ways to reduce their welfare rolls during this period.[52]

By the time large numbers of blacks migrated to the big cities, teachers, policemen, firemen, sanitation workers, and others were highly organized and powerfully independent enough to sway most matters pertaining to their respective agencies. Therefore, city political leaders did not control job entrance requirements and so forth so as to help bring blacks into the system. Eventually, excluded blacks became volatile and forced the federal government to undertake an unprecedented part in big city politics.

However, part of the federal government's motivation was based upon the fact that the big city black vote was so very important in presidential elections. By 1961, the national Democratic administration began to perceive of the need to reward blacks, who were generally excluded from the desirable slices of various municipal pies. Consequently, it was necessary to find a way to reward blacks so as not to jeopardize the administration's southern congressional support. What emerged was a series of federal service programs— delinquency-prevention, mental health, antipoverty, model cities— directed toward black natural neighborhoods. Under the various programs, federal spoils were spread in a manner similar to distribution under old big city machines. Some residents were put on payrolls to help others find employment or obtain welfare, and manpower agencies were created to provide some job training.[53]

Nevertheless, federal spoils were insufficient and impermanent. If Democrats had hoped for blacks to remain loyal, it would have been necessary for traditional big city agencies which controlled the bulk of federal, as well as state and local appropriations, to include blacks in the expanding and more secure municipal education, housing, health, and other programs.

National Democrats who administered the juvenile delinquency program hoped to use it to initiate municipal reform by requiring that local governments, as a condition to receive federal funds, submit comprehensive plans that included blacks. But paper plans were not too compelling for local bureaucrats who presided over the programs. This failure caused the administration to attempt to include change by another means.

Federal utilization of the slogan "maximum feasible participation" made it possible for natural-neighborhood organizations to receive federal funds and hire community workers who proceeded to pressure housing inspectors and pry loose welfare payments. Also, because of federal funds, lawyers were available who were willing to, and actually did, represent the interests of natural-neighborhood residents in court against various city agencies. Later, new programs made it possible for poor natural-neighborhood citizens to organize and mount offensives against such institutions as welfare departments and school systems. Thus, using federal dollars to restore to life the functions of the political machine, the federal government was able to help blacks themselves spur local service agencies to respond to legitimate black demands.[54]

The outcome was that black people secured their principal tangible gains from confrontation politics through the public welfare system. Aggregate national welfare costs increased from approximately four billion dollars in 1960 to almost fifteen billion dollars in 1970. In some big cities much of that money went to blacks and browns, primarily because other groups did not compete within the welfare system. However, if black people received a little more in the form of welfare benefit in big cities, that was just about all they got.[55]

Where black demands stuck out like a sore thumb, less obvious but much more important in accounting for increasing public service costs was the reaction of organized whites, especially those who had categorical, material stakes in the administration and distribution of municipal services. Their reactions were partly based upon the perception that black demands threatened their traditional preserves. Also, in part, they were no longer held in check by stable relationships with local politicians since the black influx and white exodus introduced a degree of uncertainty into those relationships.[56]

The organized producer groups reacted with a rush of new demands. They had political muscle to exert, not only because of expert organization, but also because they were frequently allied with uncontracted constituencies by class, ethnicity, and union affiliations. So as not to appear to be self-seeking, their demands for higher salaries, lower workloads, and greater autonomy were always concealed in terms of protecting the professional standards of the city services. This ruse helped them win broad public support. On many of those occasions when the organized producers reinforced their demands by closing the schools or bringing the subways to a standstill or allowing the garbage to pile up, many citizens were ready to blame the inconveniences on politicians.

Blamed politicians, less secure because of the black influx-white exodus, were not in a good position to oppose or greatly modify the escalating demands since the organized producer groups had enough muscle to halt services and alienate the broader public. Therefore, the politicians attempted to expand payrolls and workout contracts.[57]

Examination of the largest service run by municipalities, education, reveals the propitiatory efforts of the politicians. The educational complex was jumped on by organized groups because it offered jobs for teachers, clerical and supportive personnel, and contracts for maintenance and construction. However, before they attacked the complex, it was set upon by blacks demanding integration. Integrationists lost to local white resistance. Some idealistic blacks (former integrationists) sprinkled goober dust on integration and transformed it into the type of citizen participation demand that would lead to a black share of the jobs and contracts. The political response was to hire more black teachers and move more token numbers of blacks out of teaching up into the lower echelons of the educational administrative hierarchy. But this is well-nigh all that blacks received.

During this same period that blacks received very little from the system, organized producer groups made large gains. An estimated 80 percent of rising school costs can be attributed to personal costs. Incited by perceptions that black demands challenged and threatened their traditional prerogatives, coupled with the fact that city political leaders were generally weaker and more conciliatory than in yesteryear, organized producer groups began rapidly to augment and entrench their stakes. The strength of their demands increased to such a degree that, during the late 1960's and early 1970's, news of teachers' strikes throughout the country was not unexpected. In response, threatened city fathers usually made great efforts to increase salaries and expand jobs, programs, and privileges.[58]

The educational shenanigan was repeated in other public service agencies. Costs moved upward across the board as big city mayors strained every nerve to extend benefit of the service agencies so as to calm dissonant and uproarious groups.[59] They tried job expansion so that there would be more jobs to go around. Hence, the city payrolls expanded by 17 percent between 1964 and 1969. During that same five-year period, municipal payrolls increased by 57 percent.[60]

After several years of such political shenanigans in the municipalities, estimates indicate that black people comprise from 25 to 30 percent of the approximately two million people employed in noneducational capacities by America's municipalities.[61] This estimate may be reliable, but with few exceptions blacks are concentrated in the lowest paid and most menial categories. The agencies in which blacks are concentrated are the very ones most subject to cutbacks during financial crises. The most desirable-paying job categories in most cities are police and fire. Furthermore, these two departments are least likely to receive a blow from the budget ax and in most cities they are departments in which blacks are most underrepresented.[62]

The promise to cut the city payroll helped Ralph Perk win the mayor's office in Cleveland. In 1972, he took steps to stand by his promise by initiating reductions in departments like parks and recreation, which employed proportionately more blacks than others. In Detroit, Mayor Roman Gibbs allowed the trimming ax to hit the heavily black department of sanitation and other departments with sizable numbers of blacks.[63]

Data on black employment in city governments may thus be

misleading. What does it matter if cities employ blacks in lowly paid, highly vulnerable positions? Are not blacks better off in cities where they are involved with education and social work in sizable numbers? For these reasons, black people seeking a fairer share of the municipal pie should look for the real meanings in any employment data released by city halls.[64]

Black people in Baltimore comprise 46.4 percent of the total population and hold 46 percent of the 41,000 municipal jobs. Examination of the 46 percent shows that, if education positions are excluded, the black percent of city jobs held drops to 38.6. Sixty-four percent of Baltimore's black employees are in public works, parks and recreation, hospitals, health, social service, housing, and community development. Even among some of these departments, blacks may be concentrated in the less desirable-paying positions. Only 39 percent of the city's white public works employees compared to 84 percent of black employees work as laborers, or in those positions that are not protected by civil service rules. The percentage of blacks in Baltimore's more desirable-paying departments of police and fire are 12 and 13.4 respectively.[65]

Comparing Denver to Baltimore, one finds that blacks and browns make up about 26 percent of Denver's total population and hold 32 percent of the career service jobs. Approximately 51 percent of Denver's city-county employees are hired by the Career Service Board. However, a separate Civil Service Commission is responsible for the personnel systems of the police and fire departments. Blacks and Chicanos hold title to only about 8 percent of the police and merely 3 percent of the fire positions.[66]

Cleveland is possibly typical of what black people throughout America can expect when it comes to city employment. Most of Cleveland's less desirable-paying positions are in sanitation, transit, parks and recreation, and subprofessional hospital jobs. These also happen to be the categories where proportionately more blacks are employed. Cleveland's police, fire, and financial administration employees receive the city's more desirable salaries. These categories also employ the lowest percentage of blacks. Indeed fire and police departments in most cities employ the lowest percentage of blacks and the majority of those blacks hold the lower-level jobs.[67]

The political leaders of big cities who strained resources to expand service benefit so as to calm organized dissonant and uproarious groups and give blacks a little nibble of the pie learned that, unlike

machine politicians of yesteryear, they could not attach many conditions to the concessions they made. It was impossible to attach re-
stricting strings because the organized groups had enough political
muscle to shield most of the expanded positions, increased salaries,
and conceded job prerogatives with civil service regulations or union
contracts. Thus, the results of the political shenanigans provided
organized white producer groups with tangible gains, and blacks
gained a few low-level city jobs and a little more welfare that
is now threatened. White real gains and blacks minute gains added
up to a run on the city treasury since the budget followed political-
shenanigan trends.[68]

Francis Fox Piven believes that municipal costs in Chicago rose
at a relatively slower rate than in most other big cities, partly because Mayor Richard Daley's political organization made it possible
for Daley to play his power cards so that he would not have to
concede as much to organized blacks or whites as was the case
for most other big city mayors. But despite Daley and his political
apparatus, Chicago, like other big cities, faces a fiscal crisis.

NOTES

[1] Alan A. Altshuler, *Community Control: The Black Demand for Participation in Large American Cities* (New York: Pegasus, 1970), pp. 13–14.
[2] *Ibid.*
[3] *Ibid.*, pp. 15–16.
[4] Mario Fantini, Marilyn Gittell, and Richard Magat, *Community Control
and the Urban School* (New York: Praeger, 1970), p. 94. The authors show
how the 1968 annual conference of the National Committee for Support
of the Public Schools answered, in part, the fundamentally paternalistic charge
that low-income blacks cannot manage their own affairs.
[5] *Ibid.*, p. XI.
[6] Altshuler, *op. cit.*, p. 22.
[7] *Ibid.*, p. 24.
[8] Angus Campbell, *White Attitudes Toward Black People* (Ann Arbor,
Mich.: Institute for Social Research, The University of Michigan, 1971),
p. 8.
[9] Altshuler, *op. cit.*, p. 21.
[10] *Ibid.*, p. 16.
[11] See Fantini, Gittell, and Magat, *op. cit.*, p. 13.
[12] *Ibid.*
[13] *Ibid.*
[14] *Ibid.*, pp. 7172.
[15] Laurence J. Peter and Raymond Hull, *The Peter Principle* (New York:
Bantam Books, 1969), p. 8.

[16] *Ibid.,* pp. 24–25.

[17] *Ibid.*

[18] *Ibid.,* p. 53.

[19] John M. Pfiffner and Robert Presthus, *Public Administration* (New York: The Ronald Press, 1967), p. 45; p. 46.

[20] Felix A. Nigro, *Modern Public Administration* (New York: Harper & Row, 1970), pp. 183–84. See also Amitai Etzioni, "Mixed Scanning: A Third Approach to Decision Making," *Public Administration Review,* XXVII No. 5 (December, 1967), pp. 386–87.

[21] For ideas pertaining to pro-inertia, anti-innovation, and drifting, see Etzioni, *ibid.*

[22] See Nigro, *op. cit.,* pp. 132–35.

[23] Donna E. Shalala, *Neighborhood Governance: Issues and Proposals* (New York: National Project on Ethnic America, The American Jewish Committee, 1971), p. 5.

[24] Nigro, *op. cit.,* p. 430.

[25] Fantini, Gittell, and Magat, *op. cit.* (n. 4), p. 94.

[26] *Ibid.,* pp. 93–94.

[27] Kenneth E. Marshall, "Goals of the Black Community," in Robert H. Connery and Demetrios Caraley, eds., *Governing The City: Challenges and Options for New York,* Proceedings of the Academy of Political Science, XXIX, No. 4 (1969), p. 196.

[28] Altshuler, *op. cit.* (n. 1), p. 16.

[29] Marshall, *op. cit.,* p. 194.

[30] Irving Kristol, "The Negro and the City," in Robert A. Goldwin, ed., *Nation of Cities: Essays on America's Urban Problems* (Chicago: Rand McNally, 1969), pp. 61–62.

[31] Marshall, *op. cit.,* pp. 198–99.

[32] Edward T. Rogwsky, Louis H. Gold, and David W. Abbott, "Police: The Civilian Review Board Controversy," in Jewel Bellush and Stephen M. David, eds., *Race and Politics in New York City: Five Studies in Policy-Making* (New York: Praeger Publishers, 1971), pp. 60–61.

[33] George F. Howe, "Survey of Municipal In-Service Training," *The Municipal Year Book 1971* (Washington, D.C.: International City Management Association, 1971), p. 223.

[34] Altshuler, *op. cit.* (n. 1), pp. 156–57.

[35] Marshall, *op. cit.,* p. 199.

[36] *Ibid.*

[37] Altshuler, *op. cit.* (n. 1), p. 171.

[38] *Ibid.,* pp. 158, 171.

[39] Michael Lipsky, "Toward a Theory of Street-Level Bureaucracy," Paper Presented at the 1964 Annual Meeting of the American Political Science Association, Commodore Hotel, New York, September, 1969, p. 1.

[40] Altshuler, *op. cit.* (n. 1), p. 158.

[41] *Ibid.*

[42] Hugh O'Neill, "The Growth of Municipal Employee Unions," in Robert H. Connery and William V. Farr, eds., *Unionization of Municipal Employees,* Proceedings of the Academy of Political Science, XXX, No. 2 (1970), p. 1.

[43] James P. Gifford, "Dissent in Municipal Employee Organizations," in Robert H. Connery and William V. Farr, eds., *Unionization of Municipal*

Employees, Proceedings of the Academy of Political Science, XXX, No. 2 (1970), pp. 162–64.

[44] *Ibid.* The societies and fraternal groups include Holy Name societies for the Catholics, Emerald societies for the Irish, Columbian Associations for the Italians, Hispanic societies for the Puerto Ricans, Steuben societies for the Germans, and Pulaski Associations for the Poles. In New York, blacks have the Guardians in the police department and the Vulcan Society in the fire department.

[45] Ewart Guinier, "Impact of Unionization on Blacks," in Robert H. Connery and William V. Farr, eds., *Unionization of Municipal Employees,* Proceedings of the Academy of Political Science, XXX, No. 2 (1970), pp. 173–74.

[46] *Ibid.*

[47] Frances Fox Piven, "Who Gets What: Cutting up the City Pie," *The New Republic,* February 5, 1972, p. 17.

[48] *Ibid.*

[49] *Ibid.*

[50] *Ibid.*

[51] *Ibid.,* p. 18.

[52] *Ibid.*

[53] *Ibid.,* pp. 18–19.

[54] *Ibid.,* p. 19.

[55] *Ibid.*

[56] *Ibid.*

[57] *Ibid.*

[58] *Ibid.*

[59] *Ibid.,* p. 20

[60] Walter L. Webb, "Government Manpower: An Overview," *The Municipal Year Book, 1971* (Washington, D.C.: International City Management Association, 1971), p. 187.

[61] The American Federation of State, County and Municipal Employees—the fastest growing union—says that some 35 to 40 percent of its 525,000 members are black.

[62] "Civil Service: Municipal," *Black Enterprise,* April, 1972, p. 28.

[63] *Ibid.*

[64] *Ibid.,* pp. 28–30.

[65] *Ibid.*

[66] *Denver Post* (editorial), June 9, 1972, p. 26.

[67] "Civil Service: Municipal," *op. cit.,* p. 30.

[68] Piven, *op. cit.* (n. 47), pp. 19–21.

CHAPTER 19

Violence or Open Avenues into the Political System?

Since American big cities have reached the critical financial juncture, it is imperative that the type of urban black political power-seeking organizations that can be established and become effective in presidential, congressional, and councilmanic elections come into existence and gear themselves to effectively influencing state legislative bodies. They cannot merely try to influence state legislatures; they must do so. Their success or lack of it will partly determine whether or not black Americans will lose all hope in America. This is a heavy burden for them to bear. However, it is the price they must pay for the privilege of representing black people.[1]

Black influencing of state legislators and governors is essential because cities will increasingly become more financially dependent on state governments (and the federal government) for portions of their funds. This development will allow greater state intervention in urban politics generally, and in natural-neighborhood politics especially.

> The initiative and the massive sums of money required to improve the housing, welfare, and education of ghetto dwellers cannot possibly come from the municipal level but rather from state and federal sources, and municipal governments can only petition the higher governmental levels for necessary funds. It is the President, the Federal Congress, and in some cases, the state government that will decide the volume of dollars and the manner in which they will be spent. . . .[2]

It will not be easy for black state legislators, even with the help of other elected black officials, because state capitals are more vulnerable to suburban and small-town votes than to black votes. The decisions made by state legislators and governors will be political, based upon power, not upon some kind of public morality.

Therefore, in the state legislatures black political leaders cannot concentrate on proposals that solely benefit blacks. They must devise proposals that contain benefits for organized white groups as well as meaningful benefits for blacks. If they fail to accomplish this, there will be no meaningful state concessions.

Not only must there be increased and more effective political activity on the part of blacks, but the private sector must cease and desist from some of its practices if blacks are ever to become part of the American system. Along with those whites who moved from the various cities, many businesses and industries that have jobs for people possessing limited skills have relocated outside the city. This is a real problem confronting black people, despite any amount of political power that may be acquired. Growing industrialization of the overwhelmingly white suburbs is mostly the result of decisions made by white business leaders. The consequences of their actions is being felt by blacks, browns, and necessitous whites who live in central cities. The business-industrial movement to suburbia has become so prevalent that it is difficult to tabulate which companies have left or are planning to leave such cities as Boston, Cleveland, Detroit, Los Angeles (financial district), New York, and St. Louis.[3]

Captains of industry cite a variety of reasons as to why there is business-industrial relocation outside of the central cities. Among them are cheap land, single-story factories that are convenient for truckloading, wretched telephone service in many cities, and rising crime rates. Regardless of the reasons (and we suspect there are some which are not stated publicly), their consequences are frequently drastic for low-paid blacks, browns, and whites. In many cases, the relocation is to the most exclusive suburbs, where low-paid families cannot obtain reasonably priced housing. In many other cases, the effect is drastic because the relocated facility is so far from the central city that commuting is prohibitively expensive, monetarily and time-wise.[4]

On February 28, 1971, the *New York Times* reported what must be classified as an American tragedy. According to the *Times*, between 75 and 90 percent of all low-level workers do not retain their jobs when a facility relocates to suburbia. On the other hand, the *Times* estimated that at the executive level, 80 to 100 percent retained their jobs after relocation to suburbia. This is a great tragedy for all poor workers involved, but greater for blacks since less than 5 percent of blacks live in suburbia and, during the last 20 years, 80 percent of all new jobs—and most new production jobs—have been located in suburbia.

Does planning for and implementing business-industrial relocation include exclusion, for the most part, of blacks and browns? There are some members of the General Counsel's Office of the Equal Employment Opportunity Commission who believe it does. In July of 1971, EEOC's General Counsel's office released a draft memorandum that, if adopted (the elite will never allow this), would cause certain relocations to be prima facie violation of Title VII of the Civil Rights Act of 1964. The proposal would make it almost impossible for relocations to take place when a plant is to be moved from a community that has a higher proportion of minority workers than the proposed new location. Also, the memo implies that when relocation is more detrimental to minority workers than to nonminority workers, the relocation has the foreseeable effect of excluding minorities from employment. Under such circumstances, it would be necessary for the employer to prove otherwise. Likewise, if a greater percentage of minority workers cannot move than can move, and if that percentage is higher than a comparable proportion for white workers, the employer would be in violation of Title VII of the Civil Rights Act of 1964.[5]

The memo suggested the need for special recruitment efforts in the nearest areas of minority residence, company payment of high commuting expenses, assistance in the search for housing, and payment for moving expenses. The procedures outlined would, if adopted by the Commission, face tremendous opposition from business. The recent controversy in the Congress over a bill to give the EEOC power to issue cease-and-desist orders brought lobbyists out from every corner in the capital.

Since most whites have no profound desire to see blacks move into their neighborhoods, it would be better, no doubt, if businesses were to prepare themselves to deal with the problem by accepting the fact that they have a responsibility to their workers, future workers, and to the present and future of America itself. One way to accept that responsibility would be widespread corporate decisions not to relocate in suburbia. Although its headquarters is in Westchester County, IBM has located a major plant in the Bedford-Stuyvestant natural neighborhood (Brooklyn). General Motors is expanding its international headquarters in downtown Detroit. Business should not move out of the city and allow certain lily-white areas to reap all the tax benefits of the new industry while central cities pick up the tab for housing and education costs incurred because people who are willing to work cannot get housing in the towns where they could find employment.[6]

If America hopes for a high measure of tranquility and stability in the future, two things must transpire. White business leaders must come to recognize the consequences of their decisions to relocate in suburbia, and there must be genuine redistribution of power in the big cities. If industry continues to relocate in suburbia and if power remains concentrated in the hands of the elite and its supporters, there is a high possibility that alienation and isolation may cause most black natural neighborhood residents to become so disillusioned that the confidence in government and its services will be undermined to a dangerously low point.[7]

Seymour Martin Lipset believes that in any given democracy, stability not only depends on economic development, but also upon the effectiveness and the legitimacy of its political system. Effectiveness can be measured, in part, by the extent to which the system satisfies the basic functions of government as most of the population and/or powerful groups see them. Groups generally deem a political order as legitimate or illegitimate in accordance to the way in which its values are in agreement with theirs. Therefore, in order to be viewed as being legitimate, governments usually create and attempt to sustain the belief that the existing political institutions are the most appropriate ones for the society.[8]

Lipset says that crises of legitimacy are primarily recent historical manifestations because, with the increase of keen-edged cleavages among groups, mass communication has made it possible for groups to organize around different values than those previously regarded to be the only acceptable ones. When subordinated groups organize around contradistinct values that include points of dispute pertaining to their being denied access to decision making in the political process, there can be a serious crisis of legitimacy. Since legitimacy also partly depends on how questions at issue that divide the society are resolved, one way to help resolve such vexing questions would be to effect structural changes that would open avenues leading into the political system to those organized around variant values.[9]

Furthermore, easy entrance into the political system tends to induce the loyalty of the new groups to the system and helps the old dominating elites to maintain much of their status even though they lose some of their power. This type of resolution of a crisis of legitimacy will help effect a high measure of tranquility and stability, thus making the society more secure. On the other hand, in nations like Germany, where entry into politics by newer groups was restricted by force and denied for prolonged periods, much alienation ensued. Not only were the outsiders alienated from the system, but they adopted extremist ideologies which, in turn, kept the more established groups from accepting their political movement as a legitimate alternative for structural change.[10]

Generally, even if a political system is tolerably effective at the time, there is a threat to the influential conservative forces because access to politics is denied to emerging groups at crucial periods. In such a case, the system's legitimacy will be questioned. If this leads to a breakdown of the tolerable sufficiency—repeatedly or for a long period—there is danger to the system's stability because confidence in government and its services will be undermined to a dangerously low point.[11]

America's crisis of legitimacy can be alleviated before it becomes somewhat more aggravated if the elites and the white middle class (who can influence politicians) come to realize the results of the reforms of the 1920's and 1930's. These reforms did not eliminate politics from administration but did help to exclude the average citizen—black and white—from participating in the delivering of government services. These two influential white groups must therefore be made to see that if there is meaningful decentralization the base of participation will be enlarged and the average natural-neighborhood residents will, at least, have an opportunity to try to influence the administration of services in their communities just as most middle-class suburban residents influence services in their respective areas. In fact, in most suburban areas a measure of autonomy has long been taken for granted.[12]

Failure on the parts of the elites and the white middle class to recognize the necessity of taking steps to make local government

more meaningful for noninfluential citizens could enhance the
polarization between the races. Further polarization would be very
easy since most white ethnic neighborhoods remain essentially
leaderless, unlike the black community in which a homegrown leadership cadre gradually emerged during the 1960's. Kenneth E.
Marshall believes that, aside from focusing attention narrowly on
dollar-and-cent issues and sustaining efforts to keep the various
policy-influencing organizations as lily-white as possible, would-be
leaders of white ethnics tragically ill-served them. This partially
explains why many white workers' political sagacity is so rudi-
mentary that they erroneously blame black welfare "chiselers" for
much of the present fiscal crisis.

> Beneficiaries in recent years of full, and even overly full, em-
> ployment, working-class whites have seemed content as almost
> mindless consumers of commodities and of the arid images that
> flicker from their television sets. It has taken a regressive 10 per
> cent surtax and a growing inflation, which in the last two years
> has eaten up everything they have gained, to kindle a beginning
> understanding of how marginal their recent affluence is. But the
> white worker's political intelligence is so rudimentary that he
> blames black welfare "chiselers" for the tax vise in which he
> finds himself rather than the war, the voracious military-industrial
> complex and national fiscal and monetary policies which in the
> form of excessive interest rates, cooperative subsidies, and so forth,
> take money out of his pocket to line further the coffers of the
> wealthy.[13]

A type of leadership must emerge among the white working
and lower-middle classes that is capable of helping them articulate
their needs and ensure that they direct their energies in the proper
direction so as to effect desirable results. Misplacement of their
disgruntlements and frustrations onto the black natural neighborhoods is detrimental to blacks and whites both. Capable ethnic white
leadership could attempt to raise the level of political sophistication
in white ethnic neighborhoods to the point where the inhabitants
would understand that they, too, would benefit from meaningful
decentralization. The leadership could begin by showing how school
decentralization not only holds the potential to be a process for
strengthening black education, but that it could strengthen educa-

tion citywide and thus white ethnic children, too, would derive benefits.

White ethnics could also be shown how the municipal bureaucrats only serve them tolerably well. Their streets are more likely to be regularly cleaned than the streets in black natural neighborhoods, and they may receive fairly adequate police protection, to be sure—more than that received in black natural neighborhoods. But are their street and police services as adequate as in white middle-class neighborhoods?

White leadership must make sure that white ethnics recognize that in the past they have been in error grumbling about Head Start programs and the like. Rather than view such programs as handouts to blacks and be pleased when they are cut back, they should be viewed as opportunities to mount campaigns for such programs to serve all children.[14]

There is much suspicion that Richard M. Nixon's administration adopted a Planned Variations formula for the Model Cities program to mollify whites who opposed Model Cities because so much of the program's past thrust was directed toward black natural neighborhoods. Planned Variations extended Model Cities from geographically limited target areas in 20 cities to the entire city so that there would be citywide application of funds. There is little doubt that if this formula quiets white ethnics, it will be extended to other cities.[15]

No doubt, the elites of corporate America are anxious to see government in America move in the direction of providing more tranquility and stability. And, apparently, they are willing to see government employ "other means" to see if they work before resorting to the utilization of blatant repression. If these assumptions hold any measures of truth—and we believe that they do—then the possibility, however slim, exists that the elites can be persuaded to accept experimenting with natural-neighborhood government as "another means" because with it greater citizen involvement could cause black natural-neighborhood residents to feel less outside the system.

If and when the elites accept the concept of natural-neighborhood government, their acceptance possibly will be wrapped in high-sounding principles. However, just as moral oughts had very little to do with the fact that violent repression was not employed to effect social control in restive black natural neighborhoods with the advent of activism in the 1960's, they will not greatly influence corporate America's acceptance of natural-neighborhood government.

Corporate America came to believe that employment of violent repression to effect social control in disturbed and restless black natural neighborhoods would be detrimental to their self-interest.[16] Therefore, belief that natural-neighborhood government would lessen the potential dangers to their self-interest would outweigh any moral oughts in deciding to allow devolution of authority in the big cities. Of course, such an assessment pertaining to violent repression is correct. Repression only breeds more violent responses.

It seems clear that violence feeds on violence; a violent act tends to evoke a violent response. The goals of the two types of violence . . . violence for social control and violence for social change, stand in marked contrast to each other, yet the means by which these goals are to be accomplished are identical. It is unlikely that the use of force for social control will eliminate the desire for social change, although it may indeed suppress the expression of that desire. It is also unlikely that the use of violence for social control can be expected to teach the lesson that the use of violence as a means to an end is unacceptable. Violence for social control exemplifies the opposite lesson, and by example teaches it.[17]

On the other hand, if any members of the corporate and/or political elite do think in terms of elite retention of all authority and in terms of violent repression for social control of black natural neighborhoods, for the sake of the general society, they should think twice. For what their thoughts could accomplish in reality would be perpetuation of what some call "negative black political action." That is, black natural neighborhoods have the capacity to organize to stop a highway that is being built or to prevent luxury apartments from being constructed, or the abandonment of other projects. In other words, such actions would be viewed as negative because blacks would be reacting to actions already undertaken by elite, rather than acting to help plan and initiate projects.[18]

Elites should also think twice because once "negative" political action is in actual process, it is difficult to control. If the action involves civil disobedience, there is the great likelihood that most participants in the action believe that disobedience of the law can be justified in specific cases because every law is not just. It is also reasonable to expect that many of the participants will have joined in the action because they have come to believe that elite control of legal remedies to redress grievances make such instruments empty as they pertain to black people.[19]

If sizable numbers of the participants believe in civil disobedience and believe also that instruments to redress grievances are empty, political action could take a very violent turn. It is not necessary for a majority of a group to seek violence to cause various members of a group to move in the direction of violence. In most black political action groups it is reasonable to believe that some members lean toward violence. Recent research indicates that among black men, 4 percent agree "a great deal" that protest in which some people are killed is necessary before changes will take place fast enough. Another 6 percent agree "somewhat." Six percent agree "a great deal" that protest in which there is some property damage is necessary for changes to be brought about fast enough. A different 19 percent agree "somewhat."[20]

Elites should evaluate the above feelings before they decide to block meaningful natural-neighborhood government. They could erroneously assume that there would be no violent reaction on the part of blacks since 84 percent disagree "a great deal" that protest in which some people are killed is necessary before changes will take place fast enough and 53 percent disagree "a great deal" that protest in which there is some property damage is necessary for changes to be brought about fast enough.[21]

It does not take 84, 53, or even 4 percent of blacks to initiate violence in an attempt to effect social change. In any big city on any given day a very small band of urban black revolutionaries could ignite the fuse by strategically locating themselves during an afternoon rush hour and beginning to shoot white people. The white reaction would be so swift that no attempt would be made to distinguish the 84 percent blacks who disagree "a great deal" that protest in which some people are killed is necessary before changes will take place fast enough, from the 4 percent who agree "a great deal" that protest in which some people are killed is necessary.

Once the bloodletting gets under way, those blacks who live outside of black natural neighborhoods will be most vulnerable. This will be especially true for the few black people who move into nearly all-white neighborhoods so as to acquire better housing. However, some other so-called blacks move into near lily-white upper middle-class neighborhoods so as to get away from black people. Once a small band of black revolutionaries ignites the fuse and the powder goes off, both of the former types of blacks will be liable to injury or death. The violent acts will not necessarily be perpetuated by their immediate neighbors, but some white from somewhere will point his gun in their direction because "the only good nigger is one that stops breathing on account of being filled with lead." It would be rather ironic if the black brother who moved to acquire decent housing would have to share the tragic fate of a black face that tried to move away from black people because he so worshiped white people. Many blacks would feel sympathy for the black brother, but would shed no tears for a black face-white folks-worshiper who ran from blacks and was rubbed-out because of his black face. Neither should his white friends shed tears because he has gone to his last home. Had he lived, in no way could he have helped to lessen racial tensions.

Natural-neighborhood blacks will have a better chance of survival in such violence if only because of their heavy concentration and the presence of those blacks who in the mid-1960's began to purchase guns and cartridges "just in case" it became necessary to defend themselves and their families. Those guns and cartridges help enhance their survival chances because they ensure that some whites will die if the natural neighborhood is invaded. Most whites do not harbor desires to die. Therefore, the greatest number of whites will not be eager to storm black natural neighborhoods.

Not all black men who live in white communities disbelieve in guns and violence. In fact, there appears to be a slight relationship between levels of education and income and the use of violence for social change. White men, as their educational and income levels increase, tend to view violence for social change less favorably. On the other hand, the relationship is stronger for black men and in the reverse direction. With increased education and income there is a tendency for black men to see violence for social change as more necessary.[22] Therefore, it is highly possible that some black men who live in white communities and have above-average educations and incomes view the utilization of violence for social change more favorably than their above-average education and income white neighbors. It seems reasonable to assume that such an intelligent black man would be prepared to defend his family "just in case."

Why are some better-educated black men more prone to violence for social change than their lesser-educated black brothers? We do not know, but there are several possible reasons. There is some speculation that some of the better-educated black men feel racial subordination more keenly than do lesser-educated black men. They are impatient with the rate of social change to the extent that they are very discouraged with present efforts at improvement. Therefore, it seems reasonable to assume they are less hopeful than many other black men that change can be brought about without injury to humans and damage to property.[23]

Whatever the reason or reasons, it is highly doubtful that the elites, even with all of their intelligence-gathering expertise (including black spies), will be able to identify very many of those black men who are bent toward political violence, so as to put them under surveillance.

Most of them themselves will not know who they are until racist actions push them over the brink. Many better-educated black men hold private and public professional and/or white collar jobs. For as long as they will have held their jobs, many of them will have dressed, talked, and socialized in white middle-class style. However, some black male employees attempt what is difficult on a white job: they endeavor to maintain their cultural blackness by not aspiring for upward social mobility. Upward social mobility requires rejecting one's blackness and adaptation to values and behavior prescribed in accordance with the standards of the white middle class.[24]

These blacks soon learn that their decision to undertake to maintain their blackness represents assertive black manhood to whites above them in the administrative hierarchy. The American heritage of racism will not allow black men to exercise independent thinking that leads to self-assertion, like white men, without hazard to themselves. Since whites in the administrative hierarchy cannot view them as "boys" to be used in window-dressing roles so as to make the organization look liberal and American, they will become black men who hold positions of no authority. They will not be able to climb the promotional ladder as white men do because for them efficient performance and promotion possibilities are not positively related. These factors—holding positions of no authority and the inability to climb the promotional ladder—may trigger any potential political violence they harbor and push them over the brink.

Many black men (also black women and children) harbor feelings of resentment and grievance against white society. When some of these blacks feel the sharp pain of racial subordination's penetrating lash, the agonizing bitter sensibility that it leaves causes them to view the racist action as violence against them. They then may come under a retributory spell and utilize violence as a means of redressing their grievances.

Some people surmise that such retribution could spring from, in part, the influence of eye-for-an-eye, tooth-for-a-tooth views, or the indelible impressions made by the western movie or television western glorifying the cowboy who settles his grievances violently with his gun.[25] Eye-for-an-eye philosophy and cowboy images might have influenced some well-educated black men to come to harbor potential political violence and become a part of what the late Malcolm X called a new generation of black people that formed "a just opinion, that if there is to be bleeding, it should be reciprocal—bleeding on both sides."[26]

During the mid-1960's, blacks with a penchant toward political violence were sometimes called "black nationalists." They were considered to represent such tiny minorities in various black communities that the elite tended to classify them as insignificant. We now know that all blacks leaning toward political violence cannot be called black nationalists because some of the highly educated live in white neighborhoods. The present group, though small, cannot be ignored for the same reasons Malcolm X said black nationalists should not be ignored:

> The black nationalists to many of you may represent only a minority in the community. And therefore you might have a tendency to classify them as something insignificant. But just as the fuse is the smallest part or the smallest piece in the powder keg, it is yet that little fuse that ignites the entire powder keg. The black nationalists to you may represent a small minority

in the so-called Negro community. But they just happen to be composed of the type of ingredient necessary to fuse or ignite the entire black community.[27]

Another possible explanation for black men being more bent toward political violence than white men is the fact that all black men harbor inside of them a potential bad nigger. Even the most passive, deferential-toward-whites, proper-talking, white-worshiping black man (a "polished nigger") can be pushed by racial subordination's penetrating lash to the point that the bad nigger comes out of him and he becomes angry, hostile, and uncompromising.[28]

A wise and responsible person would avoid triggering the potential political violence that is harbored inside some blacks. Under a natural-neighborhood government system, the energy that could be spent on violence could be used participating in the planning and policy-making process. Yes, America can avoid racial violence, but in 1964 Malcolm X said America was not morally equipped to do so.

> So, in my conclusion, in speaking about the black revolution, America today is at a time or in a day or at an hour where she is the first country on this earth that can actually have a bloodless revolution. In the past, revolutions have been bloody. Historically you just don't have a peaceful revolution. Revolutions are bloody, revolutions are violent, . . . bloodshed and death follow in their paths. America is the only country in history in a position to bring about a revolution without violence and bloodshed. But America is not morally equipped to do so.[29]

We agree that morality will not cause America to take the necessary steps in the direction of meaningful decentralization to avoid violence. However, America can be pushed into that direction. Corporate America has the muscle to provide the impetus and possibly would provide it if it could be convinced that natural-neighborhood government would be less detrimental to its self-interests than centralized government.

Convincing corporate America to support natural-neighborhood government will not be easy, partly because some of its individual members are guilty of placing black people in different camps. In some of their minds many black people are fighting for integration and others struggling for separation. Separatism possibly frightens them. However, individual members of corporate America should be aware that many blacks are fighting for neither. For enlightenment on this point we again refer to the late Honorable Malcolm X: "We have to keep in mind at all times that we are not fighting for integration, nor are we fighting for separation. We are fighting for recognition as human beings. We are fighting for the right to live as free human beings. We are fighting for the right to live as free humans in this society. In fact, we are actually fighting for rights that are even greater than civil rights and that is human rights. . . ."[30]

The natural-neighborhood government plan will come closer to allowing blacks to live as free humans in this society than the present elitist-controlled system. We recognize that there is no one best blueprint for decentralization that will afford greater human rights to blacks and that would work in each of the 89 cities in which black people comprise a sizable percent of the population. In fact, in some cities it may be desirable to decentralize all functions. In other cases the interdependence of some functions (like the sewage system) within the metropolitan area may make it desirable to have areawide administration. This could work and not violate the general principles of natural-neighborhood government as long as the policy-making and administrative bodies included enough representation from central cities so as to be able to veto proposals that would ill-serve black natural neighborhoods before they are put in practice.[31]

Technological advance and the magnitude and nature of the population shifts in much of urban America help to make it imperative that existing political institutions and structural arrangements be modified to the extent that they will allow greater inputs from noninfluential and/or subordinated citizens. Inputs or legitimate demands of powerless citizens must and can be handled (under natural-neighborhood arrangements) so that such citizens will not, in most big cities, have to resort to threats or politics of violence to be heard. If there is devolution of authority along with proportionate representation at decision-making levels in America's big cities—blacks, browns, poor whites, middle-class whites, captains of industry—all of America benefits. If there are no institutional and structural changes, there can only be unfavorable consequences for all of America.

NOTES

[1] Frances Fox Piven, "Who Gets What: Cutting up the City Pie," *The New Republic*, February 5, 1972, pp. 19–21.

[2] Kenneth E. Marshall, "Goals of the Black Community," in Robert H. Connery and Demetrios Caraley, eds., *Governing The City: Challenges and Options for New York*, Proceedings of the Academy of Political Science, XXIX (1969), p. 194.

[3] Robert Cassidy, "Moving to the Suburbs: When Business Flees the City," *The New Republic*, CLXVI (January 22, 1972), pp. 19–20.

[4] *Ibid.*, pp. 20–21.

[5] *Ibid.*, pp. 22–23.

[6] *Ibid.*

[7] Donna E. Shalala, *Neighborhood Governance: Issues and Proposals* (New York: National Project on Ethnic America, The American Jewish Committee, 1971), p. 5.

[8] Seymour Martin Lipset, *Political Man: The Social Bases of Politics* (Garden City, N.Y.: Anchor Books Edition, Doubleday & Company, 1965), pp. 64–67.

[9] *Ibid.*

[10] *Ibid.*

[11] *Ibid.*

[12] Shalala, *op. cit.*, p. 2.

[13] Marshall, *op. cit.* (n. 2), p. 197.

[14] *Ibid.*

[15] "A New Look For Model Cities, Urban Redevelopment: Vanguard of the New Federalism?" *Black Enterprise*, November, 1971, pp. 17–20. The initial 20 Planned Variation Cities were Newark and Paterson, N.J.; Erie, Pa.; Norfolk, Va.; Tampa, Fla.; Winston-Salem, N.C.; Dayton, Ohio; E. St. Louis, Ill.; Indianapolis, Ind.; Lansing, Mich.; Houston and Waco, Texas; Des Moines, Ia.; Butte, Mont.; San Jose and Fresno, Calif.; Tucson, Ariz.; Seattle, Wash.; Rochester, N.Y.; and Wilmington, Del.

[16] Marshall, *op. cit.* (n. 2), p. 195.

[17] Monica D. Blumenthal *et al.*, *Justifying Violence: Attitudes of American Men* (Ann Arbor, Mich.: Institute for Social Research, The University of Michigan, 1972), p. 247.

[18] Shalala, *op. cit.* (n. 7), pp. 4–5.

[19] Charles Frankel, "Civil Disobedience: Is It Ever Right to Break the Law?," in Thomas R. Dye and Brett W. Hawkins, eds., *Politics in the Metropolis: A Reader in Conflict and Cooperation* (Columbus, Ohio: Charles E. Merrill, 1967), pp. 92–97.

[20] Blumenthal, *op. cit.*, p. 35.

[21] *Ibid.*

[22] *Ibid.*, p. 227.

[23] *Ibid.*

[24] Milton M. Gordon, *Assimilation in American Life: The Role of Race, Religion, and National Origins* (New York: Oxford University Press, 1964), pp. 46–47.

[25] Blumenthal, *op. cit.* Especially see pp. 14 and 230.

[26] George Breitman, ed., *Malcolm X Speaks: Selected Speeches and Statements* (New York: Grove Press, 1965), p. 48.

[27] *Ibid.*, pp. 47–48.

[28] William H. Grier and Price M. Cobbs, *Black Rage* (New York: Basic Books, 1969), pp. 55–56.

[29] Breitman, *op. cit.*, pp. 56–57.

[30] *Ibid.*, p. 51.

[31] Committee for Economic Development, *Reshaping Government in Metropolitan Areas*, A Statement by the Research and Policy Committee (New York: Committee for Economic Development, February, 1970), pp. 16–17, 43–45.

Index